KUSIQ

*An Eskimo Life History
from the Arctic Coast of Alaska*

**Oral Biography Series
Number 2
William Schneider, Editor**

Other publications in the Oral Biography Series

The Life I've Been Living
by Moses Cruikshank

Moses Cruikshank is an Athabaskan elder and a skilled storyteller from Interior Alaska. In his stories, Moses blends description, opinion, advice, and humor to teach the lessons he has learned from living out in the country.

Moses' stories were recorded, edited, and arranged by William Schneider, Curator of Oral History at the Alaska and Polar Regions Department, Elmer Rasmuson Library, University of Alaska Fairbanks.

KUSIQ

*An Eskimo Life History
from the Arctic Coast of Alaska*

by
Waldo Bodfish, Sr.

Recorded, compiled, and edited by
William Schneider

In collaboration with
Leona Kisautaq Okakok

and
James Mumiġana Nageak

University of Alaska Press

Library of Congress Cataloging-in-Publication Data

Bodfish, Waldo, 1902–
    Kusiq : an Eskimo life history from the Arctic Coast of Alaska /
by Waldo Bodfish, Sr. ; recorded, compiled, and edited by William
Schneider in collagoration with Leona Kisataq Okakok and
James Mumiġana Nageak.
       p. cm. –(Oral biography series ; no. 2)
    Includes bibliographical references (p.) and index.
    ISBN 0-912006-44-7 : $21.00
    1. Bodfish, Waldo, 1902– . 2. Eskimos-Alaska-
Wainwright-Biography. 3. Eskimos-Alaska-Wainwright-
History. 4. Eskimos-Alaska-Wainwright-Social life and customs.
5. Wainwright (Alaska)-Social life and customs. I. Schneider,
William. II. Okakok, Kisataq-Leona. III. Nageak, James
Mumiġana. IV. Title. V. Series.
E99.R7B675 1991   90-11246
979.8'7-dc20   CIP

International Standard Library Book Number: 0-912006-44-7
Library of Congress Catalog Number: 90-11246

Printed in the United States.

This publication was printed on acid-free paper that meets the
minimum requirements for the American National Standard for
Information Sciences—Permanence of Paper for Printed Library
Materials ANSI Z39.48-1984.

Copyediting, book design, and production by Elder Editorial.
Cover design by Deborah Grahek, IMPACT/Graphics, Elmer E.
Rasmuson Library, University of Alaska Fairbanks.
Cover photographs by David Libbey.

Contents

Foreword

I have known Waldo Bodfish, Sr. since my late teens, my reindeer herding days for Barrow Reindeer Company. He, at times,
went by or spent a night at our camp, in his travels by dog team.
I have always admired him from the time I first got to know
him, even for a brief time. He was friendly, mild mannered, and
a man with a very good dog team. That is my recollection of
Waldo when I first met him. He is from the village of Wainwright, and I am from the village of Barrow.

And now, after seventeen years as his pastor (1972–88)
and friend, in his village of Wainwright, my knowledge and
respect for him has grown. He has been a faithful member and
dedicated elder in our church. He is a man of knowledge and
experience pertaining to the Eskimo way of life. A hunter, trapper, whaler, carpenter, leader, he is a person who really qualifies
as a jack-of-all-trades, even at his ripe old age. He has a unique
and interesting way of telling his experiences that allows a person to learn about arctic survival at the same time. As you flip

through the pages of this book you will not only enjoy his life stories, but you will also see clearly the passing of the old Eskimo way of life.

—Reverend Samuel Simmonds

Preface

This book, the second in a series of oral biographies published by the University of Alaska Press, is by Waldo Bodfish, Sr., an Iñupiaq elder from Wainwright, a village on the Arctic Coast of Alaska. Bodfish was asked to share his life story because it is important to our understanding of North Slope history and culture. He possesses the qualities necessary to produce an oral biography: he is a good observer with a keen interest in people, and he has an excellent memory for detail. Perhaps most important, he has a strong appreciation for the importance of his experiences.

The Series
Individuals whose life experiences and personal accomplishments provide an intimate view of the events, personalities, and influences that have shaped Alaska history are the subjects of books in this series. Each book tells the story of a person's life in his or her own words, based on oral history recordings that have been transcribed, compiled, and edited into a

book-length account. The written text is designed to read as much like the narrator talks as possible in order to preserve for the reader the narrator's speaking style. Supporting chapters convey the context in which the accounts were shared and indicate the cultural and historical importance of the information. Authorship resides with the narrators, but the books are the result of collaboration among the narrators and those who interview them, transcribe their accounts into narrative, and research and write supporting chapters and footnotes.

The Collaborators

The collaborators for this book include William Schneider, curator of oral history at the Elmer E. Rasmuson Library, University of Alaska Fairbanks; Leona Kisautaq Okakok, deputy director of administration at the planning department of the North Slope Borough; and James Mumiġana Nageak, instructor of Iñupiaq at the Alaska Native Language Center, University of Alaska Fairbanks. Schneider recorded and compiled Bodfish's stories, while Okakok and Nageak, both language specialists in Iñupiaq Eskimo and former liaison officers for the North Slope Borough Commission on Iñupiat History, Language, and Culture, contributed their skills in interviewing, translating, and clarifying Iñupiaq concepts.

How This Book Is Organized

The foreword by the Reverend Samuel Simmonds, whose introduction is based on his many years of association with Waldo Bodfish, Sr., is followed by this preface and twelve chapters of Bodfish's narrative. Each chapter represents a major period of Bodfish's life, as indicated by its title.

Background and commentary by the collaborators follow. In chapter 13, Schneider presents a historical overview of the themes Bodfish introduces in his narrative, and in chapter 14, he discusses the collaboration and methodology used to produce this book. In chapter 15, Okakok discusses how she worked with Waldo's narrative to determine the correct English interpretation and accurate Iñupiaq spellings.

Appendices A through G follow, containing information on pronunciation, personal names, genealogical relations, and place-names. In Appendix F, anthropologist Richard Nelson recalls the types of hunting stories Bodfish shared with him. Appendix G contains a portion of a transcript from an interview with Bodfish conducted by Nageak. It highlights the richness of the Iñupiaq language and illustrates the interaction between Bodfish and a different interviewer.

The chapter notes following the appendices were written by Schneider and Okakok. The notes by Schneider are unmarked, while those by Okakok are preceded by her name.

Throughout the book, Iñupiaq terms are defined the first time they appear in the text or in the notes. Note that the singular and plural forms differ in spelling. For example, the singular form of *kayak* is *qayaq,* while the plural form is *qayat.* The singular form of *shaman* is *aŋatkuq,* while the plural form is *aŋatkut.* For more information, refer to Edna Ahgeak MacLean's forthcoming *Iñupiaq Dictionary.*

Acknowledgments

Many people have contributed to this book. Special thanks go to the faculty and staff of the Elmer E. Rasmuson Library, especially David Hales, who organized and compiled the index, photographer Richard Veazey and his photographic staff, and Dixon Jones and Debbie Grahek, who designed the cover, did the photo layout, and produced the maps. Jan Neimeyer assisted with the maps. Lisa Chavez did the initial editing, putting in many hours making corrections, and she helped research photographs. Barbara Matthews assisted in proofreading and copyediting. Joan Soutar and Anna Poe computerized the index. Lorraine Elder of Elder Editorial did the final editing, design, and production. Her cross-checking and cross-referencing helped to insure consistency in spellling and style.

Edna MacLean secured initial and major funding from the North Slope Borough, which supported travel, research, and transcription by Joan Jaspersen and Muriel Hopson. Irene Reed supervised the transcription.

Luis Proenza, vice chancellor for research at the University of Alaska Fairbanks, provided two generous grants for this work. Members of the North Slope Borough Planning Department gave support throughout the project. Jana Harcharck, liaison for the Commission on Iñupiat History, Language, and Culture, arranged financial support and coordination of the review trip. Dorothy Edwardsen researched genealogical files, and Margie Fischer lent a personal picture to be used in the book. Chris Wooley located and copied photographic collections and sent an emergency supply of cassette tapes to collaborators in Wainwright.

Joyce Justice of the Federal Archives at Sand Point located information from school records. Arthur Railton of the Dukes County Historical Society generously shared personal knowledge of Captain Hartson Bodfish and his life on Martha's Vineyard. Sandy Bodfish shared research she had done on the Bodfish family. The staff of the Whaling Museum in New Bedford searched collections, made ships' logs available, and copied pictures. Photographs also came from The Presbyterian Church Archives in Philadelphia, the California Academy of Sciences in San Francisco, and the Denver Museum of Natural History.

Barbara Bodenhorn and Yvonne Yarber generously shared genealogical research. David Krupa proofread each section of the manuscript many times and made important substantive suggestions.

Edwin Hall, Richard Nelson, David Libbey, Alan Borass, Margaret Blackman, and Ernest Burch, Jr., reviewed earlier drafts of the book. Special acknowledgement to Burch for giving time to review and comment on the manuscript and for sharing his extensive knowledge. To Blackman, special thanks for many stimulating discussions which ultimately influenced the organization of this book and our appreciation of the collaborative process in life histories. As well as giving helpful review of the manuscript, Richard Nelson generously shared a bit of his relationship with Bodfish in Appendix F.

Dorothy Jean Ray and John Bockstoce were very helpful in providing references to sources and in clarifying several points. James Corbin shared letters and field notes on house types, and Arthur Fields, Sr., provided helpful information on trading.

Special thanks go to Mattie Bodfish for helping us to complete the project. She made us feel welcome, and was generous with information, patient with our many questions, and always ready to give us a good meal and a comfortable place to stay.

Each person's contributions are appreciated, and it is hoped that this publication proves worthy of their efforts.

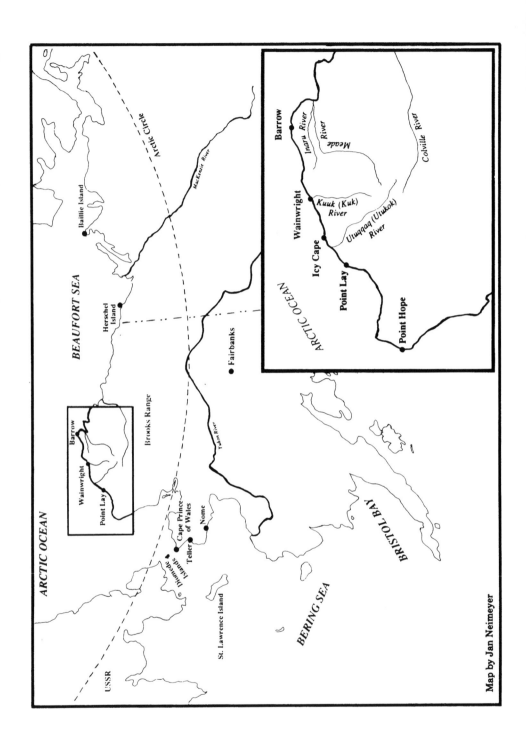

Map by Jan Neimeyer

The Narrative

1

Living at Icy Cape

I am Eskimo. I don't want to change my nationality and I like to speak Eskimo.[1] I'm a half-breed: father White man and mother real Eskimo, from Point Hope.

My Family
My mother's father was Esowana and her mother was Akutugreak. There were three girls and two boys in my mother's family. They have Fred Anashugak, Riley Ahlook, my mother, Lucy Kongona, her sister Alice Akligok, and Mary Samarona. Samarona, the woman that married Jack Hadley, was the oldest. Riley Ahlook is the next and then my mother and Alice and Fred Anashugak. Those are the brothers and sisters.[2]

They originated from Point Hope. They have relatives there at Point Hope. And while they were at Point Hope two young men, Riley Ahlook and Eluktuna, decided to learn how to be reindeer herders.[3]

They spent two or three years maybe, or four, at the reindeer station in Teller; I don't know how long. And they earned some reindeer while they were herding with Lapps. They had some government herd and there were three or four families that were brought from Siberia to teach reindeer herding. Six altogether. Four of them brought their wives, and two of them were young ones. After Riley and Eluktuna earned their own herd, they drove them all the way to Point Hope. And they spent many years in Point Hope herding.

When their herd grew, my uncle Riley moved up north near Icy Cape, and they did the herding there.[4] I was only a small boy at that time and occasionally I knew what they were doing. I saw the reindeer all the time and lived with my folks.[5]

My mother's first husband was named Kusiq, and when I was born in 1902 they named me after him, after her first husband.[6] They lived down at Point Hope just half a year and then my mother lost her husband. The shaman, *aŋatkuq,* wanted to have my mother's first husband for his son-in-law, but Kusiq didn't want to marry the shaman's daughter.[7] That's why the shaman killed him. My mother loved that man, and that's why she named me after him. Kusiq was the brother of Charlie Ned and Siuchiarook. Kusiq, I guess, was the oldest of those brothers; that's what they told me.

My father was Captain Hartson Bodfish, a whaling ship captain.[8] He took my mother up north and wintered over at Herschel Island. And the next spring they went back out. He put my mother off in Teller, Alaska. That is about one hundred miles north of Nome. And there I was born, April 1, 1902.

Jim Allen[9] told me my father was one of the best whaling captains they ever had from the company whaling people in Massachusetts. And I know that he and Captain Tilton got more whales than the other whalers put together. Jim was telling me that when it turns real foggy just before freeze-up in late fall, my father used to sneak out and get a whale before anybody went out. And by the time they found him he was just cutting the whale. That's what Jim always told me. That's the way he got more whales than others, I guess.

When I was working with Jim Allen he would tell a story about the whaling ships that came up here, how they would pick up five or six Eskimos from along the coast—St. Lawrence Island and Little Diomede, some from Cape Prince of Wales, and Point Hope. They always picked some people for the whaling ship crew when they reached our area along the coast here, when they started to winter up at Herschel Island in the latter days of whaling. That's what Jim Allen told me. He was a young man.

And they always got women that were good sewers from Diomede and Cape Prince of Wales and St.Lawrence Island. I know my mother got on the ship at Point Hope.[10] During the winter they made some clothes for that year. My mother told me they made clothing for the officers on Bodfish's ship. But they never did the work on crews' clothes. If they had other women from Herschel Island, they made the crews' clothing. That's what she told me. There's a little bay at Herschel Island, but it's big enough for several ships. That's where they wintered. They kept the stern of the ship open all year round. Every day they chopped the ice out, kept the propeller clear from freezing solid in the ice. They put heavy canvas on the living quarters of their ship, even on the side, and made it real warm. They lived in the ship. That's the way they always wintered. Some of them carried lumber from Outside and built a house for winter quarters.

Early Memories

My earliest memory was when I was a small kid. My mother told me I was born at Teller. I was born there in 1902 and lived down at Teller when I was a baby, for how long I don't know. And my mother got married while she was in Teller to my stepfather, Andrew Ahneovak. And my stepfather was apprenticed to Riley Ahlook, the reindeer herder.

I don't know how long my mother was down there while I was a baby. The second time when I went down there I learned about my father's side of the family. Andrew had one brother and one sister down there. When I got a little older I began to know everything about my parents. And that's how I got to know Teller when I was a kid.

When the herd grew bigger and they finished their apprenticeship down there, Riley and Eluktuna took some government herd along with their own reindeer, separated them from the main herd of the Teller reindeer herders, and they started driving them through Kotzebue all the way to Point Hope. Then they trained some new herders down there at Point Hope. While they were herding, when the reindeer herd grew big enough, Riley decided to move up to this area, around Icy Cape. He separated his reindeer in the fall, when they corral and count them, and they started moving up north. They must have been going all the way to Barrow that time, but I don't remember. I was a baby.

My mother told me that on that little creek where the Community Center is at Barrow, I almost drowned there when I was a kid. Fred, my uncle, was walking into the village and I started to follow him. I could walk, but I fell in that creek. It was flooding with spring water and ice. I drifted out in front of the little creek and was floating out to the ocean with my face down in the water. I was wearing some kind of parki, fawn's skin I guess. And my mother recognized my parki and ran out there and picked me up. When they brought me to the sand, they started to work on me. And my stepfather first started it and then other people that lived in Barrow. When they gave up, Jack Hadley took over and made me alive. That's my mother's sister's husband, a White man. He revived me. That's what my mother told me. I was almost drowned.

When they were living up there with the herd, they lived south of Barrow, along that bluff Imnaaguq, that bank that goes all the way down to Peard Bay, Imnaaguq. Then they moved from there, back to Avvaq, near Icy Cape. We were living on the tundra all the time near the coast when I was a kid. From there I started to learn; I was old enough, a little bit, when we were staying there. I remember one time when the moon came up, I went outside. And when I went out there I told my mother there's a lantern up there. When she went out to check, it was just the moon coming up. Those days they had a lantern with a chimney. I called the moon a lantern.

Those people we stayed with were very religious. They had Eskimo songs translated from English, and they had service every Sunday when I was small kid. They never missed it, even Wednesday service. That's how I lived with those Christian people.[11] We lived like any Eskimo.[12] We got along pretty well with our other families, reindeer herders. They never had quarrels or anything I know of. That's how we were raised when Henry Peetook and I were kids. My mother and Henry's mother were sisters. He's my cousin. And we always stay together ever since we were boys. Henry and I are *aġnaqatigiik*. We are *aġnaqatigiik* when we are related that way. That means we both have mothers who have the same mother. And when they call it *aŋutiqatigiik* that means our fathers are brothers who have the same father.[13]

When Captain Bodfish found out we were staying close to Icy Cape, he always stopped when he came up in the summer, and put ashore all the groceries for me and my mother.[14] He did that three or four years in a row, two thousand dollars worth of groceries every year. Whenever he came up, Captain Bodfish always wanted to take me Outside for education. But my mother wouldn't let me go. I don't know why. I felt bad about that. I would be pretty well educated if they let me go to school.

Before that, when I was small, sometimes our folks had a hard time feeding us when the animals were scarce. They didn't have very big reindeer herds in those days, when they first were apprentices. They only butchered so many reindeer each year. They had a tough time getting by throughout the year when there's not much animals besides reindeer.[15] But they always catch quite a number of foxes whenever the foxes come ashore near Point Lay and Icy Cape. They got lots of foxes. That way they bought some groceries and ammunition, enough to last them a whole year.[16]

That's the way they worked at Icy Cape and Point Lay. They bought enough White man's food, the staple ones like flour, sugar, corn meal, rolled oats. They bought lots of those main foods. In those days, when they sold their furs they bought only lead for bullets and black powder and primers, enough to last them a whole year. I don't know what the fox was really worth, but they always got by on those things during the winter. And besides that, I usually remember when they were short of White man's food, when they're short of flour and tea, they went down with one or two foxes and bought some from old Shaglook.

Shaglook was kind of a chief at Icy Cape.[17] It was there that I first came to know him. He was a well-to-do Eskimo in those days. He was a good hunter. He caught lots of foxes and bought some foxes besides that, and he made a good living on furs. He even bought extra lead and black powder in case somebody was short of those. That's what he always did when I was a kid.

Life at Icy Cape
Every spring we go down to the coast below Icy Cape, by that lagoon, on the point with a big sandbar. That's where we marked the reindeer the first time.[18] And the next year we went to Aqia-ġuġnat, right across from Icy Cape. That time I began to know people. Every spring after the whaling they build canoes. Stand canoes up on their sides after the hunting and the walrusing and everything else is over. They call that *qargi*.[19] They worked around inside, just below the houses on the grassy place. They put up canvas and some walrus hide for a windbreak, put windbreaks all over the canoes, whichever way the wind blows. They turn the canvases up and move them to the wind side.

They start making anything they want to make. Some people build *umiat*. They pick up driftwood that washes ashore along the coast. If it was a good piece they always save it, tow it along, even the whole tree or long log. And they use their adze, and saw it, and split it when they are going to make an *umiaq* out of it. They do that. Everybody helps. I used to watch them when I play around with Icy Cape boys.

And all the women that stay down there in the tents and sod houses, they cook. They bring food at noontime and in the evening when suppertime comes. And they have a big feast together. The only time they eat in their houses is in the morning. When they cook and bring food to the qargi, they bring all kinds: walrus meat, *kauk, ugruk* meat, duck soup, lots of donuts, everything else.[20] They have a big dance at the qargi and they have a big feast every day. Some people that have an oven on the stove, they cook biscuits. And everybody eats just what they want. That's how they live.

When they are working on something, when somebody builds a canoe, they help him. They help one another. A lot of people help when they start to lash the canoe on the upright.[21] They finish it in about two weeks easy, when the people help. The one that knows how to build good *qayaq,* he teaches the others what to do and they do what he tells them, the way the older people know how. And that's how everybody learns how to do things. That's how I learned.

When we stayed at Icy Cape in summertime, my mother always let me haul water for the old people.[22] They have a well way down there on the south side of the village. They dug two, three wells down there. There's no water at Icy Cape when the ice is gone. And they boxed the wells up with lumber all the way down to the bottom and put holes on the sides and bottom. The water shoots through, fills that up right to the brim when it rains.[23]

Us boys—Patrick Tukrook, Freddie Aishanna, Roy and William Niugalak—we always haul water to the older people like Mickey Toorak's mother-in-law, Kignak, and Attungowruk and his wife Angalik, and Angoyuk. My mother always let me do that work. She always tell me to be good to the people and help them when they need help. That was when I was a kid. I didn't like to do it sometimes, but I have to. I always obeyed my mother when she told me what to do. My mother never let me drink tea and coffee until I was twenty-one years old. Maybe that's how I live longer, I don't know. I always just drink water after I eat. That's enough for me.

I played around with other boys my own age sometimes. Carl Mukpik and Alva Nashoalook were there too. Abraham Ilannik's kids were small boys when I was down there. Carl was the youngest one of those Ilannik boys. James was there too. James Kagak, that's Nannie's husband. Roy Niugalak was my own age and we always do the work for the old people. When they wanted meat they always tell me to go and bring some meat to those people, too. Sometimes my mother did that. I was shy when I was a kid, afraid of people. I thought they might scold me, but I had to go even though I was scared of the people I didn't know.[24] Frank Long was there and Kakmak and his wife and Irene Solomon. She's Kakmak's stepdaughter. He adopted her when she was a small girl.

Trapping and Traders

When I was a kid, that time we were reindeer herders staying between Point Lay and Icy Cape in late spring, in May when the weather gets long, we always had visitors, fur buyers.[25] And one year we had a visitor by the name of Johnson Kaiyak-pak. He was buying furs, working for Tom Berryman, who had a store down at Kotzebue.[26] He brought up a load of all kinds of stuff: rifles, and pots and pans, everything on the sled. Also he carried a large amount of cash. Those days they had only silver and gold money. There was no paper money when we were kids. And my stepfather bought a .22 single shot from Johnson. It cost him seven dollars.

I was only a small kid, somewhere around seven or eight, and they cut the stock about one third from the end and fitted an iron part there. And that's the first time I started to learn how to shoot a .22. My stepfather bought a whole carton of .22 cartridges, ten boxes to a carton. And they cost only twenty-five cents apiece. When I first start using it, I used it all day, shooting ptarmigan, and only got three out of fifty shots. But later on when I learn how to shoot, I got lots of ptarmigan with that .22.

And I always kept it clean when they told me to keep it clean. I had a rifle bag to carry it on my back whenever I followed some herders and shot some ptarmigan, or any bird— eider ducks, geese, everything else. When we're fawning in the reindeer camp, we have all kinds of birds. When they see reindeer they come to the reindeer and land nearby. When there's tundra—most of it was covered with snow—the birds go to the reindeer and graze around, eat. They have a feed there by the reindeer. They are never afraid of reindeer. When the reindeer dig the moss and the grass, them geese always land between the reindeer and start eating grass. Ptarmigan do that too. They never 'fraid of them reindeer. They always congregate in great numbers—sometimes twenty or thirty, forty or fifty—by the reindeer, on the lee side, when they were fawning. They stop there and wait out a storm, those geese and ptarmigan and pintails. Even the swans and white geese, they always go to reindeer when they see a reindeer herd. That's how it is when you are a reindeer boy.

I had that .22 for a long time, until the stock was getting too short. And then my brother John Koguyuk had it. I gave it to him when I got too big for that rifle. He had it for a long time too, but I guess the barrel was worn out with use, it was used so many times. It isn't accurate anymore when you shoot it.

The first time I trapped, I was going with my stepfather down this side of Point Lay, between Icy Cape and Point Lay. That's where I got my first foxes during that fall. He taught me how to cover the traps and how to find the right kind of snow to cover the traps when there's no snowfall during the week.

When we had a snow, you could use the fresh snow that builds up, and gather it, put it over the trap, knead it just easy. Cover it up with real soft snow, scrape it from the hard snow, and make it real level. That way the trap stays a long time and the wind never blows it away. Sometimes it blows away when it's a real strong wind, before it's settled in and stuck together. I always put my big knife under the spoon of the trap and then after I covered it all up, I pull the knife out, then knead it around, smoothly, easy, all over the trap. I leave it there with what they call in Eskimo *pukak,* that snow from underneath. It's just like grain. It builds up underneath when the cold weather sets in. And you have to dig underneath the snow and get that and sprinkle it all around over the trap. It always stays ready that way when the snow settles in. Yeah, I learned those things from my father. He must have learned them from the people that trap up here.

We set the traps early in the fall when he was looking for driftwood. We went after driftwood and he found a carcass right in the lagoon, a walrus carcass that was frozen in the lagoon. He just opened up a small hole. The foxes smell it and always go there. He had three traps right there. The traps were very scarce those days. He gave me only one trap and I set it there on one side of the walrus carcass. He had three traps right there. He caught foxes every day, but I never got hardly anything. Finally, one day I caught one. And later on I got another one. We were staying at the reindeer camp and it's only about two miles away from those traps. Just right for me to walk alone.

I just trapped there and that's how I got my first foxes. One time we went up there to look at our traps and I got a black one. My trap was on one side of the carcass. I could tell right away it was my trap when we got close. And I ran over there and stooped down and caught it. I was never even afraid he might bite me. And I held on to it for my dear life, even though he was trying to get up. My stepfather reached me and held it by the neck. And I stood up. I had a hard time holding it down. That fox just lifted me up and start to move around, but the trap always stopped it. I don't know how much my stepfather sold those foxes for. There's high price for blue fox.[27] It must be about two hundred dollars or something.

And then, after that I never trapped for long time. Only my stepfather was trapping. But when I got older and we moved back to Icy Cape, that's where I started to trap.

When I first came to live in Icy Cape there was no store on the coast except at Barrow, I guess. It was too far to go up there and buy something when we were living at Icy Cape. We went without White man food all summer until the ships came. Boy, everybody always got together when they first brought the flour and baking powder. They made big biscuit and have a big feast right there at the qargi.[28]

The people down there at Icy Cape, when they bought groceries from the ship, they only had them for as long as they lasted during the winter. Tea and coffee were really cheap; they were in bulk. They bought them with their furs to last them all winter. Some of the people got a whole case of tea. A box was about three or four feet maybe. Yeah, some of them always had tea and coffee. In those days it came in a crate with COFFEE written on the sides in big letters. And that's how you knew it was coffee.[29] That was before they started to have those MJB and Hills Brothers. We never saw any cans when I lived at Icy Cape, no canned food or tea or anything.

Boy, we always try to make some kind of biscuits. My mother used to cut meat into small pieces and mix it with bird's eggs, or anything like that to make it tastier. I liked that. They're good eating but I was always anxious to see the ship come. Oh, I was hungry for White man's food. I know my cousin Henry, one time he was crying because he was so hungry for White man's food. As soon as the ships came everybody started to make donuts. Boy, they tasted good. That's the best food I ever eat when I was a young boy.

The ships always stopped at Icy Cape whenever they saw people camping there. They know they could buy some furs. We went out to the ships with a canoe, got on board and told them whatever we wanted. Yeah, I remember everybody went out with a skin boat when the boat was anchored right in front of Icy Cape. MacRidge and Charlie Nayakik and Alva Nashoalook always were interpreters when buying White man's food.

And they sold lots of Native products: skins and furs and sealskins and some reindeer meat. They always bought those from us. They always used to buy meat, fresh meat from people that live up here. Riley always sold some fresh meat, sometimes four or five carcasses, six sometimes. The most he sold, I guess, was about ten to one ship. Those days sailors always bought some ducks and everything else for the crew. We traded those for White man's food. They also brought some black powder. When we were grown up they started to come in all those ready-made cartridges, shells like .38-55 and .45-70 and .30-30, .25-20, and .32s. They started to carry them when we became young men. Before that all the people loaded their own; they bought lead and black powder.

They had that black powder in tins. They had a big tin of black powder, about three pounds or five pounds. When my stepfather bought one of those five pound tins of black powder, it lasted me all fall. I was shooting as much as I could. I never used it all up, even though I used it all the time while I was hunting.

Capt. Bodfish in full
Arctic regalia. The tusk
weighed 44 pounds.
(Bodfish Collection #41,
negative #13489:
The Whaling Museum, New
Bedford, Mass.)

They put another canoe right here and make it round, make it a good windbreak—make good place to stay sitting around. (P343: Arnold Lloyd Liebes Collection, Special Collections/Library, California Academy of Sciences.)

Supplies from the ships. (P660: Arnold Lloyd Liebes Collection, Special Collections/Library, California Academy of Sciences.)

John Peter Ahlook.
(Acc. #79-14-42 N:
Eva Alvey Richards
Collection, Archives,
Alaska and Polar Regions
Department, University of
Alaska Fairbanks.)

2

Visiting My Stepfather's Relatives in Teller

The Trip to Teller

When I was ten or twelve years old, my folks decided to visit their relatives in Teller. My stepfather was homesick for his relatives. We went out on the old *Bear*, the Coast Guard cutter.[1] When they stopped at Icy Cape we got on the *Bear* and sailed towards the south, then went up to Siberia where the reindeer herds are. The captain must have known those reindeer herders before. He wanted to buy some reindeer meat from those Siberian Eskimos. They killed four reindeer, nice fat ones, and we brought them down to the ship.

When we stopped there, a boat came out and visited us with a bunch of Siberian Eskimos, women and men all mixed together. That's the first time I saw their clothing. Their clothes were really different from ours. They have a big hood and a sack behind it on the back. That's where they put their babies when they pack them. They have a union suit with a big hood, fur inside. The women paint their clothing with reddish rocks on the skin side, after they tan them, I guess. And the men don't have any painted clothes. And I could never even understand them when they were talking.[2] They have a different language than us. But I saw the guy that sold reindeer to the U.S. He was there. He used very good English, the one they told me that sold reindeer to Alaska.

The Coast Guard sailors and the crews and one of the mates walked up to see the village. They have a school building and maybe four houses, frame buildings, and the rest were sod houses. Those people were living on the north side of East Cape, near the big river where it goes inland. It's got a big, long bay. When we left from there, we went in through that river to get some fresh water. They started pumping water to the boat, filled the boat with water, and then took it to the ship that was anchored nearby. The water was all blue and real deep.

After we got some water we started out, crossed from East Cape to Cape Prince of Wales. The water was so rough, we didn't stop there. We kept on going down to Diomede Island. When we reached Diomede it was really pretty good. The ocean wasn't so rough on the lee side. We went ashore and I went along with the crew. I followed them wherever they went; I was only a small kid. And after I saw those people, we went to King Island on the west side. The village was there. They had poles underneath their houses right on the cliff, small platforms. And we went ashore there; pulled our boat on top of the rock. We visited with the King Islanders. They have steps in back of the houses that go up to the top. I went up there because I wanted to see from the top. It was nice and flat and grassy. Short grass was growing there. Nothing but ocean everywhere. But there's lots of birds there on King Island. It's a rookery for birds, a nesting place on the south end. Boy, there's lots of birds, all kinds of seabirds, thousands of them.[3]

And from there we started toward Teller. But the captain decided to go right straight to Nome when we got close to the coast, so we got off at Nome.

The teachers also traveled on the cutter from Icy Cape.[4]

Mr. and Mrs. Geary, those teachers, were teaching in Icy Cape, but their terms were up, so they went out with us on the old *Bear* and they came ashore at Nome, too. They had two kids. The oldest girl was Anna and I forgot the youngest kid.

When we got off there, my stepfather, Andrew Ahneovak found an apartment. And we stayed in the apartment while we were in Nome for a few days, about a week anyway.

That time Nome people had a reindeer herd, big herd. The Lomens had a herd, too.[5] And we had a relative that was working in Nome by the name of Tagotak; my stepfather told me he was my uncle. He gave us a lot of reindeer meat while we were staying there. And we had that meat until we left Nome. And when we were staying in the apartment they had everything: stove, cooking utensils.

There was a gold rush in those days.[6] Miners were digging sand on that little creek in front of the Nome village houses. They dug sand and panned gold. There were some people who made thirty-five dollars a day, or if someone is lucky, they made fifty dollars a day. On both sides of that little creek the miners were lined up, a whole bunch of them.

The first time I saw that, I met a young man of my own age, Robert Mayokok; that's where I got acquainted with him. We were really pals when we stayed at Nome. We were just kids, but we worked with the miners, doing errands for them, and earned five dollars a day while we were there. That was the first time I saw money. I never saw any kind of money before. I learned from this boy, Robert Mayokok.[7] He taught me what money is worth—dollars, quarters, and everything, when they paid me. We were doing errands for fishermen, too, while we stayed there.

I didn't want to leave when I was making money, but my folks wanted to go back home to their relatives, so we had to go, and I gave in. While we were there, I bought some salmonberries. Somebody was trying to sell salmonberries, a bucketful for fifty cents.

We left on a little boat, a power boat about thirty feet long, I guess, with a house on it. My father paid the boat owner some money, I guess, to take us to Teller people.[8] We left early in the morning and we reached Teller late in the afternoon. We went to the far side, on the north end of the bay. That's where the Eskimos live. That place was called Mitchak.[9] We took our stuff—clothing and bedding equipment—and went ashore.

And we were fishing all summer.[10] When all the fish runs were past in the fall, and when the school time came, I went over to the Lutheran Mission School. My folks built a sod house there at Mitchak with their relatives. My parents were living right close. My stepfather Andrew Ahneovak's sisters and brothers were living there; they helped us build a sod house. We lived three years down there at Teller.

Teller Mission
The principal of the school was T. L. Brevig.[11] He had three daughters: Dagny, Thelma, and Lorene. Lorene was Outside at high school someplace. Those two daughters, Dagny and Thelma, were teachers at that time. They were graduated teachers.

We lived there at the school. There was a lot of schoolchildren, almost over a hundred I think.[12] We had some assistant teachers too, girls older than us. They were helpers in the school. And one of them was Emma, Emma Willoya.[13] That's who my teacher used to be when I was small kid, when we first went to Teller. She was about twelve or thirteen years old. And I went to school there for only three years and got up to fourth grade. I just learned to read a little bit. Later on, I educated myself with books while I was in reindeer camp.

The Teller Mission School had a reindeer herd there. In the fall, just before freeze-up, reindeer herders came from Marys Igloo. They butchered reindeer. We had all the fresh meat we wanted after they butchered reindeer. We even salted the bulls they butchered. After you salt them, they are good eating.

There were three buildings at Teller Mission. One was the dormitory we lived in, and the other was a schoolhouse, big one, and one was a warehouse. Us boys kept the fire going when I went there. Two boys at a time made a fire early in the morning for one week. The other boys took their turn watching the schoolhouse and building a fire every morning, the whole year round.

Older girls from sixteen on up did the washing in the washing machines that were put in the warehouses. They put all the clothes together and wash them in a big bunch. But after they put them in the basket, we always put them up on the line. They made us work sometimes when the girls got tired, I guess. There was another girl, that older girl that was never married. She was about twenty years of age by the name of Dagny too, Eskimo girl. She was sort of a boss around our older girls when she was there.

When we went to bed early in the evening, about an hour before, those girls always taught us the catechism from the Bible. Each one of us had to learn everything in those booklets.

And on Thanksgiving we always had a big feast. Old Brevig always invited the men from down at the Eskimo village and sometimes from Teller. I guess what he liked was to always invite them for a big dinner.

They always gave us a job, some of us doing the dishes, and the girls in the cook's room. Some days when my time comes, me and the other boys, we always mix one hundred pounds of flour to make bread dough. We got big sticks and mixed it up in a big wooden box, put seasoning in it. There was also a cook by the name of Miss Wiggerson. She was an old lady but she was a good cook. And the old cook, Miss Wiggerson, was bossing us around when we did things. We always kneaded that flour when we made dough—put aprons on and kneaded it on top of the table for one hour, I guess. That was hard work we used to do. But they never forced us to work if we didn't want to. My partner was Leonard Sublugak when we were kids. He was my chum.

And we were sleeping in the same bed every night. The dormitory had a partition in the center. And you never visited the girls. There was no door on the partition, but you could go down to the ground floor level and go through the door and go to the girls' room, if you had permission from that old lady, Miss Wiggerson. She really bossed us around, us boys and girls. Sometimes the older boys razzed her when we were working in the kitchen, and tied something to her skirt—tin can or spoon, whatever they had. I always had pity on that old lady. I didn't ever do those things when I was a kid; I was afraid I might get scolded. But the other boys, the older ones always did that, and they never even told her who did it. When she asked around, they never told her. Sometimes that woman was really getting mad. But every boy used to like her a lot. Sometimes she gave us a special treat, big cookies or cake or whatever she wanted. That's why I liked her.

Every Sunday all the people always came to church at Brevig Mission from the sand spit where their houses were. And after church they had a big tea. Sometimes they gave them tea or coffee or whatever, and biscuits. And after they had a snack or noontime meal, they went back home in the evening, after church. They spent all day Sunday at our place. They always came at church time, and on Saturday I went over there and spent the night with my parents, go back on Sunday evening.

One of the young men was there trying to learn how to be an aŋatkuq, that's shaman. He always listened around.[14] He just did that to impress us. He wasn't aŋatkuq, but he learned the songs that an aŋatkuq sings in those days. He always sang when he started to play. I liked to watch him. All the older boys were standing around on the side when he played in the mid-

dle of the floor. That would keep us quiet for some time. Brevig
never scolded him. I was surprised. I thought he would never
let those things happen. Anyway he wasn't aŋatkuq. He just
learned the songs and tried to become an aŋatkuq. Us boys
learned his songs. Every time he sang one I learned it myself.

On weekends we always went down to visit our folks. And
whenever they had Eskimo dances after school we visited
down there. They used to have dances there, down at the village. It was about three miles away. But my father built a house
right there—big, big room, big enough for us. And we stayed
there all the time. But when there was something going on we
went down to the village. My stepfather had a sister and brother
down there. His sister was named Kimachook, Mary Kimachook. And she's got a husband and two kids, only two kids.
And my uncle, the youngest one was never married yet when I
was down there. His name was Aseaginna. I named one of my
sons after him. And my mother named one of my half-sisters,
Mary Kimachook—that's Wesley Ekak's wife—after her.

And sometimes we had a visitor from Cape Prince of Wales
too. They brought some reindeer from Cape Prince of Wales.
And while I was there, they had a big dance one time in the
Eskimo village. The two persons came from Cape Prince of
Wales carrying messages to Teller people. That's the only time
I watched when they were telling the people what they would
bring when they went to Cape Prince of Wales. Yeah, that's the
only time I saw two messengers that came from Cape Prince of
Wales to Teller to get the men for running a race and to take
part in the big dance at the Cape Prince of Wales.[15] I only saw
two *kivgat*—that's messengers. They come and stayed with us
for one night and went to the village the next day. They came
down with a dog team from up there. They had a dog team
driver and they walked. When they got close they got off the
sled and walked to our place and spent the night.

I went to the dance when they had a dance for them two

messengers. I watched the dances down at Eskimo village and went home before midnight. That's the only thing I know on kivgat.[16]

They always told us to come home around ten o'clock, us older boys. So we had to watch the clock while we were watching the dances down there and we didn't stay very long. Had to come home. It's a few miles I guess, from the village to the Teller Mission School.

And after that, when they started back to Cape Prince of Wales, some of the people were taking their families and some food, carrying them on the sled. Berries, and wolverine skins— whatever they had—going to trade with the people at Cape Prince of Wales when they had a big dance.

They gave a big feast too, at Eskimo village up there. And every evening when we heard they were going to have a dance, we went down for that *Aqpatak*.[17] That's what they call it. That's the first time I'd seen it. That evening they brought me a plate of berries all mixed, and fat cream, and orange juice. Us kids, they always gave us all kinds of berries mixed together on the plate. And they let us eat those while we watched the dance.

That's the first time I saw motion dance. *Aniuraaq* is what they call it up here.[18] And they had that old-time dance aniuraaq at Cape Prince of Wales, but I didn't take part in it. We were in the school, but I saw it later on when they came back. They stayed up there for a long time, about a month anyway.

When we were in Teller we always went fishing out in the lagoon, made a hole when it froze up. We catch a lot of tom cod and flounders.[19]

Just before we started school, all the family men went up to the creek on the north side of us, about three miles or more from our place. And in late September they were fishing before the fish went out from that creek, just north of Mitchak village. All the men went up there to do some fishing when the weather got really cold, freezing every night. After we had fish, all the men went up there. My stepfather asked me to go with them so I went along and watched them fishing when the trout started running out from that creek.

That's where I learned how to fish with what they call *taluyak*.[20] They made the taluyak out of willows. And they pile up rocks right across the riffle of that river, heavy rocks right across, and they made a channel of three or four feet. And they put willow on top of those rocks, stand 'em up sideways, and put rocks to keep them from washing away. They put willows with an opening just wide enough for that little channel. And they put those sacks right there behind that and tied them. When it was full they pulled it out. Some of the men went way up and dropped ashes on the river, stove ashes on the riffle, and let it drift out. Fish don't like to swim through that, that's what the Eskimos of Teller said. They don't like to go through the ashes. They just go downstream before the ashes reach them. They get together, and that way people caught a lot of fish.

When the bucket is full behind the fish trap, they pulled it out and dumped it on the tundra, then spread out all the fish. And then after they worked all day, they divided those fish. We were fishing for three days, and we got fish every day. Thousands and thousands of fish we caught that way. And then they were divided among a number of men that went fishing.[21] We got a big pile for our own family, and we cut some willows around the river and covered them all up. After it was frozen good and strong when the snow comes in, we hauled them down to our camp. We got enough trout to have at our home for a whole winter, that year when I first went with my stepfather Andrew Ahneovak.

Every summer when the fish start to come in, we seine them with a net. We took what we wanted on the salmon run and got all kinds of fish—king salmon and everything else— and dried them up on the rack, on fish rack, and let the rest go every time when we were seining. Every family has a seine.

They always line up on the beach and down the coast seining. Even when they do that the fish never run away. They kept on coming, one behind the other. When we were fishing we could hardly pull the end of the seine on both sides. We let some of the fish run out before we pulled it in, there were so many fish that time.

We cleaned them and dried them just like Eskimos do. And we put the fish in with rock salt in wooden barrels, and filled it up with salt on the bottom and poured water in it. They always kept that way, anything we salted for the winter use.[22]

Grandmother Ahngulook

In Teller I saw my grandmother from my stepfather's side. Her name was Ahngulook. Boy, that woman was a really good sewer and good hunter. Every summer, late in August, she went up to the campsite in the mountains—walked up all the way, and us boys always carried her stuff. She spent two, three weeks up there trapping for squirrels and muskrats, also picking berries.[23] And weekends I always took some grub when my stepfather told me to bring some grub for her. I went up there, packing food and spending the night there, and the next day I came home.

That was about five miles up on the side of the hill. I don't know really for sure, but it's about five or six miles. Sometimes I stayed two days and followed her around when she looked at her traps. And she always carried a lot of pokes[24]—five or six, seven or eight—to fill up with berries, all kinds of berries, salmonberries and blueberries, blackberries.[25] They grow a lot on those streams up there. We had berries, all we wanted all year long when we were there, until it breaks up in the spring.

When the birds were migrating I found out that they always stop there, even geese, and snow geese, and long-legged ones—cranes. Those birds always stop there picking berries, eating berries. When my grandma wanted some, I always shot one bird and took it to her, fresh one. Sometimes she cooked it while I was there. We always had a good meal.

Boy, she really loved me, my grandma. She always made something, socks and everything, made out of squirrel or muskrat. In the evening she always sewed clothing. Sometimes she made me parki out of squirrels and muskrat and made parkis for her sons. She was always doing things all the time. She was a good, strong woman. She was not a big woman, but yet she's not too small. She had a packsack made out of sealskin, when she went out checking her traps. They put snares on bent willows and caught squirrels that way. Every time when we went there, we saw a squirrel hanging right there, choked to death. She was pretty good with those.

When I was in school, I never hardly used stockings. Once in a while I used stockings when I wore shoes, but when I wore boots, I always used those socks she made. She made me waterproof boots too, out of sealskin.[26]

Working at Nome

In the summer before fishing started, my folks and the rest of the Teller able-bodied men always went down with a boat to work at Nome. They had a small boat running back and forth all summer long. It must have been a tugboat, I don't know. It carried passengers back and forth to Teller and Nome all the time. Never stopped all summer long.

There were so many miners, they always had a brawl every night. I listened to them when we lived there, fighting and everything else. I was always afraid of White people when I was first down there. After I get to know them, I was never scared. When I went out after we had breakfast, my mother always stayed home, but me and my stepfather, we went out. And I worked around the fishermen and people panning gold, right at the mouth of that lagoon. That's where I was doing errands, me and Robert Mayokok and Dwight Tivook. He was there too. He was from Cape Prince of Wales. His folks were living in Cape Prince of Wales, but they always went to Nome sometimes to work there before the ship comes from Seattle.[27]

On the last part of August we always went home by the same boat. My stepfather made enough money to buy groceries during the summer, long before freeze-up. I don't know what it cost them to pay for the trip home and going down there, but Dad always had money to pay.

I was always glad to go to Nome and earn a little money. Sometimes I made five dollars a day. When there was not much to earn I got only three dollars or four dollars. And both Robert Mayokok and I, sometimes, when we did errands, they gave us fifty cents apiece every time we did some. And when we did that all day, we made five dollars and sometimes seven dollars, but boy, we never reached ten dollars even when we worked hard.

When we got hungry we went to the store there close to the beach and bought some sandwiches and juice. We ate on the wharf down there. After that we started looking around for some job. That's how I got to know Nome. He was familiar with Nome people, that Robert Mayokok. We were working all the time, doing some errands and helping the fishermen when they took off the fish from the net. And that way we always got free fish to take home, besides pay.

And after work we went home, eight-thirty. The policeman in Nome always told us to go home and go to sleep as soon as it was nine o'clock. Our folks never let us stay out. And every morning as soon as we had breakfast, I met Robert down near the wharf. I never even know where his folks lived, at that time when I got acquainted with Robert Mayokok. We had a lot of fun anyway. Sometimes when we couldn't find a job we just watched them panning gold. And after they got to know us we always get a job anytime. We even went to the stores to get what they wanted. They sent a note to the storekeeper to let us bring them something. When the store was a little further away, they always gave us a dollar apiece.

My folks stayed in that area for three years. And then on the third year, when the summer came, they decided to go back to my mother's relatives in Icy Cape. So we got on board the Coast Guard cutter—old *Bear* again—and started going north.

That's the boat I used to go in when we're going out to visit our relatives in Teller.
The *Bear* appears in the distance, 1921.
(BA 21-525: A. M. Bailey Collection, Denver
Museum of Natural History Photo Archives.)

John "Jack" Hadley,
Waldo's **uncle who** saved his life.
Point **Barrow**, Alaska, 1892?
(AC 10422: Sheldon Jackson Photo
Collection, Presbyterian Historical Society,
"Presbyterian Church (U.S.A.),
Department of History.")

Andrew Ahneovak with Waldo, in Teller. (North Slope Borough District Library. Picture taken by Patrick Rosenkranz in 1981 from an old picture of Waldo's.)

That's the school they have long time ago.
(P289: Arnold Lloyd Liebes Collection, Special Collections/ Library, California Academy of Sciences.)

Coastal Locations

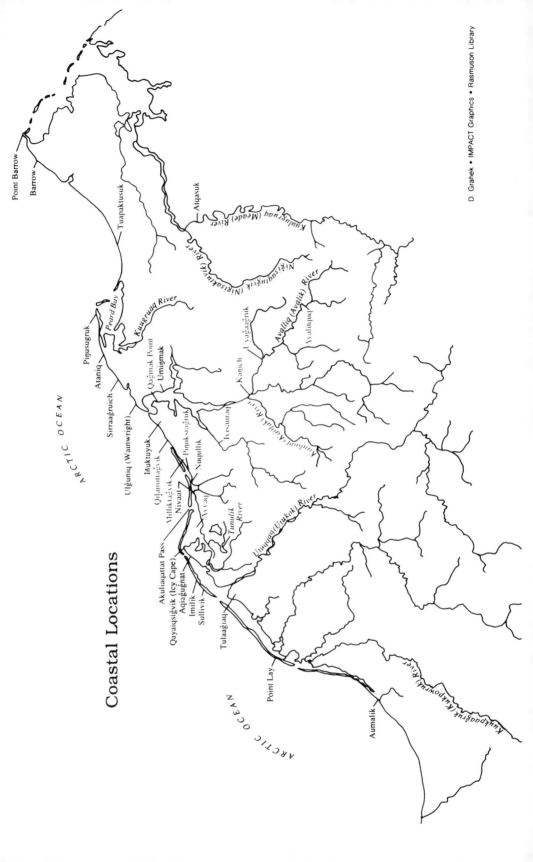

D. Grahek • IMPACT Graphics • Rasmuson Library

Point Barrow
Barrow
Tuapaktusuk
Atqasuk
Kuulugruaq (Meade) River
Niġisaqtuġvik (Niṛisaḵtiṵvik) River
Avalliq (Avalik) River
Avalitqua
Kanich
Iyagaagruk
Pigusugruk
Peard Bay
Kuugruaq River
Ataniq
Qaġmak Point
Umigmak
Sirraagruich
Kugrua
Kuqpauraq (Kuuk) River
Ulġuniq (Wainwright)
Iñuktuyuk
Qilamittaġvik
Piŋuksraġruk
Milliktaġvik
Nivaat
Nuġullik
Attaq
Tuunlik River
Akuliaqattat Pass
Qayaiqsigvik (Icy Cape)
Aqiaġunat
Imiliq
Sullivik
Unugaat (Utukok) River
Tulaaġruaq
Point Lay
Aumalik
Kuukpaagruk (Kukpowruk) River

ARCTIC OCEAN

ARCTIC OCEAN

3

Growing Up Around Icy Cape

That year the ice was thick along the coast. The old Revenue Cutter *Bear*, after it stopped at Icy Cape, it worked its way up the coast. We couldn't come into Wainwright—too much ice pack—so we went on to Barrow, and passed it. We were drifting inside the ice and it was closing in on us. And we stayed there on the ice for a long time, but it never crushed us or anything. We always stayed in a small hole. Finally the wind changed and the ice began to slacken and scatter. As soon as it was slack we worked through the ice and got into Barrow, and we went ashore there. We stayed there for two, three days and then started home. They were supposed to put us off at Icy Cape, but the captain decided to put us off in Wainwright. That's the first time I saw Ulġuniq—Wainwright—when we were put off there.[1]

My First View of Wainwright
There were only a few sod houses and one small schoolhouse on the edge of the bank. There were only two frame houses

33

when we got there. The one belonged to Adam Nikkaktoak, Ben Tagarook's daddy. Martin's mother inherited it when her father died. And the other one, I think it belonged to Tagilook. Later on, Charles Nayakik's father owned it. It's still down there, used for a warehouse.

All the houses were on the edge of the bank. And there was grass in front of two little creeks. That big sand grass was growing all in front of the village, both ends of the village. Later, the high wind made waves that washed that land from below the bank. The Uḷġuniq people were camping in their tents below the houses on that bank.

They had a store there, run by Charlie Hanson, I guess. He moved from Icy Cape to there, to run a store for Backland. James Angashuk had a little store too, in his house, what is now his son Oliver's old house down there. Angashuk had a house, and a little store with supplies from Captain Backland. But it never lasted. He ran out of food before the winter was over; it was so small. That's what I heard, but I never saw him myself. And the school building was already up too.

My stepfather bought a canoe from old Agnasagga. He was living here in Wainwright at that time. We sailed down the coast with Susook's dad and his family, the Pootkakroak family, and old Neakok. Neakok was a funny man. He made us laugh all the time when we were traveling. We traveled down there around the first week of September, before freeze-up. The reindeer herds were down at Nuqullik when we passed them.

My father bought a house from Peter Panik there at Nuqullik on that point. They had a good house there, and they figured they were going to winter at the Nuqullik River, way back up there. That's where they wintered when we first came back.

Whalers Adrift from Barrow

I remember, later in the spring, two boats came ashore when the whaling season was open. I didn't know where they came from. These two canoes had drifted out when they were whaling at Barrow earlier in May.[2] And they came ashore just a little this side of Point Hope, in front of two mountains that stick out close together on the coast called Iviaŋŋiik. They call them Iviaŋŋiik, which means woman's tits. They spent a month out there on the pack ice. And after they hit the coast at Iviaŋŋiik, they started to work up north pulling their skin boat. They came ashore right there and worked all the way up to the reindeer camp.

I remember them when they were approaching. Later on, my mother told me they drifted out from Barrow when they were whaling, and they had been out there for a whole month. They came ashore there in the late spring. When they first drifted out from Barrow, they drifted way down—almost reached Cape Prince of Wales. When the ice started working north they lost sight of land until they hit the coast there near Point Hope. That was the first time they saw land. Some of the men, they recognized the place down there, that place called Iviaŋŋiik. They knew Point Hope was close, but they kept on moving toward Barrow, where their home was. Jack Hadley, my mother's sister's husband, was with them.

They were real hungry people. All the hunters looked around for food. Sometimes one guy got a seal. And they cooked a meal there, used the blubber for fire. They just skinned the seal with the blubber on, and spread it on the fur. And they built a fire right there in the center and ate boiled seal meat. They were out of White man's grub, and that's the way they were living.

They always moved back out to the pack ice when the storms came, moved to solid ice and lived in snow houses.[3] They got a polar bear while they were drifting out there on the heavy ice. One day a bear came. They shot it and cut the skin to make soles for the bottom of their boots. They lashed it on their boots while it was raw. They used that polar bear skin to keep them from making holes on the bottom of their boots.

When the storm was over they packed their things, pulled

their sled with a canoe, and started going to the lead way up there.[4] But they never saw the land until they reached that Ivianŋiik. That's the first time they got close to the solid ice that was stuck on the shore, and crossed there through the young ice.[5] That's the first time they tried to come ashore. Before that, when the sea was rough, they had to go back out to the solid pack ice again. They spent a whole month out there, over a month, I guess.[6] They came ashore in June.

And when they reached us, the women of the reindeer herders fixed their boots, patched them up and everything else. They gave them grub: reindeer meat, birds and anything else. They got their food from Icy Cape people: whale meat, maktak and everything else. They were really hungry for tobacco, them people that smoke. That's what I heard afterward; I didn't know anything about it when I first saw them. When they reached Wainwright, they sailed from there to Barrow after the ice went out, going back home to Barrow. I didn't even know when they left our camp. I must have been playing with Henry, or sleeping.

Traveling with the Reindeer Herders

Wesley Ekak had a position then as a reindeer herder. Riley apprenticed him when Mickey Toorak's term was expired. Those people became regular herders: Mickey Toorak, Michael Keogak, MacRidge Nayakik, Charlie Nayakik, and old Riley Ahlook, Fred Anashugak, Henry Peetook's daddy Thomas Tazruk, and my stepfather, Andrew Ahneovak. I was the one that was herding for Andrew, my stepfather. I just followed the reindeer herders; I was big enough to do the herding. My stepfather always gave me one reindeer a year while I was doing herding for him.

Just before the freeze-up we went to Nivaat and built sod houses there. At that time, Henry, old Riley, and I, we sailed down to Piŋuksraġruk with a whale boat to get a load of coal from that coal mine there. It's a little bit south of the shelter cabin. We got a load of coal and hauled it back to Nivaat for the fall and winter fuel. There was a lot of driftwood on the north side and south side of the lagoon, on the sand spit. That's where we built our sod house, dug in through the sand, lots of loose sand; that's why they named the place Nivaat.[7]

When the fawning time was getting close we moved down toward the Uqsruq River. We went over that big hill and camped on the river. Tunulik, that's what they call that river. They started fawning and we followed the river down to the mouth of Tunulik. We followed the Avvaq River down to mouth, to Qiuġruaq. That's the narrow place on the Avvaq River where they used to get spotted seal. That's where we stopped. Before the river broke up we moved down to the coast again, south of Icy Cape on the point there. Several years before, Riley built a frame house down on the point down there. That's where we hit the coast and stayed before the reindeer marking time comes. We just herded them there on that peninsula and kept them from crossing the Avvaq River. We watched them regularly.[8] And when the marking time came we moved to Shaglook's place.

We were marking fawns on the sand spit toward Icy Cape, on that beach. Shaglook always followed us when we started marking. That's how I got acquainted with him and he began to like me real well. Old Shaglook.

Old Shaglook

I learned lots of things from old Shaglook. He always told me what to do on hunting trips. That's how I learned from him— part of my experiences. He told me how to build a snow house real quick and things like that. He taught me to make a spear and a dart for birds.[9] He had all kinds of equipment. I watched his tools and equipment. That's how I learned from him to build my own when I started to go hunting, when I was old enough to hunt. I made *unaaq,* trying to follow his equipment.[10]

Shaglook was a big trapper of white foxes. He told me he went inland when the trapping season opened and also trapped along the coast. And he went up close to Utuqqaq, way up there at the headwaters of Uqsruq. That's where he trapped. He spent the winters up there and then he came down and watched his traps on the coast. Sometimes he made a trip down the coast with his two daughters and looked after his traps.

He always set a big bear trap on the ice in the middle of winter, around March. He put a big log standing up, put a marker on it. It was about a quarter of a mile from the beach, on the coast so nobody will be in danger unless they go out there. When I went to see him one time, he was marking all around the place of the trap. He had a big log standing up, right on the edge of the rough ice, and marked it, and had three short ones right around the trap.[11] He put blubber in there and set the trap. That way he always caught a bear—one or sometimes two during the winter. That's how he hunted.

He always told me that sometimes he got over four hundred foxes and he was buying furs at the same time from his friends around Icy Cape. People gave him furs in exchange for ammunition: black powder, lead, primers, loading tools, and everything else. Those days people had loading tools. All the families that lived around there had loading tools for their rifles. They used black powder and primers. They bought enough to last all winter long. They loaded all year round when they were hunting. Old Shaglook had a lot of those supplies. Some people, when they couldn't find any black powder and lead and primers, they went to Shaglook and bought all they needed. That's how he got rich, I guess. He always had something whenever someone needed food. He always gave them food without it costing them anything, but he always bought furs from them whenever they had a fox skin to sell.

And then when the ships came, he had a partner by the name of *Karluk,* the small schooner with two masts. The ship always brought some supplies for him. He made orders before the ship went back Outside, and when the ship came back he traded for what he wanted. Sometimes he got two and three boatloads when they lightered supplies from the *Karluk* to shore. They sometimes had to make two boatloads.[12]

He bought some lumber from that ship too. That's how he built that lumber house. He built his house himself, and he used to have a small warehouse to keep the flour in when I first came to know him. He always had an automatic rifle, but he had all kinds of other rifles too.

Shaglook's wife was quite a trader. She ruled her husband when he was trying to sell a fox. If she wasn't satisfied with what the guy offered, if she wanted more, she kept trading until she satisfied herself and sold all the furs they had. That's the way she was, old Shaglook's wife, Mayaroak. Shaglook called her Mayak and some other people called her Mayaroak.[13] She ruled the business whenever she started buying something from the trader. When the price for fur was getting low, they were broke too, just the same as anybody else.

He was smart, that old Shaglook. He was a good hunter all around. And he was kind of a leader to the Eskimo people. He was kind of *umialik,* chief, around Icy Cape when I used to know him.[14] He was a good athlete when he was a young man. He was one of the best runners of Utuqqaġmiut people, when they raced from Ittutchiaq, that high hill way up there on the east side of Point Lay. People all the way from Nuataaq came to that place and visited Utuqqaġmiut. They started racing from there. Normal travel, it was a three day run to the mouth of the Utuqqaq, but Shaglook made it in one and a half days when they were having a foot race. When he stood around his heels never touched the floor. He stood on the front of his feet, never touched the floor with his heels, even though he was an old man. I liked to visit with old Shaglook when I was reindeer herding.

Marking Reindeer

When we were about to start marking reindeer, we made a kind of corral. There's a big roomy place on the north end of the Aqiaġuġnat on that sand spit, near Shaglook's place. That's where we marked them. We let them in and followed the edge of the coast, and drove them over there, and left them there. We had sticks standing up with a rope around them, right around that corral. And when we started to lasso the fawns, they never went away. Some of the people that lived there went around that corral and watched the herders lasso the fawns and mark them. They had a lot of fun themselves too, watching the marking. All the young people always came from Icy Cape to see the reindeer. Every time we came to the coast we had a lot of visitors, people that walked up there.

Whenever my parents needed meat I always butchered one reindeer and took it down to my family at Icy Cape. And then I went back home to the reindeer herd. Whenever I wasn't herding I walked down and stayed with my folks, visited all day there. And I came to know Freddie Aishanna, Roy Audlakroak, Pigaaluk, and Amos Agnasagga, Kanayuk family, Ahloak's family, Ehlook's and Kutuk's family, Ilannik's family, all those people, Panik family. I got to know them when I started visiting them down there when I was a teenager.

Whaling Time
When the whaling time came, Riley sent two reindeer herders to each of the different crews to go whaling for one week at a time. When the week was up, another two took their place when they came back. That's the hardest time I ever had. That's the first time I had a hard time. I had warm clothes, but not warm enough. When I first went out whaling in Icy Cape with Kakmak, we had no tent. We only had a windbreaker made out of canvas and poles, and snow blocks on the east end piled up as high as your shoulder. That's where we always slept.

Boy, when I tried to sleep and the wind blew, I was really cold. Cold got right through me. Sometimes when our cook was sleeping, we didn't drink hot tea. I didn't know how to start the fire by myself. This boy by the name of William Niugalak, he was pretty good at making a fire. Sometimes me and Frank Long had to wake him up in order to start the fire when we wanted to have a meal, some kind of a meal—seal meat, whale meat, maktak, duck soup.

We had a fire pot from a sailing ship. It was sort of a pot, about a foot and a half long and a foot and a half wide, and it had a cross bar right in the center. They built a fire right in the center and put blubber inside and cooked our meals. They made soup in a big pot that stands on top of the fire pot. It really cooks fast, that kind of stove. It makes seal meat, whale meat; whatever you cook, it takes no time to boil.

That time we were out whaling, we didn't get a whale. The other two boats got one each, that was enough. They didn't want to get any more. That was enough for the whole winter they said. Whales came up every day while we were waiting down there on the edge of the lead. Big ones came up but they never bothered to shoot them. The only one they were looking for was a small whale.[15] Every day whales came up in front of us and we never went after them. I always wondered why they never went after those whales. And later on I found out.

Those days they had no block and tackle. They used rope, tied to ice blocks, and they pulled together when they cut the whale. They cut the maktak about three and a half feet wide, put a hole in the center, put the rope in the maktak and pulled it while the people were cutting it loose, rolling the whale as the maktak comes off. They cut the meat off too while it was in the water. That's how they cut whale in those times. Young people pulled the meat up quite a ways, sometimes a hundred feet away, there on the ice. Older people cut it down there, tightening the ropes at the same time. And they cut the whale up, and then they sawed off the head.[16]

We were only teenagers, but we went out with them when they went out paddling in the canoe, the skin boat we call umiaq. They made us paddle too, and when we started to let up they told us to keep on paddling. That was a tough one; I got tired of paddling sometimes. We hunted around for ugruk. When ugruk is feeding right in the middle of ocean he makes music. They make noise when they are feeding on the bottom and they call it *aviuqtaqtuaq*. Eskimo call that aviuqtaqtuaq.[17] We stopped and listened to find some ugruk. As soon as we heard it, we went toward them. And we got our bearings, where it was, and found them and got them.

Whales were still running but we never bothered to hunt them. We got all the ducks we could with shotguns. We had only one shotgun, so people took turns shooting ducks. And we boys, every time we came back to the camp, we hauled them into the Icy Cape village. And after we took loads of ducks to the Icy Cape village, we went right back out to the whaling camp.

Frank Long and I, we were the mess boys when we were whaling, and we helped the cook. We had a cook, a regular cook there to make our meals, but we always helped him get some water and snow and blubber and everything else. We always were helping him.

My First Kill

That's the time I got my first seal too, that same year when I was first whaling. This old man, Kakmak's father—his name was Kupaak—he had a rifle, .38-55. And he told me when the seals go on top of the ice, late in the whaling season when the weather gets warmer, to shoot that seal over there lying on top of the ice, on the flat ice. He didn't think I would get the seal. I went up there, walking on the edge of the lead with his rifle. And when I got abreast of the seal I started crawling up there. Kupaak was watching me with his big telescope. When I thought it was close enough, when that seal put his head up, I shot him and hit him right smack on the neck. And Kupaak was surprised, I guess. And the next day, Kupaak told his grandson, Frank Long, to go and shoot some seal whenever seals came up on the ice. And Frank went, but he missed the seal when he shot at it. Boy, he started to kid his grandson about missing that seal. He's not like me, he told him.

I gave that seal to an old woman by the name of Angoyuk. This very old lady lived down there. She was one of the first people at Point Lay. She was the mother of Johnson Tuginna and Neakok Knox. Anyway, she was the mother of those people. And my mother always let me give what I got—when I started to hunt seals and birds and things like that—to that old lady.[18]

She was living in Icy Cape. And that old lady, she made me a net for ptarmigan, a long one braided with sinew. Put the sticks on so far apart, put it in the snow. It was about fifty feet long or more. She made that, braided it all winter, and in the springtime she sent it to me. I was really proud of that old woman when she gave me that ptarmigan net.[19] I had it for a long time too. Whenever I went to Icy Cape while she was living, I always gave her some meat. I loved that old lady. She was a good old woman, Johnson Tuginna's mother.

Knud Rasmussen's Visit

When the whaling was over, Rasmussen came to Icy Cape from Wainwright.[20] That time at Icy Cape, I got to know Knud Rasmussen and a young boy who was traveling with him; Mitiq was his name. There was also a woman—Agnagolook, that's the woman—and she was sewing boots for them as they traveled west from Greenland. I just talked to Rasmussen once in a while, when I learned a little bit of English. He was telling about how he made the trip all the way from Greenland. The young boy, Mitiq, was a good hunter. Mitiq was the same age as we were, little bit older. He became a friend with Wesley Ekak. They went out hunting with a dog team while Mitiq was resting his own team. Mitiq had a little sled about from here to the couch, two or three feet long. It was a light one. And it had poles on the side and they put a white canvas up. That way they could sneak up on seals and shoot them. They got dog feed that way, easy. That's what we learned from Mitiq, how to use that hunting equipment. And I built a little sled like that one time and used it in Wainwright here after I was married. They're good—you can sneak up on a seal even on the flat ice. Just cover the top of your sled. Even if the runner shows, it doesn't bother the seal.

Rasmussen and those others stayed all spring. They stayed there till Nalukataq was over.[21] And I heard they moved south and reached Point Hope.[22] They left their dogs down there. Upicksoun got some of Rasmussen's dogs, and Wesley Ekak got some too. I always thought he hired a boat from Icy Cape to take them down all the way to Point Hope. My stepfather and I, we went back to the reindeer herd. And I didn't know what was going on there when they left.

Knud Rasmussen and his travelling companions. (Acc. #78-14-393 N: Eva Alvey Richards Collection, Archives, Alaska and Polar Regions Department, University of Alaska Fairbanks.)

That's a typical Eskimo, Mayaroak.
She's a shrewd trader, and a great cook. I used to love to eat her donuts.
Icy Cape, 1921.
(BA 21-025: A. M. Bailey Collection, Denver Museum of Natural History Photo Archives.)

4

Mastering Adult Skills

I really loved my parents when I was young kid. I always did whatever they told me and tried to do what was right with my reindeer and my friends at reindeer camp. That time I could watch the herd just as good as any man, even though I was a teenager. I never was afraid of anything. Once in a while I took some reindeer carcasses, butchered them and hauled them down to my parents to have meat besides brants and ducks.

Sometimes we had a hard time when my stepfather began to weaken. He got sick one year for a long time, and then after he got well he was kind of like he used to be. He quit herding, and I started herding then. He and my mother lived all the time at Icy Cape while we were there. But whenever I caught a fox I always sent it down to them to buy White man's food. They bought groceries, staple foods, like flour, sugar, tea, and coffee, and rolled oats, and things like that. They bought them all with furs. I don't know what they paid for fox at that time. I never found out. I never did business with people—I was only a kid.

When my parents lived down at Icy Cape, I always stayed with my uncle, Fred Anashugak, and Cora, his wife. I stayed with them all year round.

Kupaak's Brant Snares

One year I was at Aqiagugnat, down near Icy Cape. Frank Long told me that his grandfather and grandmother were going to Nivaat to hunt brant before they started migrating south. He took them up there. That time we had no outboard motor. He towed the canoe with dogs, then sailed across to Nivaat.[1] His grandfather was Kupaak. That's Kakmak's father. And his grandmother was Akamalutuk.

Kupaak had a rifle but no shotgun, and he had hunting equipment made by himself. He made several snares—put a flat piece of wood underneath and put a peg on the end and made baleen snares. He put them right in the center of the wood, so far apart, and made them pliable so they can be open all the time, even if they were in the water. They sink them down about two or three inches under water, those snares. And they put bait on the seaweed up there on the beach, on the slope of the beach, and spread them around. And when the brant came and saw those, when the brant were hungry, they landed there and started swimming over to the seaweed. And then while they were swimming along, they got their feet caught in the snares. Sometimes he got two or three from one bunch of brant without using anything else. They snared those brant all the time when they were there at Nivaat.

Just before freeze-up Kakmak asked me to go up there to help Frank Long visit his folks up there, to see how they were getting along late in the fall. And we went, me and Frank Tukumik and Frank Long, to bring some White man's food and some whale meat. Maybe, Kakmak thought, they were out of whale maktak.

When we arrived, there was a lot of brant hanging around on the rack. And I was surprised they got so many that way. I never thought they could really get that many. When I counted, it was over four hundred brant hanging there. And also they had a lot of ducks besides that. Eiders, all kinds of eiders—Pacific or King Eiders, or Spectacle and Stellar Eiders. They swam around and fed right on the edge of the water and got caught on those snares Kupaak put in the water during the night. That way he got all kinds of duck, even Pintail. Boy, I was surprised.

We stayed overnight and watched him when he went to check them. He said he always pulled his snares every night and put them in early in the morning at daybreak when the brant begin to fly. And they sat around outside their tent and watched. His wife was there too, on the edge of the beach, watching those snares. If they were closer, he told his wife to go get it. If they were farther out he went in a qayaq.

Afterward, I learned that everybody made snares down at Icy Cape when they gathered together at the qargi. But I never figured out what they were going to do with them—how they worked—until I went to Kupaak's camp that time.

Uncle Fred Anashugak

I was following Fred for a long time when I was young. I began to know what's going on, down there between Point Lay and Icy Cape. That's where I found out that he was my uncle, Fred Anashugak. He stayed with his brothers and sisters all the time while we were reindeer herders. When I was old enough I followed him around and learned a lot from him. And that's why I tried to imitate him. He was just like an older brother to me. I learned how to herd from him mostly. I followed some of the herders too, once in a while, but I never went with them often. Only Fred and I were real pals. Fred was a real pal to me.

He was married down there at Icy Cape on the last part of our stay. They had a triple marriage down there. MacRidge Nayakik and Charlie Aguvluk and Fred Anashugak. MacRidge married Samantha, Charlie married Grace Kelignik, and Fred married Cora Ayalgook. That was the first time I saw people married in a schoolhouse. And that's the first time I saw a preacher who married people.[2]

I never thought about Cora—that's Mark Kutuk's daughter. I never knew she was to be the wife of Fred. When I went down to Icy Cape and visited with Icy Cape people, she was always good to me when I met her. That was to be Fred's wife! I didn't know that. I didn't even suspect. And after they married, when I became a teenager, I always stayed with Fred and his wife until I became a young man.

Fred, he was young teenager when I was small kid, a few years older than me. He was a pretty good Eskimo songmaker. Fred always sang all the time and made new songs, Eskimo songs. And sometimes when we went to Icy Cape, he taught them to Icy Cape people, dancers. They used them all the time too! In the early days of my life I used to remember them, but I hardly sing anymore. Mattie remembers them pretty well; she's a dancer.[3]

Snow Houses

My uncle taught me lots of things. When I was a kid growing up at the reindeer herd, I learned how to build a snow house from my uncle and other people, just watching them. When we were going to move we always went from the reindeer camp and built a snow house.

We always moved inland in January. The first thing when we were going to move, old Riley sent men to build the snow houses. They fixed snow houses with a tent inside. All you had to do was put your tent inside when you reached there. All the family men went up there. When we were old enough to keep the reindeer herd, they left us young people to watch the herd.

When you make a snow house, you have to have a saw, a shovel, and a big knife. That's all you need. When you are fitting snow blocks in the wall, you fit it with a big knife. You put the blocks flush against the other blocks that you put on already. Then put soft snow between those blocks and fill it up from the outside. You have to put soft snow on every seam so it will be nice and cozy when you go inside. The wind or draft won't go in through the seam on the snow blocks you put up.

When you have no *talu* for an entrance you have to build a new block of snow to cover it, put the hole in the center. And pull it in after you go in, close it. We put a rope in the center and pull it in when we close it. And in the morning, just push it out and go out. That's the way we used to do when we built snow houses. But sometimes you have a bearskin—those bearskins were just the right type—or a caribou skin. We call them talu in Eskimo. Put a stick right across, on the center of the caribou skin, and put a string on the top and hang it in front of the talu. Keep the fur toward the inside. I always carry a bearskin, brown bear, that I shot years before, and use it for talu. I carry it around all the time when I go trapping or somewhere.

We always put a tent inside, no matter where we are. If you live on the coast, when you go up inland or down the coast, you build a snow house. After the stores got canvas from the States, we always made a seven-by-five tent for ourselves, each trapper. And we put up a tent every time we reach the place where we got a snow house. It's nice and warm as could be, just like any other permanent house. Before canvas, I used to have a caribou skin to cover the top. It was always warm that way too, until the snow house got very old.

When ice forms all around inside, the snow house always gets cold, no matter how you heat it. When you sleep, boy, it's really cold, always cold when you put the stove out. But it's always warm when the stove is going. You have to make another house when it gets like that. Too icy, thick ice. You can use that old one for the hallway.[4]

Sod Houses

Afterward, I started to build sod houses. It's more comfortable when you live in a sod house. I use a frame of willows, big wil-

lows in the Kuulugruaq River. I mean Niġisaqtuġvik, Meade
River way up there.[5] There's a lot of willows around, nice and
straight when I cut those, enough to build a house. I frame it
with big willows, long ones. Tie them together and put them in
the ground. After I lash every willow, then I start to put the sod
around it. You start it from the bottom all around and then go
to the top, until you finish the top part of the house. Cover it all
up and then you put another layer on top of that *ivruq*. I cover it
with nice soft...what you call that? *Nuna,* we call it nuna, ivruq.[6]
We use that soft ground, soft sod about four inches thick. You
cut it in blocks behind the willows. They always have that ivruq
sod, sod that is good for building houses.

Boy, it's really warm that way. I cover it with soft snow all
around, on top, everywhere. Boy, it's really warm there, that
top snow, when you put *niñŋuq* on top of it.[7] That's what they
call it in Eskimo. Soft snow, when you are putting it on top of
the sod, is niñŋuq. Inside that house you could dry everything—your clothes, harness, whatever you have. Your canvas
cover, your tent, you could dry it up in that place. I stand up
inside, walk around without my parki. It's a big room. That's
how I build my sod houses.

Caring for Reindeer

Sometimes when I was herding and the herd strayed, I went
after them and spent the night without anything. I just cut the
snow blocks and made a windbreak, spent the night with the
herd. And the next morning when the day came, I went home.
But my mother never worried about me when I stayed overnight out there without anything to eat. I survived all right.

One time when I was herding at Qilamittaġvik, I was
watching the herd right at the edge by Aulataġruaq River. And
the darn reindeer, some of the herd crossed the river, swam
across. I didn't know it until they had crossed already. The
river was narrow on the south side of the bay, but wide enough

to swim across. That's where they went across, on the point, on the sand spit.

I took all my clothes off and tied them with my lasso in a bundle on the top of my head, and I swam after those reindeer. They were going up the hill, quite a long ways away. When I saw them the next time, I sent my reindeer dog, and he caught them and brought them back to me.

I drove them out to the edge of the lagoon. And I did the same thing, took my clothes off and put them on top of my head and started to swim across with the herd following me. And when I got to the middle, a spotted seal pup was alongside of me and scared the heck out of me plenty. I thought he was going to bite me, but he never touched me. Sometimes he went under me and came up on the other side. I swam across holding on to the reindeer's tail. I didn't have hard work. But I was scared like anything from that spotted seal. I thought he was going to bite me on my leg or on my arm or belly. When I reached a shallow place he went off. Boy, I was scared!

The reindeer herders were very strict in those days about taking care of a herd. You had to learn all the things that the reindeer herders were supposed to do. When I was a kid I used to watch people. I used to watch reindeer herders when they were taking care of the deer in fawning season. They carried a little stick when fawning was going on in the middle of May, and they checked all the reindeer fawns that were born in the herd that day.[8] They checked to see whether it was a male or female, and they recorded it on the paper.

They always told us not to touch the baby fawns with our bare hands or mittens, because the mother will desert him and leave him if he smells of a person.

And when a storm came, some herders used to take care of the ones that were on the windward side of the herd, where the storm was drifting snow into them. If they were young fawns able to walk, they moved them to the inside of the herd so they had a windbreak. But if they couldn't walk, they always cut blocks of snow and put a windbreaker on them. And that way you save the fawns from freezing when it was stormy.

We even helped the reindeer when they couldn't have a baby—when the fawn had trouble being born. We pulled the baby out. That way you saved the mother, but the fawn always died before it was born. And some of the reindeer used to have stillborns, and premature ones, little fawns that were born and died.

I found out that fawns that were born in the last part of April and the first part of May were always the healthiest. Those that are born later are weakest, even though the weather is warmer. They begin to grow more slowly than the ones that are born in the cold weather. That's what I found out when I used to be a reindeer herder.

You have to keep your herd moving around all the time. You never let them stay in one place. Keep on moving to where there's good grazing. If you let them stay in one place they eat all the grass. If you let them stay too much, the fawns always start to weaken; their mothers don't have much to eat on the tundra.

When the young fawns get tired they stop and stay in one place for a while. And after they rest up, they move back to the herd again. They always come back. They never try to stray off away from the herd. Only the yearlings and the males do that. They are really wild when you're fawning in late May, when the bare spots begin to show up on the tundra and the wind is blowing gently. When they smell something, they run off like anything. And the last part of May, first part of June, they always have buck fever. I call it spring fever. They want to run off every direction, those yearlings and the bulls and others. They keep you on your toes all the time, running everywhere. If you have a good Lapp reindeer dog you don't have to run after them, but when you have a bum reindeer dog you have to run and try to keep them together.[9] When old Riley Ahlook was learning to be a reindeer herder, they had a lot of reindeer dogs down at Teller, where they put off the reindeer that time. And when he came up, he brought four reindeer dogs, two female and two males. And every spring he made a litter of reindeer dogs from those reindeer dogs he had. That's how he kept a new reindeer dog all the time.

He bred and raised them. And the ones that didn't work good, not smart enough, he always killed them. And the ones that were smart, they always kept them, even though they had four, five, or six. And when they had a new apprentice, he gave the herders a new dog. We were never short of reindeer dogs back then.

Later on when our reindeer dogs were getting old around here, and I was herd assistant, I asked the reindeer superintendent—Sidney Rood, who had an office down at Nome—I asked him to order six reindeer dogs from Siberia. And they told me they would bring them up on the *North Star* on the summer voyage. So I waited for them and got them as soon as the *North Star* got here. And I sent them up to the reindeer herd. They were all trained. And in the fall, after the lagoon was frozen up, I went up there to check on how they worked, those reindeer dogs we got from Siberia. I stayed about a week there, going out with the reindeer herders to check which was the best reindeer dog. The first day I used two, then the next day we used the other two. And I found out there's only three that were trained to be reindeer herders; the other three were just breaking into being reindeer herding dogs. Two of them got to be pretty good after they were trained.

We had three females and three males, the reindeer dogs that we got from Siberia. And they worked fine up here. They had long black hair. Two of them had spots on their neck. And boy, they turned out to be good reindeer dogs. We had them for several years, until I started working for the Weather Bureau. Some herders had a tough time when they herd, taking care of the herd in winter. While they were fawning, herders always have hard time keeping the herd together. That's the reason I ordered the dogs.

They used to castrate the bulls in summer at the marking times for young fawns. The chief herder used to talk with the boss at Wainwright and determine how many bulls to castrate. So they castrated in summer while they were marking the fawns. They kept a good many bulls for the breeding stock in the fall. All the reindeer herders know the good bulls. They picked out their best bulls for breeding stock. The ones that always get real fat quick in the spring time, we always kept those bulls. They're healthy bulls. Some of the bulls are always poor every year, all year long. They never get fat, even in summer. So we castrated those poor bulls, every one of them. They breed just as good as the ones that are real nice and fat, but we never kept them. That's the way you can have a good strong herd.

They had several ways of castrating in those days. One was where you lasso the bull and knock them down and you chew the testicles of the bull with your teeth, and chew it up. If you don't chew it good, the deer always breed in the late fall. And besides that, his testicles will swell up real big. I don't like that kind of castrating. It was introduced by the Lapp when they first came over I guess, when they brought the reindeer to Alaska from Siberia.[10]

Another way is to take the testicle of the bull and split the skin lengthwise, flip it off, and when the testicle is on the surface you cut the layer of the outer skin of that testicle, and then peel it back. Then you cut the end of the vein that attaches to the lower part of the testicle, cut it with a knife and pull it out until you reach the end of the veins in the testicle, to where there's a clear spot where there's no vein. You cut it there and throw the testicle away. I like it better that way. That's the best way to castrate. The bull never breeds after you castrate it.

When I used to be a reindeer herder I kept track of all the herd before they grew big. I always knew when one of the reindeer was missing. I was raised with the reindeer and got to know all of them. They usually have leaders, some female, some bulls, that wander off every time you go after them. Before they grew big we had about five thousand in the herd at Ivisauraq, and I always knew when some of the reindeer were missing. I knew it right away. And we started looking for them and always found them. I got to know them real well.

Every time when marking time comes, I kept track of all the fawns there too—which is the oldest and which is the youngest. I knew all about those fawns when they were growing up during the summer. When their mothers were missing from the herd, I always knew.

It used to be a lot of fun when you started marking fawns. Boy, we used to build a log corral—short logs, stand them up on the beach down at Qiḷamittaġvik, at Iñuktuyuk, wherever we stayed, Piŋuksraġruk. We always built a driftwood corral, stacked up wood all around, except on the ocean side. They won't swim off; they don't try to swim out when you have a corral. And they had one entrance, and us boys that did the lassoing, we lined up near the entrance of the corral and let the reindeer run out a few at a time. That old Tookaloona used to be our driver when he lived with us, when he was a reindeer man. John Tookaloona, he was a reindeer herder for a long time. And when we were marking down there he let them out to us, and we lassoed the fawns.

The first day when we started, we always had a competition with one another to see who got the most lassoed fawns. Sometimes I got one hundred and ten the first day, before we marked all the fawns. When you first start there's a lot of fawns to be marked. You can throw your lasso anyplace and catch fawns. A lot of herders always got one hundred in the first day, when we started lassoing. But after a while, we never got that many. And we had a hard time finding ones when it was almost over; you have to look around, walk around between the herd, to find the fawns that weren't marked. That's the way we finished all the marking.

Those times Michael Jimmy was my partner. We used to stay together for a long time when we were reindeer boys. All the young people, able-bodied boys, were reindeer boys in those days after the old reindeer herders retired. Michael Jimmy was one of Samuel Agnasagga's brothers. I used to call him partner when we were reindeer boys. He was not real strong, but he was strong enough to be a reindeer herder until later years. We were reindeer boys together at Ivisauraq. We always went together and traveled together, and we traded by ourself once in a while. When I got something he liked, he always tried to buy it from me and I did the same thing. That's what they call partners.[11]

My Stepfather's Death

I guess my stepfather had TB. We were staying at that point beside the mouth of Avvaq. He really got sick and we got left behind. Reindeer herders moved down in Avvaq and left us, and I stayed with my folks there. I was hunting all the time. My father was really sick and finally he died one day while I was hunting brant. When I got home I found out.

We had a floor of lumber, made just like the dimensions of our ten-by-twelve tent. And I made a coffin out of floorboards. We didn't have any place to get wood. Me and my brother John Koguyuk, we buried him there. I was still young. My brother was not strong enough. So we put him on a walrus hide, split walrus hide that we used to have. And we put the casket on top of that. And we pulled it all the way up there and buried him after we dug for two, three days all by ourselves. We didn't have any pick. All we had was an ax. We chopped it there. We chopped it every day with ax until it was deep enough, about four and a half feet down. And we buried him there. Then we went up there and had a short prayer meeting. I put a log monument there, and stood it up. The last time I went there, when we were at the Avvaq mouth, I walked up there and tried to find it, but I couldn't find it. Somebody must have cut it.

My stepfather never talked to me when he really got sick, but when he was about ready to die, he told me to raise my brothers and sisters any way I know how. And I raised them, all by myself. When I learned how to trap, I kept them supplied with White man's food, until my mother remarried to Walluk.

She was a widow for several years before she remarried. Those days they never had any welfare or anything. The women, when they became widows, they had to remarry in order to have some man take care of them. I was only a boy, but we didn't starve. I learned how to hunt early when I was young.

I inherited my stepfather's hunting gear and used it until they were worn out. He had a .38-55 rifle, a brand new one. And boy that rifle, when I used it, it shot accurate. I loaded it myself too, after I learn how to load shells from him. He had all the loading tools and everything for the rifle, even the ramrod to clean the barrel with.

That time Riley was about to retire and he wanted his children to go to school. He wanted to retire and live in Wainwright. That's why he brought us up. And I brought my mother up and let her stay in Wainwright. I was fifteen years old, getting strong. I could herd like any man, in night herding or day herding. And I stayed at the reindeer camp and trapped. Every time I caught a fox at the reindeer herd, I sent it up to my mother so she could get food for my brothers and sisters. I never saved any fox skins for myself. I only got a few when I first started trapping. And every time I got one or two foxes, I sent them up when somebody was going to Wainwright.

Later on my mother stayed with us, but it was too much for her, moving around, so she decided to stay at Wainwright. So I took her down there to Wainwright. We used the house down at that creek in front of the post office, on top of the bank there. It belonged to Okeleak, Weir's granddaddy. She rented that house when Okeleak and his wife stayed upriver on the Ivisauraq, fishing. Okeleak and his wife stayed upriver all winter long, and when the spring came, when whaling started,

Okeleak always came down for the whaling time. It was pretty good weather then, so my mother always stayed in a tent in summer.

And after about two, three years my mother remarried Walluk. He was a widower too, and his first wife was Innuksuk. Walluk was the youngest brother of Attungowruk that lived in Icy Cape. I stopped supporting her as soon as she got married. Walluk was a really good hunter. He always got lots of foxes when he trapped.

Hunting Seals at the Breathing Hole

One day I decided to bring some fresh meat for my folks. So I butchered one steer and next morning I took it down to Ataniq and spent the night there. In the morning when we woke up, the weather was on west wind. And I asked Walluk if I could go along with him when he decided to go out hunting out on the ice—we might see some bear. So I went along with him. He had a dog team, seven dogs. He had nine altogether, but he left two, and we went out.

When we reached the edge of the lead, the young ice was already closed in. And on the edge, ice was crushing and making ridges here and there. And Walluk tested it. He put his sinker right on the edge of the shore ice and tested which way the current was going. And the sinker was going right under the shore ice, so he told me it was all right if we went out there; it wouldn't break off. The tide was running in from the ocean current and we went out. It was thick enough to walk out on.[12]

We were about three miles from the edge of the shore ice when we reached rough ice where the young ice was thicker. And while we were going through the rough ice we found a hole, right in the small flat ice, in between that little rough ice that was frozen in. And when he looked at it, it was open. It was not even frozen underneath that air hole. So he got ready, and he told me to walk up north. When I walked far enough, he told me he was going to put his arm up to let me stop. If he raised his hand, he wanted me to stop. And he told me to go around, same distance all the way around him. So I did. I walked around, going round, and I reached the place where I started. And then I started the second round. I was about three-fourths of the way when I heard the shot. I was maybe four hundred yards away from him. He waved at me to come so I went over there. He got the ugruk, big one too. He shot him when he came up in the hole. And we got one ugruk that day.

He told me every time when the hunters were two, they always did that when they found a seal hole or ugruk hole, in order to keep him running all the time so he would be winded and want to come up in one of those holes for air. That's how we got that ugruk. That's the only time I ever watched Walluk, my stepfather.

And we pulled that ugruk all the way up to our team where they were tied on the edge of the lead, and we loaded him up. It was the middle of the day, about noon. And Walluk told me he was going to look around some more down south, so I brought the ugruk in all by myself on the trail. And later in the evening, when the day was kind of twilight, almost dark, Walluk walked back home. That's my first experience shooting seals or ugruk at the seal hole.[13]

And that evening he was telling me what to do. He told me when the ugruk first comes up through that hole he just breathes one time and then he goes back under, and the second time he always goes into the dome of the hole, and breathes and goes back again. But the third time he fills that hole up. He fills that up and starts to breathe when he doesn't hear any noise from the top of the ice. He starts to breathe for a long time. That time you can shoot him. You can look at him from the top and point your rifle and pull the trigger. Every time you get him. And that's how they hunt on the seal hole. But he told me when you are alone, you have to wait a long time. Sometimes you get a seal without anybody, and sometimes you never get nothing, even though when you watch it, ice forms on the water underneath the air hole.

Every time when ugruk or ringed seal has a hole, when it's frozen, he scratches it up, scratches it from the bottom side and opens it. After he opens it, he shoots out water from underneath through that hole and builds it bigger and bigger. Through that hole he makes a hole about one and a half inches, about that size. And then he shoots water through there. When it lands on the side of the hole it forms ice. It builds it bigger and bigger and then he scratches it again and enlarges it all the time. So that's how they build their seal holes, them seals.

One seal always has several holes around that neighborhood where he is wintering. If you find him, you'll be lucky. If you got somebody else, then you watch all those seal holes. That way, you catch the seal in a few minutes. They got to have air in their lungs when they're under the ice.

Corralling in the Fall

At that time I was with the number one herd in back of Ataniq on the Kuugruaq area. We always got together and corralled in the fall, around November, first week of November. And every fall we did that before we became the Wainwright Reindeer Association. All the owners got together and built the ice corral. And when they got together, they kept the herds in different locations. One was on the northeast of us and another one was way up Igluqpauraq, and another one was down south of Qaġmak Point. And all the people, all the reindeer herders and their families, came to Wainwright, spent two, three weeks of round-up in those days before the reindeer were growing big.

And they always had a good time when they congregate. They had races after the corralling. They were always playing games and having sled deer races right in Wainwright.[14] They always congregated in front of the old schoolhouse. And all the reindeer herders went up to their herds and picked up their best sled deer, and had races down to the inlet or further down. We used to have a lot of fun.

When I learned how to drive sled deer, I was in the race. One time we reached the marker where we were going to turn around on the inlet, on the back side of the inlet at Tut-tuaġvik.[15] The sled deers were galloping real hard. There were four or five sleds with sled deer pulling the people, going real fast. They were almost abreast of each other, little lag, about a sled length. When we reached that little valley over there, south end of the village, Joe Aveoganna was in the middle and we were getting close to the line. It was only a little more than two hundred yards, and he let his sled run over in front of my sled, and we both lost. Edwin Anaktook and Harry Koochik, they were first. I would have been first if Joe didn't run over my sled. I always thought he did that on purpose.

And then the next year we came and we had another cor-ralling up at the mouth of Umiŋmak.[16] Jack Anakak was chief herder at that time, before I was appointed.

We built an ice corral down there at the water lake south of the village. They always built ice corrals in those days. We had no lumber. Boy, it was pretty good too. You can always use that ice corral for ice water. You don't have to chop ice from the lake. You just knock off what you want from the corral that's standing up all around. It's got a chute and everything. We ran the reindeer through there. And after we finished they use the corral for ice water.

All the people went up there, walking, when we used to have corralling. Everybody went up there, all the villagers. Even the teachers went up there with their families, hired somebody to take them out. Some teachers learned how to drive reindeer too, but the middle-aged teachers, they didn't drive reindeer. I always drove with them.

Separating the Herds

And that year, when I was herding at Kuugruaq, I was an apprentice with Edwin Anaktook. That year they sent us up to Barrow to pick our reindeer that were mixed in with the Barrow herd. So William Penn, Wesley Ekak, and I, we made a trip up there. One man from each herd. Number one herd was there on the Kuugruaq side, sometimes on north side of Kuugruaq. We had a boundary that time with the Barrow herd. Sometimes the reindeer got mixed up. So we made a trip up to Barrow to get our reindeer. We took two sled deer apiece and traveled three days to get to Barrow. And after we talked with the teachers up at Barrow, we went up to the reindeer herd. They had three herds up there, all scattered everywhere. That's the first time I saw those two Leavitt boys, Herbert and Adam. They were boys then. And when we got there, we built a snow block corral to put our herd in. Dug it way deep down to the bottom, about six or eight feet high.

All the reindeer herders helped us when we built it. And every day we lassoed the Wainwright herd that was mixed in with the Barrow herd. And we put them in that pocket. They never tried to go out. After we lassoed about twenty or thirty deer that were mixed with the Barrow herd, the Barrow herders drove their deer about a mile and a half away, out of sight. We let our deer out and drove them down towards the west, and one of us watched them during the evening, while they were grazing. Then when we couldn't find any more Wainwright herd among their herd, we moved down to the next herd. But we always watched our herd every night. We did the same thing—built a big snow fence, made a place for them. We did that every time we got to another herd. Lassoed them and put them in there. We did the same thing every day.

After we found all the deer that were mixed with the Barrow reindeer herds, we drove them to our herd and got them together. We got over two hundred reindeer from number two and three that time. We drove them home, camping on the tundra every time it got dark. Sometimes we kept on going while it was dark, and then made camp. The deer grazed around all night. They never moved away after we drove them, they just grazed around there all night. The next morning we picked them up and drove them and camped again. When we reached number one herd, that's where I stayed. We put them there with our own herd.

And after we put them on the number one herd, I went to Wainwright with my own sled deer. After I stayed in Wainwright one day I moved up to Milliktaġvik and stayed overnight there at John Peter's house. Two families were living there, John Peter and Akuklook, and Ahgoruk, father of Joe Aveoganna's wife, Carrie. Next morning when I woke up, after we had breakfast, I found out two of Ahgoruk's dogs were loose. And those dogs made my sled deer run off. They never try to break away unless the animals go for them. They broke that halter rope and got away.

Caught in the Storm

I left there that morning with a Crescent Baking Powder can of water on my back and pulling my sled. When I got thirsty I would drink water from the can. When I got close to Ivisauraq, it got dark. A storm came up from the south. Boy, you couldn't see a thing. I kept going, pulling my sled. Nobody tried to help me.

The deer must have stopped someplace up there. I didn't see them. That evening, I built a snow house, just big enough to sit in, just like a big chair with snow on the side. I used my harness to sit on, and spent the night there. After I drank that baking powder can of water, I refilled it with snow and put it inside my parki. After I drank that water in the morning, I filled it again with snow and put it inside my parki, and my body heat melted it when I slept.

Next morning I couldn't see a thing. I went out for a little while and stood my sled up, but I didn't recognize anything. I spent the next night there. That was a whole day and night without anything to eat. And when I got cramped up I went out-side and warmed up, limbered up my legs. That evening, on the second day, the storm was so thick you couldn't see ten feet away.

On the third day, in the afternoon, the snowstorm let up. I was about three miles away from the reindeer camp. When the storm let up a little bit, I found I was camping on a little stream that I recognized. Finally I reached the Ivisauraq River below Ivisauraq, where the reindeer camps were. I followed the river up and I began to see smoke. That was the only time I started to get hungry. I never thought I could spend three days with-out eating, but I did. Boy, the food really tasted good when I started eating. Cora was making reindeer soup when I reached there. Boy, that was the best meal I ever ate!

Reindeer herders. From left to right, Weir Negovanna, Fred Anashugak, Waldo Bodfish, and Henry Peetook. (Acc. # 78-14-405: Eva Alvey Richards Collection, Archives, Alaska and Polar Regions Department, University of Alaska Fairbanks.)

Old Kakmak, when we went hunting. Icy Cape, 1921. (BA 21-044: A. M. Bailey Collection, Denver Museum of Natural History Photo Archives.)

Those are the furs Walluk got, blue, white and silver fox. Those are baby fawn skins, reindeer leg pieces sewn together in his parka. Wainwright, 1921–22. (BA21-333: A. M. Bailey Collection, Denver Museum of Natural History Photo Archives.)

5

Responsibilities of Adulthood

Marriage

I used to meet girls when we were corralling. That's how I got
to know Mattie. And I decided to get married when I went to
the village at round-up time in the fall corralling. I asked her to
marry me and she said yes. That's how we got together. We
went up to Barrow in January and married in the middle of the
winter, 1925. We went up by dog team with two other couples, a
triple marriage. William Penn and Bessie Kanayuk, and Jessie
Panikpak and Tagilook, that's Ethel Papiklook, Mattie's sister.
We were married together, a triple marriage. It's been over sixty
years we've been married.

That time I got married, I got one of the reindeer herders
from Kuugruaq to come down to Ataniq with me. When I
reached Ataniq I sent the man back to the reindeer herd with
my sled deer, and we used Walluk's dogs to go to Barrow. Walluk was married to my mother then.

He had a good team. We had nine dogs when we went up
there, and we made pretty good time. We went up there in

three days and came home in two days. In Barrow we stayed at Bert Panigeo's house, that's Mattie's relatives. Nellie Panigeo is Mattie's cousin. Her father and Nellie's father were brothers. That's where we always stayed when we went to Barrow.

From Barrow, after we were married, we came back to Peard Bay. There were three houses when we were there. Michael Keogak was there, and his wife and their daughter and son-in-law Ernest Kignak. Ernest was married to Michael Keogak's daughter, the youngest one.[1] And Lloyd Ahvakana's daddy's folks were there. They had three houses, sod houses. They were trapping down there. We camped that night there.

When we got to Wainwright, I went back to the reindeer herd. I left my wife with her folks. Her father was Joseph Papiklook and her mother was Mary Oenik. They had a house in Wainwright down near the creek there, an old-fashioned house, *iglu,* with fireplace in the hallway and a storage place for clothing, equipment, and food.[2]

In April, towards spring, after we were settled way up there, I went down and picked up Mattie and brought her to the reindeer camp. I trapped up there and got enough fox to buy a big ten by twelve tent, and I bought a Yukon stove, everything she needed, cooking utensils and everything.[3] I bought a lot of stuff for her after we were married—new dresses. When I was first married to her I spent a lot of money. And that's the time I took her up to the reindeer herd. We lived in that tent up at the reindeer camp.

When we were traveling together, I always tied a rope from her sled deer to the side of my sled and took her along when we were moving. She's strong all right, but I don't know why she never wanted to drive the reindeer. When we were fawning there, I told her to drive reindeer, but she wouldn't do it. I don't know why. Sometimes when the weather was real good, I took her along when I went after reindeer, and we used one sled deer. We were pretty well clothed. We had warm reindeer-skin parkas. I like that, and she likes that too. Sometimes we had an argument too. But we never did argue enough to leave one another.

She likes to live in the tent. When we were up there, Nannie Kagak always stayed with us when she was a little girl. She liked to stay with us. One year I took her up and she spent the fawning time with us, all spring. I guess Mattie was kind of lonesome, little bit. She told me to bring Nannie up. I said, "Okay, if you want her I can bring her up." She was related to my wife. That's why we took her. She never wanted to go home. She spent the whole summer with us when I first married Mattie.

They always help around, them women, when they have nothing to do, when we're marking fawns. Some of them push the herd toward us. And when the herd runs between us, we lasso the fawns that were marked and we put them in the corral.

And then I made an agreement with Jim Allen, the trader, to order me a house, ready-made, cut up, ready to put up. That's how I got that little sixteen-by-twenty house. And they priced it at one thousand two hundred dollars when it landed here. They gave me a good deal, I always thought. Jim Allen was doing pretty good when the price on fox was high. He made pretty good money. I got a lot of fox when they were forty-five dollars a fox. And that's how I paid for the house I ordered through him.

It came in on the Liebes and Company ship, *Fox*, I guess. That was Pedersen's ship when he was working for H. Liebes and Company.[4] That was about 1926 or '27, when we were first married. I put it up all by myself. Once in a while Upicksoun helped me.

Turning the Reindeer Loose

The spring after we were married, the herd became a company herd, Wainwright Reindeer Association, and we turned the reindeer loose like the cattle do.[5] That was a big mistake. The superintendent down at Nome introduced it to the unit manager, and the unit manager talked to us. And we decided to try it.

They introduced that idea of turning the reindeer herds loose all along the coast, all the way to Barrow, and up at Cape Halkett. They had a herd up there too. That's how we started to lose all our herd. They were getting too many. At the same time, the wolves that had been breeding with dogs up at Herschel Island; they came around. They roamed around, worked their way down, and they reached us at that time. Lots of wolves all over, everywhere—black ones, gray ones, reddish ones—just like dogs.

If I'm right, when the whaling business turned real low they had four, five hundred dogs up there at Herschel Island. When they wintered there, they always sent out some hunters with thirteen or fourteen dogs each, whatever they have. And they send them out to hunt caribou. And after baleen was getting real low in price, the whalers stopped coming. When they quit coming, instead of killing the dogs, they turned them all loose. They got mixed with wolves and bred and made all colors of wolf. That's how that happened.

And when they got too many, the wolves must have worked down south through the tundra until they reached us here, because there were lots of black wolves mixed with a pack when we came across them sometimes, lots of black wolves and reddish and everything else. Very few gray ones. That's how the wolves got to be many around the coast here, all along up to Banks Land. And they killed lots of musk ox up there, them wolves. The dogs, when they chased them, they run 'em off of the cliffs on those rock ledges up there. That's what I heard from the old-timers.

Our herd was getting smaller. Every time when we rounded up, they were getting smaller and smaller.[6] After they got up to twenty-two thousand that year, they were getting fewer when we round up. And in the meantime, the reindeer herders always quit, and we had a hard time keeping them with the herd, even though we furnished them with food and everything else. They were having a hard time. In July, herders always lose the herd, when mosquitoes and flies are getting thick. Every year the reindeer were getting smaller and smaller, then someone else took over.

That person had them for two years, '44 and '45, and then he lost the whole herd. When they were at Ivisauraq they quit their herd and left them at the mouth of the river and went to Wainwright. The next fall they started to look for them, but they never found them. As soon as they left them in July, they swam across the inlet and headed up the Kuugruaq, way up there toward Atqasuk. People saw them go through and they went right straight past Kuugruaq, I don't know where. They got mixed up with the caribou. That's how they lost them. They never recovered the herd.[7]

The first three years after we turned them loose it was really good. When we rounded up the deer we had a big herd. They stretched all the way from here to that tank over there, all the way to the end of the lake down there. The reindeer would cover all that up when we first brought 'em up.

Boy, when we counted them, they were eighteen thousand, nineteen thousand, twenty-two thousand. That's what we counted those years when we turned them loose. Of course, they mixed up with a lot of the Barrow herd too. And that year Jack Anakak was the chief herder here, and we had a corralling up there at Umiŋmak. The next year they gave me that job. When Jack Anakak's term was over, when the next year came for election, they picked me up for chief herder. And shortly after that, one or two years later, they picked me up as reindeer assistant.[8]

The Native Store
And that time we saved all the Native products in our herd and we started to sell them.[9] The selling of reindeer products grew out of the old Native Store and the Wainwright Reindeer and

Trading Company. That was the early years. I was still down at Icy Cape with the reindeer herds at the time the Native Store got started. I didn't even know how they started but later on I heard—it was started by collecting foxes from trappers. When they talked about a Native store, putting up a Native store here, they decided to use foxes to buy shares from the store, stocks. And everybody started buying stocks, ten dollars a share, with white fox they trapped.

And when the foxes got as many as maybe fifty or more, when the stockholders got a lot, they started to ship out those furs. And at that time the teacher was taking care of those fur when they were buying stocks. And that's how they started in. They shipped the furs every year. The teacher wasn't taking good care of the furs that they were going to ship, and was taking some, a few foxes from the bunch that they were going to ship. And when they found out, the Bureau of Indian Affairs made him pay back what he took.

That's how it started. Just before I came up to Wainwright, I heard about it. And they had Alva Nashoalook run the store. Only a few years after that, maybe one or two, three years after, the reindeer got involved with the store. They changed the name from Native Store to Wainwright Reindeer and Trading Company. And when the Native Store started to lose on the Native Wainwright Reindeer and Trading Company, they changed it again to Wainwright Cooperative Store.[10]

When they put the reindeer management with the store, they figured they were going to make pretty good money, selling Native products and meat. But Native products didn't sell good in those days. We didn't know where the outlets were. I never made very much, but I always made about three thousand dollars every year in order to feed the reindeer herders. We always sold Native products to the trader, Ira Rank. He used to come up here with the schooner, two-masted schooner named *Trader,* and Pete Brand too.[11] Those two always bought Native products when they came up here. Every time when they came up here they bought sealskins, reindeer skins, mukluks, boots, fawn skins, everything else. I even sent some skins to Fairbanks and Elim. After they found out I was selling skins they always ordered baby fawn skins and everything else.

In the summertime we always butchered three hundred fawns when the skin was really good, when the hair was just right in August. And we shipped them out, sold them down at the Yukon River. People liked to buy those skins. Individual people that need them always ordered some skins for clothing. Even the White people that live around the Fairbanks and Anchorage area, they order them. That way I made some money for the reindeer herders. And I sold a lot of baby fawn skins locally around in the village here, even Barrow.

I used to have a lot of reindeer meat in the ice cellar, even fawn meat, and I sold them to the people around in town here locally, and got a few, quite a few dollars on them for the reindeer herders. I made money, sometimes three, four thousand dollars a year, and I used it for reindeer herders, to supply them. We weren't paying much to the herders, but they were getting their shares of reindeer all the time.

The *North Star* had a storage room on the lower deck and they hung them in there and kept them nice and frozen all summer long while he was cruising out, going back home to Seattle.[12] That's the only time I shipped reindeer meat. And the third time I asked them if they were going to have meat shipped out, but they said it's hard to sell. White people don't like to buy them when they reach Seattle. The last time I shipped out five hundred they were stuck with about ten or fifteen carcasses. And so selling meat to the Outside was stopped then.

Return to Close Herding
Later, after we turned them loose—it was over five years I guess—the deer were getting smaller and smaller every year. So the reindeer company decided to have herding again. When

they got too small we started to put reindeer in herds and watch them more closely.

In the fall, as soon as it freezes up on the first part of October, we started to round up. We had a big meeting. All the owners met in the schoolhouse, and then we asked able-bodied men to help round up. That's how they earn their reindeer. The reindeer company supports the people that go out with their dog teams, feeds the dogs, and gives them grub and everything else. And everybody went out and looked everywhere, on the Utuqqaq, way up to the foot of the mountains. We traveled up there fishing at the same time, and then we brought the herd together. Some people built a corral. They got the corral ready to use as soon as we came back. That's how we worked it. And we had to put down all the owner's names and divide them into groups and watch the herd day and night in shifts. While herders were in town, we had shifts to watch the deer.

In the first years, when the ice on the lake was eight inches thick, we used to build an ice corral every year. We built it down south of us about a mile, on a big lake. That's where we put the corral every year.

When I became a herd assistant I ordered lumber through BIA and they brought that up on the *North Star* and we hauled it up to Qaġmak Point. Then the director and I, we hired Weir Negovanna to build a corral on Qaġmak Point up there, right across from the village. Weir Negovanna was the boss. Before freeze-up we picked some carpenters from among the owners in Wainwright and took them across with canoes to build that corral. And we used that corral for about three or four years afterwards.

After we got together all the herds that we brought in, we put them together. Some people brought in more than five thousand deer, some people brought two thousand. It depended on where they went and where they found the herd. It was quite a sight. They extended from the oil tank up there all the way down to the inlet [about three miles]. And after we cut enough for one day's work—we cut about two, three thousand reindeer—we drove them towards Siñgauraq and let them stay up there. The owners and I watched the reindeer, day and night, twenty-four hours a day while we were corralling. And all the owners that didn't watch the herd, they went up with their dog teams. And we put the herd inside the corral and started counting for that day. I always was wishing we had a camera to make a picture, but I was poor that time.

Sometimes when they brought too much, we worked until midnight, until we finished all the reindeer. Boy, we used to have a lot of fun. We also have two people to wake everybody up. We appointed two men. Every morning at eight o'clock they hammered on the house, told us to wake up. Even though I was really tired, I always woke up at eight. And then I got ready and started up to the corral, driving five dogs.

I had a cook up there doing the cooking, and waiters brought meat or coffee, biscuits, everything, while we're doing the corralling. Boy, the old people like that. They have a great time when the corralling time comes. They wouldn't ever like to miss it. When they are camping down at Icy Cape, Ataniq, or somewhere in Nuqullik or Avvaq, they come down before the corralling starts. They want to see the reindeer corralling. We used to have a great time!

I always had a white snowshirt on over my parki and had button right here. And the unit manager and the teachers always came from Barrow checking on their own herd. And when we're corralling—if they have a representative—five or six Barrow boys, we separate their herd and keep them away from the main herd. And every time after corralling, we kept them together until they drove them away. They drove those Barrow reindeer across the lagoon and as soon as they are far enough away from the herd, they kept them there. We always do like that.

When we finished the corralling, we drove all the herd back up to the good grazing areas and left them there. They started to graze all by themselves, like cattle do. Once in a while when we were up there trapping and those deer got too far up, we drove them down. We kept tabs on them. All the trappers, all the old reindeer herders, used to keep tabs on them, whichever way they went. You could drive them anyway you want to; they were tame. I used to drive from way up, from above Saaŋiaq in the south, or further south above Sanniŋaruq, that big river. Sometimes I found reindeer up there. And I drove 'em to my cabin and kept them until I finish my trapping. And then, when I started home, I drove them down to below Niġisaqtuġvik and left them there with my two brothers. Whoever had a trapline someplace in a different direction, when he sees that a big herd got too far away from the village, he drove them back down, let them get closer, and left them there, let them roam around.

When they elected me as herd assistant, we hired six herders for each herd and paid them with reindeer, supported them just like businessmen do when they hire somebody, paid them with reindeer. And we had four herds: one at Kuugruaq, one at Kuuk, one at Ivisauraq, and one at Icy Cape. That's four altogether. My responsibility was to look after those herds. I had to visit them every month, once a month, in order to check them out and see how they were doing. And I also brought the herders food for a month. We supplied them every month with flour and coffee and tea, rice, anything we got on hand down there. They got their pay. And I did that all year round, once a month. Sometimes the teacher followed me when I went up to the herd to check them. That made a long trip. I went up to Kuugruaq first and then cut across to Kuuk, and from there I cut across toward Point Lay, then to Ivisauraq and back home. It took me more than a week sometimes to travel to all those places. They did the same thing at Barrow with their reindeer when Alfred Hopson was reindeer assistant. The last time I made a trip to the herds I took the unit manager when he came from Barrow.

A Trip with the Unit Manager

They had a guy named Jens Forshaug.[13] He was unit manager stationed at Barrow. And one year, he came down late in June and asked me to take him down to Point Lay to check on their herd. Every year, in the spring, those unit managers go check on the herd. We started down from Wainwright to Point Lay. And the trip was fine all the way down to Icy Cape. The trail was good up here, but down on the other side of Icy Cape everything was rotten,[14] late in the year. The rivers were already broken up, but we went on the ocean side, on the outer side, around that rotten place in front of the inlet. We got to Point Lay okay.

I left my dogs with the Point Lay people and hired another team from Samarualook. I used his team and went down with Tony Joule and his family to see the reindeer herders down there at the end of the lagoon, a place called Aumalik, thirty miles down the coast from Point Lay. Boy, the ice was all so rotten we had to find a place to go. There were lots of holes close to the beach. And after we checked the reindeer herd and looked them over—Tingook and his family were reindeer boys down there—we spent the night there. And the next morning we started home. We got all the eggs we wanted,[15] and also I butchered one reindeer from that herd. Halfway back to Point Lay we had a picnic, a big feast, broiled the ribs on open fire, and had a good time. And late in the evening, when the sun was going down, we went home to Point Lay and spent the night there.

Next morning we had to start home. The ice was melting fast and we couldn't stay very long. When we reached about three miles this side of Point Lay, boy, we had a hard time crossing the inlet. It took us about an hour and a half to cross that rotten ice. Forshaug was steering the sled. I led the dogs, going around here and there, trying to get to the other side. Finally we made it. Boy, the ice was rotten, even out to the edge of the lead. The lagoon was filled up with water all the way to the end of Icy Cape that time.

While we were going along on the flat ice, we found a big crack, big wide crack about fifty yards wide, frozen, made in early fall; nice and smooth all the way to Icy Cape. We followed that, and it was a good trail. Seals were lying on the ice on that flat spot, all the way to Icy Cape. One time, when we went around the point, there were two of them there, and when I put my brake down, the dogs, they jerked on the traces and broke loose after those seals. One seal was asleep and before he could get away, two of my dogs grabbed him, bit him on the flippers, and dragged him backwards. We used the seal for dog feed when we got to camp.

The Native Store,
Alva Nashoalook,
storekeeper on the left.
(BA21-068: A. M. Bailey
Collection, Denver Museum of
Natural History Photo Archives.)

*That's Wainwright herd there. That's
a wing of an entrance. Those sled deer
are real nice and fat. They got velvet
on their horns.*
Reindeer round-up with ice corrals,
Wainwright, 1921–22.
(BA 21-080A: A. M. Bailey Collection,
Denver Museum of Natural History
Photo Archives.)

Reindeer herders
building an ice corral.
(Acc. #78-14-438 N: Eva
Alvey Richards Collection,
Archives, Alaska and Polar
Regions Department,
University of Alaska
Fairbanks.)

Corralling time.
(Acc. #78-14-744 N:
Eva Alvey Richards
Collection, Archives,
Alaska and Polar
Regions Department
University of Alaska
Fairbanks.)

6

Conducting the 1940 Census

When I was herd assistant I could go anywhere. I only had to check on the reindeer herds once in a while. That's the time I used to go way up inland trapping. I used to trap up the Meade River, near the headwaters. Every year, for five, six years, I went up there all by myself and checked if there's any furs at the foot of the mountains. And I found there was a lot of red fox up there. I got quite a few every time I looked at my traps. I went up one whole week, traveled by dog team to the end of my trapline. Then I had two lines, on the north side of Meade and on the south, right on the main tundra away from Meade River. There was a lot of fox around, even white foxes up there. It's easy to catch them when you have bait of caribou stomach. Mix it up with caribou guts and fox urine. That's how I always make trap bait.

I used to find a lot of traps that were left out on the trapline. I used to find several traps every time I saw a caribou skull on my trail. Those people that trapped way before me put traps there and tied it to the caribou horn. When I pulled it there's a trap right there, tied up to the horn.

One time I went up there and spent the whole winter trapping. I only got three foxes, one red and two white. That was a bad season, no foxes anywhere. I went way up trying to locate any foxes around that area where I used to go. There was none. But the next year was when I got about a hundred and thirty-four, I think. A lot of them were eaten by other foxes too; I would have gotten more than that.

Traveling at Fifty Below

One time, in 1940, we got strangers coming from Kotzebue, taking census all the way from Kotzebue to Wainwright.[1] I was herd assistant then and I went along with them upriver to show them where the reindeer herders were. There was Mr. Wilson, the census taker, and a teacher by the name of Richard Webb. Their dogs were traveling all the way from Kotzebue and were pretty well worn out. They couldn't keep up with us, and we had to wait a long time before they reached us.

Wilson was supposed to take the census. And after he saw my team, he wanted to hire me to work from here to Barrow. We started from Wainwright and followed the coast up to Peard Bay and then cut inland from there. Boy, that was the coldest time I ever traveled, fifty below zero every day for a whole week in January. When we first started from Peard Bay there were three families there. After we recorded them and all their children, the next day we went up inland. And that day when we camped, I cut snow blocks while he was trying to keep warm. After I built the snow walls around the place where we were going to put up a tent, I put canvas over the tent and we went inside, took the mattress in, and put little floorboards down. We tried to put some kerosene in the stove but it was frozen solid, wouldn't pour. We had to light the kerosene lantern and thaw that can of kerosene on top of the lantern. Boy, he was really cold, that guy. He couldn't stand the cold. After we warmed up and drank coffee and tea, I fed my dogs. It was late in the afternoon around four o'clock, and we camped right there, before daylight was gone.

The next morning we went up inland. There was supposed to be reindeer herders located somewhere south of Atqasuk, but we didn't know where they were. So we carried a map and we found the place where they pointed. By the end of the evening I saw some reindeer tracks and I knew right away we were close by the reindeer herd. We looked around for them and finally we saw the herd.

That time the people were living in different places. Two, three, families were living in Tikiġluk, and two families were living in Atqasuk, one on the south side and one on the north side of the Meade River. We stopped at Tikiġluk and camped there. The next morning, after I fed my dogs, I went down with an empty sled to take census of the two families at Atqasuk. One of them was Bob Akpik and the other one was Henry Nashaknik and his family.

Next day the weather was the same. It was real cold. And there were some families further up there on that part of the Meade River, so I started out all by myself. I left Wilson at Tikiġluk with the people, and I took census way up there.

Simeon Akpik was staying with his grandparents down at Tikiġluk . He was homesick for his parents so I put him in the sleeping bag on the sled and I took him along. Boy, he was very happy. When we reached Itqiuraq we stopped and took census. Spent the night there. And then I cut across to the north fork of the Meade River just below Saaŋiaq and got to the reindeer camp there. Bob Akpik, Simeon's father, was telling me where they were on the map. And I hit it right smack when I went there. Every time I came to a camp I inquired where other people were.

I overnighted there and then cut across to the reindeer

herd that was located on the Isuqtuq River way up there. I never
had trouble finding them. The weather was clear that time, but
it was really cold. You could see way off in the distance.

And after a night up there, I went back to Tikiġluk on the
third day, after I took all the census of the people that lived up
there. Then we went down to Qagluġruaq, downriver from
Atqasuk, and stayed overnight there with Ekosik and Roxy Ekowanna and their families. They were fishing there.

At Qagluġruaq I bought forty whitefish, fifty cents apiece,
to feed my dogs on the way down. And next morning we started
to cut across to Inaru River. There's some families fishing there
in the winter. Egowa was his name. He and his wife lived at a
fish camp there, all by themselves, isolated, a long ways from
the Meade River.

It was a nice, calm day when we started down, but it was
really cold again. That cold weather never let up. The first day
we missed them by a little more than a mile, but I saw smoke
coming out from the tundra when I looked with my field glasses.
They were south of us, so we turned around and went over
there, stayed just long enough to register them on the census.
Then we went on. Late in the afternoon the wind started to pick
up. It was a real cold head wind. We kept on going even though
the weather got worse. A really heavy wind began to blow from
the northeast. I tried to keep on the side of the Inaru River when
I followed it, but sometimes I lost track of it. And there was no
dog team trail anywhere. I tried to find some trails, but I never
found any. Once in a while I checked the map, but after we traveled about four or five hours, I decided to make camp.

I made Wilson work so he could warm up a little bit. I told
him to warm up by helping me. He started to carry snow blocks.
He couldn't stand the cold. He had good clothes all right, but
he never kept warm. His blood must have been too light. We
built a camp, and after we finished we put the tent up and
cooked our supper. I cut up whitefish so all the dogs could eat.
When I stood up and started to look around, I saw a skylight

right abreast of us to the west. People were right there. I missed them. They were close, couple hundred yards. But I didn't walk down there even though I knew where they were. Early in the morning, before daybreak, we had breakfast and then loaded up, and we went down there.

Boy, that old Kalayauk was a worker. They had a hallway made out of ice that they cut in the fall. It was nice and bright when you went in and out of there.

After we took census we cut across to Meade River. There were two families living up there. We got there before they woke up. We woke them up! Toovak family was there and Takpak was there too. He had two boys with him, his grandsons. And after we took census with them we continued down river, following the Meade River down until we reached Pulayaaq. Three families were living there: Oneuk and his wife, and Michael Keogak and his wife, and one other one—Numnik family. Yeah, that was him. That old man, his son used to attend the elder's conference. I know him pretty well, Jean Segevan Numnik.

Then next morning when we're done we headed for Barrow and reached there late in the evening. We had a heavy load going down, and we rested in Barrow for two days. That time there was a village up at Point Barrow, right on the spit. They call that Nuvuk. There were fifteen families living there when we took census at the Point. And after we took census we went back the same evening to Barrow. I spent one more day and then headed home to Wainwright. Alfred Hopson took over from that end.

Qaglugruaq, the Good Fishing Site

That's the first time I've traveled without knowing where the people lived, just go by map. And after I learned about that area and the people, I went up there to buy fish every fall when I didn't go fishing. I always bought some fish from Roxy and Ekosik. That's the closest people from Wainwright. They live at Qaglugruaq, that deep water place, good for winter fishing.[2]

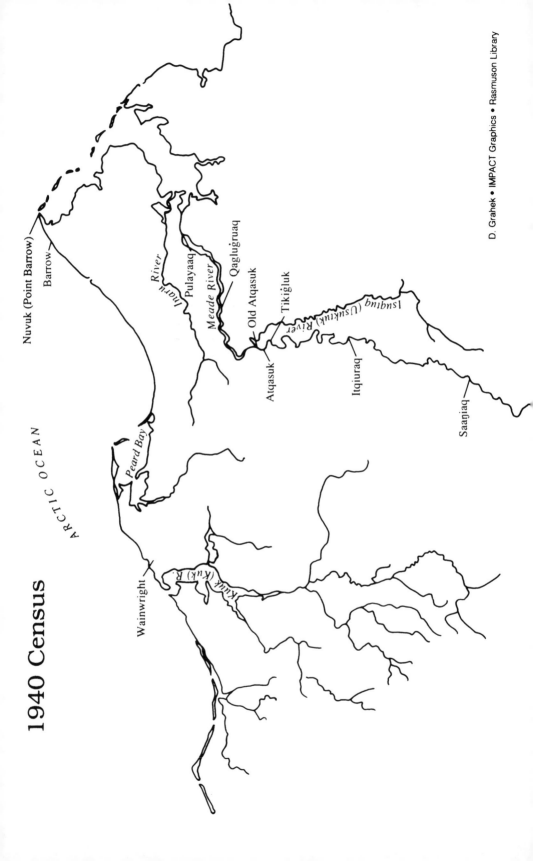

1940 Census

ARCTIC OCEAN

Nuvuk (Point Barrow)

Barrow

Inaru River

Pulayaaq

Meade River

Qaglugruaq

Old Atqasuk

Tikigluk

Atqasuk

Isuutuq (Usuktuk) River

Itqiuraq

Saaŋiaq

Peard Bay

Wainwright

Kuuk (Kuk) R.

Kuuk (Kuk) R.

D. Grahek • IMPACT Graphics • Rasmuson Library

Another time, when I was working for Jim Allen, I went up the Meade River to Qaglug̣ruaq to buy fish. Wesley and I went up with our dog team. When I got there, there was Ekosik and his wife and Roxy and his family, and we stayed there. Ekosik's got a big house.

I brought flour, sugar and tea, coffee, baking powder, lard, what they need for making biscuits. And I traded for a hundred *aanaakłiq,* one hundred whitefish. After I traded him he gave me twenty more. That was a hundred and twenty, and besides that I had a sack of *sulukpaugaq,* sack of each. And besides that I had a *tippun* net, for small whitefish. I set it out when Ekosik told me you could get smaller fish with that net. While I was staying there I got almost one hundred fish with that net. I got *qaaktaq, pikuktuuq,* and small aanaakłiq, and grayling too.[3] They had over two thousand fish, yeah. *Arraa!*[4] And he had three nets. The first one always got almost one hundred fish every night.

After we got the fish we started back home. Boy, my sled was really heavy. Wesley got a lot a fish too from them. I don't know how many, I never counted them.

7

Learning from an Old-Timer

One year I took old Ootoayuk up trapping for a whole winter. His wife died that fall and he was lonely. And when I started to trap up there I decided to take him along. I built a sod house big enough for six or eight people, framed it with willows. And after I finished it, on the second trip, I took old Ootoayuk up to trap with me. He was well enough to travel, but he was a very old man. He had warm clothes on so I took him up. We went all the way up to Saaŋiaq setting traps.

Harold Killbear was a teenager at the time, learning how to trap, so I took him along too, and taught him how to trap, how to build a snow house, and everything. He followed me. That's the way young boys always learn—when they follow older people. And Harold was just a real good companion on the trapline when he started his first long trip. He was not good trapper, but he learned. He started to catch foxes after he learned how to set traps.

Ootoayuk set traps once in a while. Boy, I found out he was slow setting a trap. He always covered it with moss or light grass that was dead, covered all around it. He covered the whole area and sprinkled it with snow, real soft snow on top, and kneaded it a little bit on top, and then he left it that way. He never replaced that cover the whole year. That's the first time I've seen a person trap like that.

I trapped with Ootoayuk all year long. Boy, that old man was always up early. He never missed six o'clock in the morning when he woke up. He had to go out every morning, no matter how bad the weather was. That's his custom ever since he started living. He was always up early in the morning.

Ootoayuk's Stories

And old Ootoayuk always told a story in the evening time. He told me all about everything old-timers used to do, and I learned quite a lot from him about the laws of Eskimos, what they would never do while hunting.[1] He said when you kill a male wolf or male wolverine, you never go out hunting for four days. You stay home, never go anywhere. There's power in that, in that hunting in the early days. And I always call it Eskimo law. You would never break it. If you break it, you get sick; the power is so strong. Before Christianity they never dared break it. And when you get the female you stay home five days without going anywhere. That's their law.

He told me how when a woman is pregnant, there is a law too. When she wants to go outside, she has to go straight out without looking around. And when she reaches the door, she must not stop, even when she goes in. That's law in the early days. And Ootoayuk told me when the woman breaks the law she has a hard time when the baby starts to be born. It takes a long time to be born. He said babies always follow their mother, whatever she did while the baby was growing in the womb.

In those days they always built a snow house for the woman that is pregnant. When she is about ready to have a baby, they put her in the snow house and let her live there. And her family always brings her some meat when there is no other woman in the house. They always bring her food in the morning and in the evening, but they never go in. They are not allowed to go in before the baby is born. After the baby is born, it's all right. That's the Eskimo law. And they really obeyed those rules in those old days. The people always followed those rules.

One night while we were camping he told a story about the snowy owl and let me learn it too. When you see an owl, you got to watch him. Some of the owls have young ones in April. They have eggs in the middle of April or May. I saw one owl that had a baby chick on April 15, when I pulled my traps out. I always saw that owl in the same place every time I went by there. I didn't know he had eggs. He always flew around above me, circling around when I came. And the last time when I went through there, he swooped down, and he bumped me on the top of my head and almost knocked me down.

Ootoayuk told me, "You have to watch when owls stay around in one place. In the springtime they have young, they have eggs nearby. When he fly around, all of a sudden he might swoop down and hit you on the head, and knock you down when he hit you hard."

That's what I learned from Ootoayuk. He taught me those things that I never knew before. Even my folks never told me about it. He was a good companion. He always told me about his hunting in the early days, a lot of stories. But I never paid much attention to it, and when he just told a story, I never got all the story he told.

Ootoayuk and Caribou
He told me one time when food was scarce, he was hunting and he saw a bunch of caribou. He went after them twice in the same day and got the whole bunch. After he shot them in the first place, he didn't kill all of them. He got half of them. He started to go after the rest after he put all his caribou down and put their legs underneath their body and slit the belly so the caribou wouldn't bloat while he was away. He caught the rest of

them and shot the whole bunch. That's the way he did when the animals were scarce. He always went after them twice, until he got them all.

And he taught me how to prepare meat when you are going to cache it. After you skin it, you cut it in half right through the middle of the backbone, and put the hindquarters inside the cavity after you clean the ribs inside. Take the lungs, heart, and liver out. Then you put the hindquarters in there. It makes a small hump when you put it together like that. You cut the neck and cut the horns off and put them right close together and cover it with the skin, fur inside. And get it down to the solid ground and knead it on the edges all around. And after you knead it, put tussocks all around it until you reach where you started. And then pour water on it. After it freezes the fox or wolverine never touches it. And that way you always get your meat when you go back. That way you could save all the meat you got in the fall. And when you have several caribou you put them together and cover them with skins.

I better tell a little more about Ootoayuk. One time when he was hunting close to Kirgavik, a big bunch of caribou were milling around. He had a brand new rifle, the kind you can put fifteen shells into the magazine. And he shot sixty caribou right there, in one day. And he did that skinning for a whole day and whole night, and the next day he finished them without sleep, skinning all the caribou. When he stopped skinning all those caribou and looked in the water, his eyes were all swelled up from stooping down. And he just laid down there and slept all day, resting. The next day after he ate, he started to put them away, gathered them together. And after he hauled them all he was pretty tired, but the next morning he went home. He didn't even bury some. He just put them together in one place and left them. And the next day he took all his family up there to bury them underground.

They carried as much as they could to the canoe and they went on up to Aviŋŋaq at the foot of the mountain, and they built a sod house and lived all winter there. Once in a while he went down and hauled some meat from that cache he had, all those sixty caribou. When the time for whaling came, he told me he saved the best caribou for the big feast at Icy Cape. And he brought them down when they went down for whaling.

One time, he was telling me, he was living on the Colville River with other families of Utuqqaq people, and he saw a big bull caribou on the side of the hill, way up there. That time, Ootoayuk was living with Kakmak's family up on the Colville River. He was trying to get as much caribou as he could before they started rutting, while they were real fat. When he reached that caribou, he shot it. It was a big bull, a real fat one. He just left it there and went to pick up his pack that he always carried. When he got back to where he shot it, the caribou was gone. He didn't know where it went. Finally he found the place where he knocked him down and gutted him. And he looked around. Something had dragged that caribou towards the river. When he walked along and followed those tracks, they led to a little ridge, a little ways away. When he got on that little ridge he saw a wolverine was starting to eat the caribou. That wolverine carried it on his back and dragged it all the way down there. More than four hundred yards he dragged that big bull.

The wolverine never ran away when he saw him. He wanted to keep that carcass. And when he got real close, Ootoayuk shot him. But after he shot him and skinned him, he went home and had to spend five days without going anywhere. He had to obey law of Eskimo. He was mad. He was sorry he shot that female wolverine. That's what he told me.

8

Being Around Jim Allen

Jim Allen was just like my own father, when I was really acquainted with him, after my stepfather was gone. I remember he used to tell me about my real father and those other White whalers up at Herschel Island.

He said that one time when they were coming home from Herschel Island, it started to freeze up on them. They didn't want to winter there, so he and Charlie Brower and Jack Castel[1] and some Point Hopers started home from Herschel Island with a dog team, going all the way from Herschel Island to Barrow. They had a boat from the ship, a whale boat, and dogs to pull the sled. They used little runners down the sides, a little bit higher than the level of the keel, so it wouldn't tip over. When the wind was right they put a sail up to help the dogs. When they got close to Barter Island they saw a lot of polar bears that were eating from a whale carcass. They were almost short of dog feed too. And one of the Point Hope Natives, them guys told him to go and shoot one bear so they could have dog feed. There were so many polar bears they were afraid. Finally they decided to go for them. They walked up to the whale, but one of the bears came to them, and they shot it right there and pulled it to the whale boat. They skinned it and used it for dog feed, and then went on.

When they reached Harrison Bay—it's fifty miles across— they ran ahead of the dogs, taking turns. Two men, that Castel and Brower, could outrun all the crew. That's what Jim told me. He found out that time that Brower and Castel were the toughest men that ran ahead of the dog team. They ran a long time. The other guys ran about an hour or so and went back to the boat and ran on the side. All of them White guys were young, Charlie and Jim Allen and Castel. And those two were the toughest characters he ever saw, that ran over the ice ahead of the team. They never got tired.

Finally they reached Barrow, and they traded that whale boat for one of Brower's canoes. They left from Barrow and sailed all the way down to Wainwright and Icy Cape, and all the way to below Icy Cape, and finally reached Point Hope, before the ice formed on the edge of the beach. It was freezing every night, but they kept on going, sailing night and day. And that's the story I got from Jim Allen.

Selling Fox Skins
My best years for trapping were right before I started with the Weather Bureau, early 1940s. That's when I got over one hundred foxes every year. At the peak of the white fox price I got one hundred and thirty-four foxes. That's the most foxes I ever got in one year.

I was trading with Jim Allen. He gave me about fifty traps, and every time I caught a fox with those traps I always sold it to him. I kept the foxes I caught with my own traps. That's the way I always do, so I could sell those fox and buy what I wanted when the ships came in the summer. Captain Pedersen used to work for H. Liebes and Company. That's where I sold some of my foxes. Everybody always did the same as I did. There was a lot of people that lent traps.

After Jim Allen started working here he bought lots. He ordered traps and he never sold them. Every time you caught a fox you had to sell it to him. That's how he bought a lot of foxes from different trappers. There were more than thirty or forty trappers at that time. If you lost one of his traps you had to pay for it, seventy-five cents a trap. That's cheap enough. Later on, I bought all the traps that I used from Jim Allen. When Dick Hall came from Kotzebue and put up a trading store at Wainwright, he had a lot of traps too. He lent them to different people, but I insisted on buying my own traps. Every time when he wanted to lend me, I never accepted it.

There were three stores at that time in the 1930s and 40s: Native Store, Jim Allen, and Midnight Sun Trading Company run, by Dick Hall. I used to get a few Native Store traps too. They put the initials NS on top of the spring. And Jim Allen put JA on his traps. And Dick Hall used to put DH. You always looked when you caught a fox.

Working for Jim Allen
Whenever something came up, Jim Allen always called me to come down and he told me. One time when we were short of flour in Wainwright, we started hauling freight in the early spring—last part of April or first part of May. Tommy Brower and his brother Bobby Brower, their daddy sent them down with a load of flour. Then Jim Allen, and Sheldon and Sammy and Freddie, we went up there to get a load of flour from Brower's Store. The trail was really good by that time. No snow on top. The snow was going fast and we left Wainwright and got to Peard Bay and camped over night.

The White people slept in the sod house there. And Tommy and I, we made a snow house. And we spent the night there. Next morning I thought they would wake up first, but we woke up first and started to get ready to go ahead of them. And Jim Allen told us to wait. Boy, I was mad at him, but I never said anything. He told us to wait until they got ready so we could go

ahead the same time. So we waited until they had their breakfast and then we started together. When we got further up they
started to drag behind. We stopped and waited. By the time
they reached us, our dogs were rested and anxious to go, and
we left them real quick.

When we reached Barrow, people were working there for
Ben Eielson, making an airfield. Ben Eielson was the pilot, and
the other one with him, an explorer. They were going to Spitzbergen through the North Pole.[2] So people were taking the
snow off the lagoon all the way to the end. Tommy told me to
go to work, so I did. And I asked his father if I could go to work
for a few days and he said go ahead. Everybody was working,
working to get ready for the takeoff, but they had too much
load. After I worked six days I quit and we decided to go home,
Jim Allen and I.

People were short of flour. I loaded on one thousand
pounds—ten gunny sacks of flour—and I bought two hundred
pounds of flour from Brower with the money I earned. That's a
twelve-hundred-pound load. Boy, that was really heavy, but I
had a big sled. Every time I stopped, my sled stuck. It was hard
to shake it loose when we first started to go. After it got loose it
was all right.

When we reached Ataniq we left four gunny sacks so I
could go faster. I was anxious to get home. I thought my dogs
would go faster, but they never did, even though I left four hundred pounds of flour there in my parents' little storehouse. I
made it back to Wainwright without any trouble.

Another time when we heard they were short of tobacco
up at Barrow, I took two cartons of Bull Durham and two or
three cartons of Tuxedo and Dixie Queen. Those Dixie Queens
come in a box, one pound tin. It's pretty big. I took two of those
that I bought from Jim Allen. And Jim Allen must have taken
some too when he went up.

That time, we had Jim Allen, Arthur Upicksoun, and Alice
Killbear, Jim's younger daughter. I took Arthur and Jim took

his daughter along. First day, we were going fast without any load. My dogs were rested after trapping season. And when Jim caught us he told me to stop when we got abreast of Skull Cliff, Tuapaktusuk. When he put a flag up, he wanted me to stop. So we stopped when he put up the flag. He told me to take Alice on my sled too. Still, he never kept up. My dogs always left him right away. They had good dogs too, all right, but not as fast as my dogs. Boy, Alice was kicking, trying to get to Barrow quick. She scolded me and everything, but I never paid any attention to her.

When we reached Barrow, we heard that Ned Nusunginya caught a whale, just about six hours before. They told me to go and try to get some maktak, so I went out there. They had already cut the whale up and started to divide it when I reached there. I took a whole carton of Bull Durham, and I gave them away free, to let the people who worked have a smoke. Boy, they were really happy.

I told Ned I wanted to buy maktak. He told me I wasn't going to buy any maktak from him. He said he was going to give me some maktak. And all I did was give him some Durham to smoke. And everybody was smoking and feeling real happy when they divided it up.

If somebody wanted to buy tobacco, I told them to bring me a small piece of maktak. So the young boys, lot of young boys, got shares in there and they gave me some maktak. I filled the box I was carrying right to the brim. I trimmed the blubber off and got all I want in trade for those tobaccos.

Up there I was staying with Bert Panigeo, and I gave Bert one whole carton and one pound of Dixie Queen, and I left a lot of my maktak in their icehouse. I had more than I could carry the second time.

When Fred Ipalook got a whale, I went down there too, and helped the people cutting up. Then I got all the maktak I want. It was a good whale too, small one, one of those small whales Fred Ipalook got below Nunavaaq. Just before I started home another crew got a whale again, but I didn't go out. I just traded my tobacco and Bull Durham to the people that had coffee.

We were out of coffee down at Wainwright. So I got about five pounds of coffee, trading my tobacco that I bought from Jim Allen. Jim Allen brought maybe one or two cases of tobacco to Brower's, I'm not sure. Those days when they were short of something they always divided it, distributed it among the stores so everybody could have some. They even did that with flour, anything.

The Baychimo Incident

When Jim Allen found out the *Baychimo* was stuck up above Ataniq, he asked Sheldon and Freddie and I to go up and check on that ship with him.[3] So we went up there and found *Baychimo* was icebound, couldn't work through the thick ice. Jim Allen went along with us to see what was wrong, and when we reached opposite the *Baychimo*, we stopped there and checked the ice, to see if it was strong enough to go out on. We took an axe and checked how thick it was. It was about four inches thick, five inches in some places. So we drove out there and stopped our team right on the young ice. The *Baychimo* crew came down, some of the officers, and talked with us a little while. And then they told us to stay overnight if we wanted to. So we took all the dogs ashore and left them on the tundra and walked out and spent the night there. Jim Allen made arrangements to supply meat for them if they were going to stay there a long time. That's how I got involved with them.

They told us to bring some deer meat for the crew, the captain did. We made a deal to haul meat and they were going to pay us ten dollars a carcass to haul it up. So we went back, and a few days later we killed the reindeer and then hauled them up, two carcasses each, six carcasses in all. On one trip, some of the crew members—the captain, the engineer, and two other sailors—decided to come to Wainwright. I took a guy named

Murphy along on my sled. I got to be friends with him. Those men were pretty cold; they didn't have enough warm clothes on.

After we were visiting, about one week after—it was late in November—they were getting ready to take off, and they cleared the lagoon back there where they could land a plane. Part of the crew was supposed to stay all winter.

Almost at the end of November, the wind came up from the south, just before we went up there to 'Chimo camp. They had a camp on the shore. It was a strong wind next day. Ice began to crush, break up on the shore ice, when the high tide came in. And it started drifting north after it broke up. That's the time during the night when the big storm came up. It took the *Baychimo* along with it in the ice. Boy, everybody felt pretty sorry about that. It drifted out, but it came back two more times. One time we were able to salvage lots of good stuff: lifeboats, chairs, mirrors, and compasses. Finally that ship disappeared and we never saw it again. That was the end of the *Baychimo*.

Hauling Coal

After I quit herding and became herd assistant, whenever there was a job coming, Jim Allen always called me up to work for him. I always did the job. Whenever he wanted somebody to go coaling, he always called Sheldon Segevan and I, and we hired some of the boys to help.[4]

He had a big whale boat about thirty-five or forty feet long, not like the ones the whalers use. Bigger one. He had that for a long time. When Jim went out the first time he bought that one from Seattle, I guess. I don't know where they built those boats. I still have the mast down there in the old house. And after that, Jim bought a launch with a twenty-horsepower engine. We always towed that big whale boat, and we towed six canoes when we went up there.

We went up to Coal Mine Number Three, camped there

with our families, and filled up sacks of coal. After we got his coal first, Jim always let us sack up four hundred sacks. Every year we always sacked up about one thousand sacks of coal in all. We sacked them, piled them right on the end of that coal bank, and hauled them from there. We put a name on each sack of coal, and piled them there in one place. We were doing coaling for Jim Allen, and all we did was pay him with coal. We gave him so many sacks for each canoe load of coal for ourselves. It depended on what he asked for. And when we hauled some coal for him he always paid us seventy-five cents a sack. I was a young man; a one-hundred-pound sack was nothing to me. Sometimes when the lagoon was rough like anything when we were unloading, I always unloaded two sacks at a time, holding a hundred-pound sack of coal under each arm.

Getting Stuck on the Ice

I worked with Jim Allen for quite a while, doing things like hauling freight down to Icy Cape. And we went whaling and walrusing. We always went with Jim Allen's boat. Hunting ugruk, boy, we always got a lot of ugruk in those days before airplanes started to fly back and forth on the coast. Sometimes we got over twenty ugruk in one day. The most we ever got was thirty-two.

I was whaling for Jim Allen for over five years. One time, the lead was way out, more than ten miles, maybe twelve or thirteen miles out. And we were whaling there. The whales were running real good the first ten days of May. And one day we chased a whale, almost got it every time. It had a calf on it, big bowhead. She was smart though. We got on top of her, but as soon as we reached her, when she came up, the baby was right on the back of the mother. And we never shot it. So we followed her, way up north of our camp, in two boats. That whale came up to breathe right in the center of our canoes. That baby whale never stayed under long. When he had to come up to breathe, the mother waited for him while he was breathing and then she went down without coming up. That mother stayed under for a long time, almost half an hour every time. She only spouted once or twice. She was from here to Dempsey's house, that far away when she came up, couple hundred yards.

But sometimes she came up right alongside of us. I was in the bow and wanted to strike that whale. She had big baleen. But she was really smart. And Ootoayuk told me if you miss the mother and strike the baby, the mother will crush our canoe; don't strike the baby. So we gave up when she went to the young ice.

Our camp was way down there, and the ice started to get closer and closer while we're working our way towards camp. Finally, it closed in on us about two miles away from the roughest part on the shore ice. Boy, that place was really rough.[5] And we had no sled for that canoe.[6] We had left our sled down there at camp, and we had to wait till the young people went to get it. We could pull and break trail at the same time if we had a sled. It took them young people about four hours to return, breaking trail at the same time. Then we started down to camp.

When we reached there we saw the water opening up inside. That happened while we were traveling down to our camp. When we looked from on top of the high ice, we saw a big open lead up there between our position and the shore. Boy, we were really hungry. We started to load up while they were making hot drinks for us.

We had left old Ardgailuk, Charlie Ardgailuk, down at the camp while we chased that whale. And the ice would have crushed our camp if he wasn't there. He moved all our gear up to the safe place while he was waiting for us at camp.[7] He was taking down the tent and packing it up, ready to put it in the canoe, and he was making hot tea on the stove. After we drank tea, we started to cut across, but there was no trail.

That time, we had Kakmak and Charlie and Ootoayuk and Jim Allen, those older people there. And only four of our young people: me, Sheldon, and Freddie, and Sammy Pameok. Boy,

we started pulling our canoe all the way to the lead by ourselves. The old people were walking behind us. Once in a while
when we got stuck, they helped us. That's the only time they
helped us, when it got too rough. Boy, we pulled the canoe, two
on the front and two near the stern, the gear and everything
loaded there. I took my shirt off.

Finally, we reached the edge of the lead late in the afternoon. And we were watching for our friends. That's Okresak
and his crew. They were not in the lead yet when we reached
the edge. After we put in the water, it took us about an hour to
pass through the young ice, slush ice that accumulated on the
edge of the lead, on that offshore ice. We were pretty safe.

We were lucky we had a sail on that canoe. We didn't have
to paddle. When we got to the middle of the lead, after we
passed that slush ice on the edge of the offshore ice, it was
rough water, a little bit. We crossed that lead way up, little above
Piŋusugruk. That's where we hit the shore ice. We recognized
that place. And soon as we hit the shore ice, we followed on the
edge and sailed down.

We were pretty tired, so we camped on a nice flat ice, on
the edge behind the icebergs. And after we had coffee we went
to sleep there. That was hard work, when we pulled through
rough ice.

After we had a good sleep, and lunch, we started going
south, following the edge, and finally reached in front of Wainwright and stopped there. That was the end of our whaling that
year.

Jim Allen's Movie

One time a movie man came from Hollywood, and he wanted to
make a movie up here. They decided to move down to Point
Hope; maybe Jim Allen talked with them. They went down there
to Point Hope to whale, and Jim instructed them on what to do.
He told me and Sheldon to take care of the store while he was
being a star on the whaling down there. Sammy and Freddie

went with them. Sheldon and I were left behind with Alice. And we put out a boat and caught a whale while them guys didn't get any down there. I never saw that movie. When I had a movie house in Wainwright I always looked for it, but I never could find it.

When they came back, Jim Allen was really sorry he didn't go whaling here in Wainwright. Most times you have a better chance in Point Hope,[8] but the ice conditions weren't right down there. The ice was closing in all the time. And about the end of May the manager of that movie crew got anxious to go back home. Jim coaxed him to stay one or two more days, but the big boss of the movie people, he wanted to quit.

As soon as they got in, Kunaknauruk took that place out on the ice. And that same evening, he got a big whale in that place. Kunaknauruk killed a whale right there! If that big boss waited one more day they would have gotten that whale. If they caught a whale they were going to pay Jim big money. But they didn't get a whale, so he only got paid his salary. That was the end of the movie star of Hollywood when he came back.

Raising Dogs

When Jim Allen went Outside I had to watch the store for him. When he came back he brought me a pup from Nome. That dog was from a guy named Fay Delzene, a winner of the four-hundred-mile race from Nome to Candle.[9] That guy gave a female puppy to Jim, he gave it to me, and I started to use her from then on. Next year I got another two dogs from Aaklu to make my team nine dogs. From then on I started to have pups every year, raising two or three pups with my female dog.

I got another female from Upicksoun and I asked him if he could give me a pup when his female dog had a litter. He had a dog from Greenland when he was in Icy Cape working for Jim Allen, doing trading down there. He got dogs from Rasmussen that time when Rasmussen made a trip down the coast. He and Wesley got dogs.

I got a female dog from Upicksoun, and I crossed that female with husky dogs. Boy, they really made a good team. I had a leader named Tony, really fast. And later on when I stopped using him, Jim Allen always used that dog. He liked fast dogs. He always trapped around here, around the village. And he always took one of the kids on weekends to look at his traps, so he took my leader when his own leader got too old. Sometimes I used some of Jim Allen's dogs too. That way we worked it out back and forth.

I got to know some prominent people through Jim Allen. That's how, I guess, they know me. I always talked to Jim when we went out to the ships. Most of the captains knew me and Sheldon were working with Jim Allen. I guess they did the same at Barrow too. That's how Tommy and his brothers learned all those prominent people in the early years—they always came on the *North Star* before planes started flying up here.

Walrus Hunting from the Boxer

One time Jim Allen asked the captain of the *Boxer* if he wanted to take us out walrusing.[10] The ice pack was a long ways out. We headed almost straight north, and we caught the ice close to Barrow, I guess. We hit the ice right smack where the walrus were. The ocean was real rough there. Old bulls were laying on top of the ice, and we shot seven.

Then the ice that drifted out from the pack came in and surrounded the ship. We could have towed those walrus out to the edge of the ice ourselves with a canoe, but the captain got the ship too close. Boy, it took us quite a while to get out through there.

We backed up and then went full speed and hit that ice, trying to break it. We never did for a long time. We ran up, pushed up almost to one-third of the ship in the ice sometimes, but the ship never broke that small flat piece of ice. Finally, on one of the tries, we broke it and got through. That was a close one. Boy, that captain, Joe Bush really got worried. He stayed up on the crow's nest on the top of the mast. The boat was lopping from side to side, but he never paid no attention to it. He hollered to his sailors down there and engineers. Boy, he really got worried. And besides that, ice was building on the outside while we were there. Finally, we got through. I was in the pilot-house after we passed through, and I told Bush not to go too fast. If we hit the ice, we might break the ship. Boy, when he passed the edge of the ice, just before it got dark, it was really rough. That old *Boxer* was rolling like anything.

The dead walrus were sliding back and forth on the bow deck there. One of the crew told us they got loose, and to go out there and tie them up. Nobody wanted to go. Everybody got seasick. And me and Charlie and old Nayakik, those are the only ones that went out there and tied those walrus. Seven walrus, over a thousand pounds each. When the waves hit, they went right across the deck and hit the rail on the other side. We tied them on the neck with a heavy rope and tied it where they tie the ship up when they get to a dock. We even lashed down the canoe on the side of the ship so it wouldn't move.

We traveled all night to get to Wainwright at nine o'clock in the morning. The captain asked me to steer the boat right toward the village. He wanted to let his other crew rest a little bit. I steered the boat right smack to Wainwright from the edge of the ice. Boy, the ocean was really rough. When the waves hit our ship from the side, the water flew over the side. Arraa!

Stormbound at Icy Cape

Another time Jim Allen made arrangements for us to take a load of supplies down to Icy Cape with Pete Strand in his schooner. We started in the afternoon, after we loaded up the ship with groceries and everything else for Icy Cape store.[11] He had a powerboat, two-masted schooner, and we sailed down.

But on the way the weather got worse and we had a real strong wind. The beach was really rough. Surf was high and

we had to spend the night on the boat. Me, Upicksoun, Sheldon Segevan, and Sammy Pameok went down there, four of us,
to put up the store's supplies in the warehouse. We couldn't
land the stuff. We waited there two or three days for it to let up,
but it was still rough.

Finally, the captain couldn't wait any longer and we started
to unload near the inlet, a little more than a mile from Icy Cape.
We went in there with our launch and a canoe. We made two
trips out, full loads, and went into the entrance and unloaded
them there on the high spot. Then we waited at Icy Cape for
the weather to calm down. While we were waiting during the
night, the wind shifted to the west and went around to the
south that day, and began to blow hard. Every day we went
down there and packed some stuff, all we could carry. We
packed them up to the store and put them in, but there was a
lot of stuff still down there. When the high water came, we
could see empty cartons of cigarettes all the way to Icy Cape,
spread all over there—wet, spoiled cartons of cigarettes. I
guess we had three or four cases, and lots of calico and flour
and coffee. Good thing we carried the sugar up first thing.

We saved a lot of the cargo, but they had saltwater on
them. We lost a lot of stuff, but we saved a lot of it too. After the
calico dried, we folded it back and everything was fine. We got
canvas and covered it up; that's the way we saved the flour.
Upicksoun was helping us too. The last time we hauled from
down there we were walking on top of the beach, right up to
our ankles in water. Boy, it was a strong wind, but it was always
a fair wind—behind our back—and we had an easy time when
we were packing. But when we went back with nothing on our
backs, it was a hard head wind.[12]

That time we put our boat on the back side of Icy Cape, on
the back side of the lagoon. That's why we saved it. We turned
it over and tied it. After the strong wind had let up, me and
David Brower went down there, and when we reached our boat
it was gone. Sometimes we saw it come up right in the river at

that entrance. It would go under for a long time and then come up again someplace. The anchor held it. When it got close, I asked David Brower to swim out and put a line on it when it came up. But he was afraid he might drift out.

I told him, "I'll put rope on your middle. You can swim out." He knew how to swim. He'd been Outside before and was educated there, and he knew how to swim in the swimming pool out there. But he wouldn't do it. He was scared. So I decided to try it.

He put a line on me and I tried to go through the breakers. They were high too. I dove in underneath a big breaker, came out on the outside and started swimming towards the boat. I swam as hard as I could. Finally, I grabbed the stern, and held onto the rail there. And when it came up, I took my rope off and put a knot on it and tied it right there. When the boat went under, I went under too. I was without breath for as much as I could stand, and pretty soon the boat came up. I held on and started to breathe on top. Finally, I tied the rope.

I couldn't tie it real quick. I tried to tie it underwater, but something was running back and forth hitting my hand. Stuff on the boat, tools and everything, were running back and forth on the bottom. Sometimes I lost the knot. There was a big ring on the keel below the shaft. That's where I was trying to tie it down. Finally, I got it tied. And then I told David to pull me in.

We picked a big log and hammered it down on the top of the beach and tied the boat there so it wouldn't go away. And when the weather calmed down, we went there to pick up the loose pieces from that launch: parts of engine, wires, and everything else. Magnetos were taken off. The distributor was broken off. I didn't know the sea was that strong. It could pull out the wires and everything. We found the carburetor top with the wires on way up there behind that point, inside the lagoon.

We stayed down there at Icy Cape all that time, cleaning the boat and drying everything that we saved. We put all the supplies back in the warehouse. Candy and chewing gum were spread all over the high water mark, every place. I don't know how many dollars they lost on that trip.

We started to fix our launch—made a mast and tried to go home by sail. But just when we were about ready to go, the rescue people came. We saw the launch way up there. Mr. Paine was the teacher at that time. He came along with Jim Allen and Charlie Aguvluk and Grouse Akudrigik. When we never came home for long time, they were looking for us. We had a house there, Upicksoun's house, and all the grub we wanted. They had maktak in the icehouses. We lived really well down there. We had maktak any time we wanted to. And lots of White man's food. But boy, we were happy when the launch came. We got home all right. Maybe Mattie was happy to see me when I came home.

Jim Allen's House

You've seen that old house of Jim Allen's down there? Our son Homer stays there now. After Jim passed away, I bought that house from Jim's daughter Kate. I decided to have a bigger house, so I sent a letter to her in San Francisco, where she stays with her new husband. And I asked her if she wanted to sell that house. I told her about the windows, how kids were breaking them, and that I wanted to buy the house before the windows were all broken to pieces. So she wrote me and told me to buy it if I wanted to. So I bought it from her.

I wanted to use that other storeroom they had on the north end for a movie house. And I fixed it up, put new windows in, painted it, and put a new floor on. After I fixed it, I opened the movies there in 1956. And I paid her a down payment on it. When I made money I paid so much a year until I finished paying it, and I had it for my own. We used it for a movie house, and we used the living room part and upstairs for ourselves. I was doing pretty good making money when I first started. And after I had competition, I just broke even.

Later on, my wife didn't want to have movies. When people started to drink I never allowed them to go in, but when they started drinking they made trouble, broke doors and everything when they had a fight in the hall. She wanted to quit the movies. So I closed it. People were disappointed, I guess.

Hauling coal from behind the lagoon. That should be Jim Allen's whale boat. Wainwright Inlet, 1921-22. (BA 21-205: A. M. Bailey Collection, Denver Museum of Natural History Photo Archives.)

9

Bringing Up Our Children

I learned it all when I was married. I was good and strong then, learned all the tricks—how to live on this coast, building snow houses, and everything else—all I could learn.

Training Kids

I trained my kids every time I go hunting. I always took the older boys so they could learn. I even told them how to put traps on, how far ahead you shoot when hunting ducks, how to judge how fast the duck is going when you are going to shoot. David learned all by himself from me, when I'm shooting geese and everything else. He always cried when I didn't take him. He was a really small boy when I first started to take him. When I went out to go round up the reindeer herd, when I become herd assistant, that's the time I always took him out, when the weather got warm in May and June.

He always rode on the sled, and when I told him not to leave the sled when I left him behind, he always stayed there. He was a really good boy. He minded me pretty good; that's why I always took him. When we were alone, I told him not to leave the tent, and he always stayed there.

When we had several children, I took all my family down to Ivrit one day. There was a big bunch of caribou milling around at back of Tingook's old house there, and we shot those. There was a lot more caribou but I didn't want to shoot more than I could carry. Homer was big enough to shoot that time. And Eddie was only a baby next to him. I told Homer to shoot only one. But when the caribou went by him real close, he started shooting, emptied his rifle. When I went down there, he got three caribou, small ones. I told him to skin all those caribou. Boy, he was really tired. He wanted to quit, but I told him, "Next time when you shoot caribou, you have to shoot only what you can work on." I tried to give him a lesson. And after that he doesn't like to shoot more than he can take.

The only time I taught the kids was when I was sealing, when the ice broke up in early spring. I took Nimrod and Dempsey. David was staying over at the time in Jim Allen's house.[1] He always stayed down there. I took those younger boys hunting in front of the inlet, sealing. I bought a .22 for Nimrod. Boy, Nimrod loved to hunt. I always carried him around when I went hunting. And we spent the night down there. Sometimes we got about ten or fifteen seals during the night when the seals were running good. And once in a while we got one or two ugruk and some spotted seal, during different summers. And he learned pretty good. Isaac, my half-brother, always took them along too, when they went hunting. Isaac always stayed with me in our house when he wasn't doing anything.

Isaac wasn't married then. He taught my kids a lot, those boys, Dempsey and them. Barry and Wayne, they learned it all by themselves following us, hunting. At that time, after the kids were grown up, we used to go upriver fishing with my big canoe. The boys always went trapping around here, close around the neighborhood at this side of inlet. They went Saturday, weekend, always looking at traps. Sometimes one of them caught a fox. Wayne got a fox behind that graveyard there. They saw how I kill the fox and they learn. I always carried a stick when I used to trap, and when the fox bites the stick I just step on him and kill him. Those kids learn.

Supporting a Whaling Crew

After Jim Allen died in 1945, around there, I decided to start whaling myself. I used the same people almost every year, except sometimes one of them didn't go whaling with me. I had my own boys whaling too. Dempsey, Wayne, Barry, and my son-in-law Billy, he was whaling with us all the time too.[2] We were always lucky.

I had a crew from Wainwright and some from Barrow. First time I started whaling, I had Ahngogasuk, one of the Barrow boys that came up a few years before, and Pete Sovalik, Issac (my brother), Frank Tukumik, and Dick Thomas, that's the youngest brother of Henry Peetook. One of the crew members was Byron James. I collected all the whaling gear, buying from different people and some from Captain Pedersen and the *Arctic*. And I became captain then, when I started whaling with the people in Wainwright. I was whaling for six years, and I got six whales. One year I got two, but on the sixth year I didn't get anything. Then I stopped whaling. It was hard work taking care of the whaling crew and the Weather Bureau work. So I quit whaling and started working with the Weather Bureau. My wife wanted to do some more whaling, but I quit.

That was the end of my whaling days on my own, but then my son Barry took over whaling. The other boys I had weren't too interested, but they went out with the crew every time the springtime came for whaling.

Naming the Children

All our children have Iñupiaq names.[3] When we had our first daughter, Minnie, we named her Ahneovak, after my stepfather, even though she was a girl. I named her after him. And when

David was born, I named him Aseaginna, Eskimo name. That's my uncle, that's younger brother of Ahneovak. I named him after that man. And when Dempsey was born, we named him Utkusik. That's a relative, I guess, of Mattie's. And when Wayne was born, we named him Tagarook, Ben Tagarook's name.

Amy, we named after Siuchiarook's wife, Atkilak. Siuchiarook, my mother's brother-in-law, is the brother of Kusiq, younger brother of Kusiq. When I went down with Charlie Ned, she was really good to me, that woman. That's why I named Amy Atkilak, after Siuchiarook's wife. She's a good woman, pretty woman too.

Barry, we named after Nakaak, stepmother of Mattie. When she died we named Barry after her Eskimo name. And Betty, we named her Sikrikak. She's a relative of Mattie's I guess. I never knew that person.

We named Eddie Shoudla, after Edna Shoudla's daddy, William Shoudla. We named him Shoudla. He wanted to be Shoudla.[4] He liked the old man Shoudla, and Mattie liked him pretty well. That's why, when he died, we named Eddie after Shoudla. And Waldo junior we named after Mattie's mother, Oenik. Homer is Kayalook. That's Jennie's sister's husband, Kayalook. He's half-brother of Mattie's daddy.

We were living for a long time before we named anyone after my mother. And my sons and daughters passed my mother's name on. There are a whole bunch of Kongonas here in David's kids, named after my mother. Amy and Billy Patkotak named one of their daughters Kongona, too.

My mother was a big woman. When she got old, she was kind of slim. But she could run real fast and she was strong. She always helped me when we made a house, when I was big enough to work. She always helped me, putting studs and everything in it, hammering them, everything else, just like a man.

Mattie and I, we always took care of her, even though she was married. She liked to have a new dress and new snowshirt on Christmas and Thanksgiving.[5] So I bought a calico dress for her long before, and put them away so she wouldn't be disappointed when Christmas and Thanksgiving time came.

The Motion Dance

She loved to dance, and I don't know why I never like to dance. She was a good dancer too. That's why the Wainwright dancers have good recommendations from outlying villages. She taught them when they were learning to dance, Mattie and other guys. That's where Mattie got good dancing, from my mother. My mother taught people those motion dances when we came back from Teller and start living in Icy Cape.

She taught Clara Forseland and Roseanna Negovanna too. They all were learning from my mother how to dance, and a lot of other people. My mother learned those motion dances from Teller people when we lived down there. I never learned them down there, but she did. She taught them to younger women when we moved up to Icy Cape and Wainwright. That's why they learn all those dances from her.

When we lived at Icy Cape, when they had a big dance, that's where she taught those young men and women how to dance. And then when we moved up to Wainwright, she did the same thing. So our younger girls, those Mattie's age, when they were young, she taught them how to do those motion dances.

After they learned them from my mother, they took them up the coast. At Barrow they danced with them too. Once in a while, when I go to a dance up there, when they are dancing, I see them. They use it, too!

10

Meeting People
through the Weather Bureau

In fall time, 1942, I went up the Kuuk River to go fishing with my family, around September. We went up there with a skin boat, umiaq—I didn't have any power that time—and we sailed all the way up to Kaŋich, then we went on to Uyaġaaġruk, a place where my family used to fish. We stayed there about two weeks. Then a canoe came from Wainwright with Richard Webb and Dr. Sinefelt.[1] Dr. Sinefelt was giving typhoid and diphtheria shots to all the people up there.

We decided to walk upriver to visit the reindeer herds that were at Avalitquq. I was herd assistant at that time. When we got halfway up, Dr. Sinefelt was tired and we had to stop once in a while to give him a rest. He was using the wrong kind of boots for tundra. Webb went on and got there first, before the doctor and I. We stayed overnight, and the next day they gave diphtheria shots to those reindeer herders and their families.

We forgot to take spoons when we went up there, so we whittled some spoons out of willows. We used those spoons, and every time after we ate, Dr. Sinefelt burned them up on the gas stove in order to kill the virus. We always laughed at him without letting him know, Mr. Webb and I.

That time they asked me to work for the Weather Bureau, to be a weatherman. So my family stayed up there fishing, and I went back to Wainwright to learn to be a weatherman. I went to school as soon as I got back to Wainwright. Mr. and Mrs. Webb were the teachers for Sheldon Segevan and me. They gave us the test and we passed. Those two teachers worked with us when we were sending the weather and coding. We had to change codes every month. That was during the Second World War, when the Japanese landed at Attu. I picked up the signal when the Japanese were talking, when they lived in Attu. Not always though. After I caught on to the old code real good, then they would send us a new one from Anchorage. I hated that. We had to study that new one before we started sending. Sometimes we talked in Eskimo, to send weather. Every three hours, twenty-four hours a day, that's what they told us to do.

We started working weather in twelve-hour shifts. One of us did the work in the daytime and one at night. That's the way we start working the first time. We had a transmitter and radio receiver, wind vane and anemometer, everything the Weather Bureau used to have. We were sending balloons when the weather was cloudy, to determine how high the ceiling was from the ground. We did all that work. And then, when we wanted to make a shift change, one of us worked for twenty-four hours, took turns.

We had a headquarters down at Anchorage. When we sent the weather, we tried to get it through wherever we could contact, either Nome, Kotzebue, or Barrow. We tried to send it to Barrow, but sometimes the reception was really bad, so we sent it through other ways. Bethel, Hughes, Nome, and Fairbanks, those were the best places to send it when we couldn't get through to Barrow.

We had forty-watt transmitters that time when we first started. And then Stanley Morgan built a thousand-watt transmitter while we were working and sent it down from Barrow.[2] Boy, after we got that big one it worked good. He built that himself. He was the first radio operator they had at Barrow. We put it up, connected it, and tried it. We had it for more than five years, and we could reach anybody. We could reach Anchorage. Sometimes we talked to them directly when the reception was good.

We had a generator in the school to power that transmitter. The Weather Bureau sent us supplies: oil for the generator, balloons, and helium to send the balloons up.

We always contacted airplanes and received messages from all over for people in Wainwright—teachers, anybody, even the ships. Some of the ships got their telegrams through us. We always had contact with ships, Coast Guard icebreakers, the *North Star.* That was our work. They sent messages through the wire all the time. My ears were pretty good, no trouble receiving messages, seldom missed a thing. But we never got paid for receiving messages.

Communication

We were the communication and we knew when things were happening anywhere. When the *North Star* came, as soon as they reached Nome, the radio operator started to contact me and Sheldon Segevan, and we talked every day. They let us know where they were, when they were unloading, when they were going to finish. We all knew about that when we were radio operators. Sometimes I told Barrow, when they couldn't reach *North Star.*

When I was working for Weather Bureau, I met a lot of people with higher education that came up on the *North Star:* the reindeer superintendent, and the big boss on the school, BIA personnel, and also some doctors. They always came up by ship before the airplanes started flying up here. They moved around all over the villages, trying to get acquainted with Eskimo people, I guess. That's how I met them.

While I was doing the weather, I got involved with the doctors and scientists whenever they came. Sometimes when we had an epidemic, I took care of people before they sent a nurse. I was just a health aide at that time; I wasn't a doctor.[3] But I did help quite a lot of people here, giving serum when I learned how to do that. And any kind of shots, diphtheria, and giving doses of medicine to the people when they got sick, before we had a nurse here. That's what I got involved with when the Coast Guard cutter came.

Working with the Doctors

I was doing the weather work, and when somebody got sick, they always got me to come over. Sometimes the teachers treated them. But when the reception was good, I talked to the doctor up at Barrow. And when I couldn't get through to doctors up at Barrow, I tried the Nome doctor or Kotzebue doctor. That way they always gave me prescriptions, told me what to do.

One year when they were taking tonsils out, I helped Dr. Waugh take tonsils out for the kids, about twenty children. I opened their mouths and he cut the tonsils, the skin on the inside of the throat. After that, he squirted it with medicine to make it numb. I just did that one year when he came with the Coast Guard.

And then after they brought them in, I watched those children in the schoolhouse. I put them together, made a bed on the inside of the schoolhouse. I watched them during that night. Boy, them kids were hollering, crying, and everything else. They wanted to have a drink of water, but Dr. Waugh told me not to give them water until daytime. They had to wait twelve hours in order to drink some water, then a little bit at a time. I always gave them two spoonfuls each, while they were hollering for water to drink. But after you watch them for two days they begin to heal up, and no more hollering. We sent them home after two days.

And from then on, every year they gave me some medicine, and I used it for Wainwright people during the winter. Once in a while a traveling nurse came here and instructed me in what to do, when I was a health aide. And in the wintertime, when the mail started to run by airplane, I always got a lot of medicine from Kotzebue, when Dr. Rabeau was there.[4] I used to get involved in some other things about doctoring. I always pulled teeth too, in those days. The Coast Guard and Dr. Rabeau from Kotzebue, they give me dental equipment and toothache medicine, cocaine, and everything else.[5] I did that work until 1960, I guess. That's the end of my pulling teeth, around 1960.

In those days we didn't have any penicillin, but we had sulfadiazine—three, four different kinds—and aspirin, cough syrup and things like that. But when a person had an accident or was really sick, I called the doctor and got the prescription he gave me, and we ministered it to him what the doctor said. Sometimes, when the airplanes start flying around here, they picked people up and took them to the hospital when they were really sick.

Native Healers

In the early years before White doctors, we used mostly seal oil for medicine, and those Eskimo doctors feel on the human body. That's the only doctors we had when I was a kid.[6] They always say "saptaq" when they were going to feel inside the person that was sick. They can tell, too, what was wrong with that guy. *Saptaq* means like that, try to find sickness inside a person.[7] John Peter could empty an appendix when that thing is filled up, empty it without busting it. Those Eskimo doctors, those feelers on the intestines, they can do that. They are really very good doctors.

John Peter was good with his hands. He always felt everybody when they got sick, and he made them well. He never tried to help people when they weren't sick. But when somebody got really sick, he went and felt their belly and stomach, intestines, and liver. And he made them well when he put it right.

That's what he did to me one time when I was up at Kuuk River. I really got sick, and good thing John Peter was up there with MacRidge Nayakik. I couldn't eat anything. Something was wrong with my stomach. It wouldn't stay down when I ate something. And I told one of the guys to go get John Peter to feel me. And after he felt my stomach, boy, it really got well real quick. I was real thin before he came. He knew what to do with intestines, and stomach, and liver.

When your intestines tangle on your kidney or something, that's what he fixed. One of my intestines was tangled on my kidney, and blocked the bowel's movement. I was pretty weak. My stomach was going up and touching my liver way up there, couldn't go down. And after they felt it and put it back, he told me not to do anything, and then the next day he was going to protect it, if they went back again. After he fixed it, I never had trouble no more.

Ever since people were living together, they had certain people among them that knew how to feel the human body. They learned it from way back I guess, from the ones that had it years ago. And also there was a doctor here, woman, Mary Patik, mother of Nannie Kagak; she was pretty good too. And also I've seen several people that know how to do that at Barrow too. They had about four feelers up at Barrow. They were really good, every one of them. One of them was Patugnak, and the other one Amikak I think, and Ooyogoak, and Illiak. I heard those people were good feelers up at Barrow.

Airplane Pilots on the Coast

Those days, when we first started weather work, there were not many airplanes. Sig Wien started coming in, but he only had three pilots working.[8] One of them was in Kotzebue and two were in Barrow; that's where Wien was stationed. Mail schedule was far apart those days. It never came regularly. It depended on the weather. Those days they had no hangar or anything to keep the airplane warm, so they had to use those heaters with canvas covers over the engine and warm it up that way. That's what we always used here when he stayed overnight. It was between 1940 and just before I start working for the Weather Bureau that those pilots start coming in with mail in the airplane. When they started carrying mail with airplanes they probably wanted the weather work up here in Wainwright. Some other pilots sometimes brought mail from Kotzebue once in a while, whenever they made a trip with hunters. They all brought mail.

Sometimes after we had supper, we had to stand by for pilots when they started to go in the nighttime, and they kept us awake, standing by until they came in. Those airplane people wanted to have contact with every station when they started to fly the mail, all the way from Barrow to Kotzebue.

Before airplanes they used to do mail delivery with dog teams three times a year; that was in the 1920s. They used reindeer the first time, and later on they used dog teams. We had several mail carriers from Barrow. They started first in November, then the second time they left was in January, and third time they left was in April. They went all the way to Kotzebue from Barrow; that's a long trip, a four-hundred-mile trip with a load of mail. Those days they had stores around here and people were selling a lot of foxes.

Delivering Mail by Dog Team
Then the post office decided to make a place to meet from both sides when they carry mail. They had a stopping place at Pitmigiaq, between Cape Lisburne and Tatchim Isua, below Point Lay. That was the meeting place. The Kotzebue mail carrier ran up there to Pitmigiaq and waited for the other guy if he got there ahead of him. The mail carrier from Barrow went down there, and if he got to Pitmigiaq before the other guy, he waited

for him. They changed the loads and the guy from Barrow, he went back with the load from the Kotzebue mail carrier.

Store owners shipped out fur as soon as they bagged them up, twenty in a bundle. I know Jim Allen always sent about ten or fifteen bundles through the mail. That sled was really high. Sometimes the mail carrier hired another man when they had too many foxes to load up. They're bulky to load on a sled.

Bert Panigeo and Johnson Kaiyakpak were the first mail carriers when I was a young kid. And later on Engnavina used to carry mail from Barrow to down there, after Bert Panigeo did. And then later on Ned Nusunginya used to carry mail from up this far north.[9] And then Sikvauyugak and Ahalik were the last people that used to carry mail, I guess. Those people carried mail every year with dog teams. And right after that they start carrying mail with airplanes. Sig Wien was the first one that started carrying mail. Once in a while John Cross brought mail from Kotzebue too, before he started working for Wien.[10]

In summertime they carried mail from Nome by boat, Nome to Barrow. The guy that brought the mail was Castel, that same guy that Jim Allen was talking about from the whaling days.[11] I don't know for how many years he did that—maybe two, three, or four. He had a big launch, real fast one named *Nanook*. He went all the way up to Barrow every summer, as soon as the ice went out in July. Then he went back to Nome.

Big Game Hunters

People from the States used to go bear hunting every spring, and they wanted the weather all the time. Those pilots used to come often in the later years, last part of the 1930s and 1940s. After airplanes start coming regularly up the coast, White people started hunting polar bears and I got into guiding. In those days I always got a guide license from Juneau.

One time I guided a guy who came in May. He was a preacher. We traveled around all over at Point Franklin, out to the lead. We spent the whole week there; never had any luck. And we camped out on the edge of the lead waiting for bears, but they never came around. He was a good sport, a middle-aged man. He shot several times at seals. He had a scope on his rifle, big rifle, a .300 magnum. But he always missed. I don't know why...maybe he was cold and shivering when he shot.

Another year, another man wanted to go bear hunting. That time we only saw a bear on the offshore side of the lead, but we had no way of crossing, so we just watched him. We would have gotten that bear if he was on the shore side. We waited for two days, but he never crossed the lead. He was hunting seals, in the hole, I guess, watching seals, but he never seemed to get any while we were watching him.

Then two years later, another guy came from Michigan. He was a farmer there. Walton was his name. We saw a lot of bears, but the bears didn't come across the lead. Every day we saw polar bears. Boy, he was anxious to shoot a bear, but they never crossed that lead. I was hoping that bear would come across to the shore ice, but he never did. One day we saw four bears nosing around where the offshore ice was broken, making a lot of holes looking for seal, I guess, laying down on the edge of the water waiting for seals.

So finally we gave up and went ashore. I was going to have a boat ready to go whaling so I wanted to work on that. He was paying me a hundred dollars a day, but after two, three days he moved to Oliver's house. He's got more room there. Oliver's kids were out in Fairbanks, going to school. I told him to go ahead to Oliver's house and said he could eat every day at our place if he wanted to. So we worked it that way. And I worked on the boat and paddles and got ready for whaling.

When they were ready I sent the crew out. And a few days later they came ashore with two bear cubs. They shot the mother because she came in and tried to steal all their meat. I put those cubs outside our house, made a snow house for them, and I kept them there while we were whaling. When that sport hunter came over from Oliver's place, he told me I was a lucky fool cause I got those bears.

A few days later, MacRidge was scouting around south of Wainwright, and he found a bunch of belugas. Walton asked me if he could go down there with those guys that went beluga hunting. So I said, "Go ahead." Albert Driggs took him down. And they got seventeen belugas altogether. There were a whole lot of them, but they didn't want to get more than that in case the ice started to break out after the storm is over. They might lose some of the meat.

So Walton went down there and stayed with people in a tent down there when they butchered belugas. Pretty soon a bear came through where they killed and butchered the belugas. Walton was there all right, but people beat him to it. One day a bear came in real slow. Finally, he got about four hundred yards away and stopped behind the ridge. Sometimes that bear stuck his neck over the ridge to look at the people. He was watching people walk back and forth in that place and watching dog teams. Albert told Walton to lay down on top of the ridges where they were cutting belugas and to get his rifle ready. And when that bear went on top of the ridge and started to look around, Walton aimed, and real steady, he pulled the trigger. The bear flopped down. And when they went down there to investigate, the bear was laying down behind the ridge already dead. He hit him right smack in the center of his neck, broke his neck. Boy, he must have been really steady when he shot. Boy, that man was really happy! He got the bear! And as soon as he got it salted and everything he went back home. He was a happy man when he got that bear.

I really liked that old man, Walton. He had a big farm someplace in Michigan. And he had three or four sons down there taking care of the farm. He wrote me once in a while when he got back home.

Another year I started guiding a walrus hunter from the

Seattle area. He was a farmer too, a middle-aged man. He brought his wife along. When the walrus came we went out there, Homer and I, and Alva's son, Alva Jr. We went out there with umiaq, and we cruised around way off in between the ice until we were opposite Point Franklin. The first day we just saw one walrus swimming. And he shot it and killed it, but it sank before we reached it. On the way home we saw another one swimming in the water away from the ice. And he hit it right smack on the head.

That man was a really good shot. I could never beat him when we were shooting. I had a .30-.06 that time and he had a .300. When we practiced shooting one day, he would always beat me when we had three shots apiece. He always hit the black spot where the ice was grinding. I shot way under, a foot under the target, but he hit it every time.

We had a rough time when we were out in really rough ice. After I made the trail he walked along behind me, but he never complained! He was a good sport.

Then we found about a thousand walrus laying on a big cake of ice. Homer was running the motors. When we got really close he got scared and turned around. I want to get really close to them, but he was afraid, there were so many. Two times we went around them, trying to spook them with the smell of gasoline, but they never did. They just sniffed at it and went back to sleep.

So I decided to get on the ice about a hundred yards away from the walrus. It was a good-sized cake of ice. And that ice where the walrus were kept moving toward us, until it was flush on the windward side of us.

Boy, his wife was shivering like anything from fear, shaking all over her body. And I let him shoot right there on top of the ice when the big bull stuck his head up in the center of that big cake of ice. He knocked him down, but the other walrus never started to go down in the water. They just put their heads up. There was so many; they were never afraid.

Finally, we took a cloth, soaked it up with gasoline and burned it right there alongside of them. The walrus were about from here to the window, that far away [about three feet]. And when they smelled that soaking sack with gasoline, they gradually started going down into the water, one at a time. Sometimes two or three jumped in the water. Finally, the whole bunch started going down. Boy, there were lots of walrus. I was worried about that. If they started down, they might climb up on our place; they might get to us.

Finally they left us, and we got the walrus he shot. After we took a picture of it, I opened the breastbone and punched it with my pocketknife and started to blow it up right through there. When it's full of air we put it in the water and towed it all the way back to Wainwright from up there.[12] I had fifty horsepower. We just towed it all the way to Wainwright, pulled it up to the bank with the tractor, and butchered it right on top of the bank here.

And after we pulled it up, I cut it and salted it and shipped it out when the airplane came, and that couple went home the next morning. He had a big farm down in the Seattle area. I guess he was making good money. I sold him some foxes and he paid me one thousand and four hundred dollars. I make four hundred dollars on that fur he bought.[13] He said he was going to give them to his daughters and relatives when he got back home.

And a few years later I took another guy out, a walrus hunter by the name of Albert. On the first day that Homer and I took him out, we cruised around all over without getting one walrus. We did see some walrus, but other hunters beat us to them. On the way home we saw a lone walrus, good sized one too. And he was in the bow and I was just right behind him. He got buck fever; he shot but missed it. Boy, I scolded him. I told him, "You get ready when we get real close."

But the next day we found five walrus on a cake of ice, and we walked over on the ice and got really close to them. He was going to shoot the biggest one, facing the other way from us. When the walrus put his head up he shot him in the back of the neck and hit him right there. But the bullet of his rifle went right through the neck and hit the ivory and smashed it all to pieces. So I shot one just before they dove in the water, and I gave him the one I shot.

A few days after he got the walrus, he took part in a beluga drive into the inlet. Boy, he had a great time. He made a lot of pictures of those belugas.

I met lots of people through that Weather Bureau work, and had lots of chances to guide.

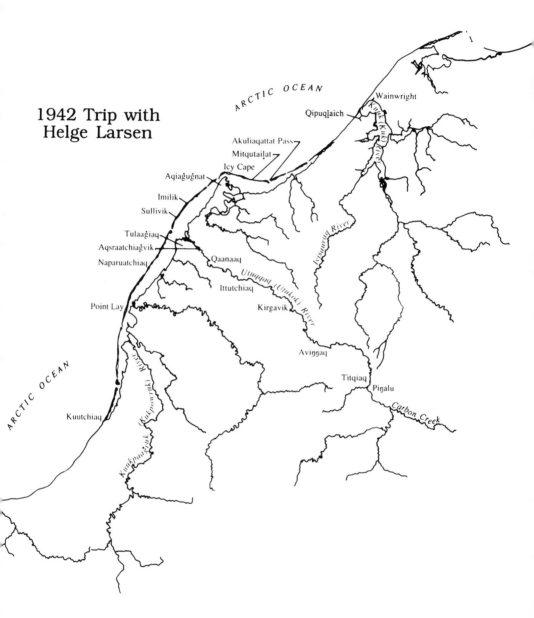

1942 Trip with
Helge Larsen

ARCTIC OCEAN

Wainwright

Qipuqłaich

Akuliaqattat Pass

Mitqutaiłat

Icy Cape

Aqiaġuġnat

Imilik

Sullivik

Tulaaġiaq

Aqsraatchiaġvik

Naparuatchiaq

Qaanaaq

Ittutchiaq

Kirgavik

Point Lay

Avinnaq

Titqiaq

Pinalu

Carbon Creek

ARCTIC OCEAN

Kuutchiaq

Kuk (Kuk) River

Avsuvuaq River

Utuqqaq (Utukok) River

River (Kukpowruk)

Kuukpaayuk (Kukpowruk)

D. Grahek • IMPACT Graphics • Rasmuson Library

11

Documenting Old Sites

A Trip with Helge Larsen

One summer, in 1942, I worked with Helge Larsen on archaeological work at Icy Cape and up the Utuqqaq to Piŋalu. That time we spent a month and half traveling around, even down to Point Lay and back through the lagoon until we got home here. Larsen found out about those places when he was digging at Point Hope with Rainey, and he wanted to check them out. That's why we went up.[1]

I really enjoyed that trip. There were a lot of mosquitoes though. When we were up inland we didn't have any mosquito repellent. We had a hard time, but we never had any shortage of food or anything. We were living on the animals, caribou and belugas, berries and things like that. We also gathered a lot of eggs when we first started, from the sand spit all the way down. I really enjoyed that. I learned a lot of things from him when we worked together, like how to dig in the houses.

We started out the last part of June or first part of July. Jim Allen took us all the way down with my canoe. I took a bag and my clothing and a rifle. Larsen had a shotgun, single shot, in case we needed some birds.

Before we left, we were digging down at Qipuqlaich, five houses right on the spit, on the lagoon side. That's right across the inlet, that high bank across there. That's where the people were always camping on the ocean side in early spring.

Three men went that time, me and Stanley Katuak and Norman Grouse. I took my canoe; I didn't have any outboard motor at that time. And I only took three dogs. If there was a head wind, they could tow the canoe on the beach if the weather was good. And Jim Allen took us down to Akuliaqattat. We started down from there when the ice started to break out. The ice was still stuck down at Akuliaqattat; but on the inside, near the beach, it was all water from here all the way down to Aku-liaqattat. And boy, there were lots of seals when we reached that big flat ice down there, the grounded ice. People were shooting ugruk that were laying on top of the ice close to the edge. We had three boats, including mine. And we camped out at Akuliaqattat when we stopped there.

The ducks started to move. They were running from the north, going south, flock after flock. And we were on the edge following that water. And some of the boys started shooting with that single shot shotgun. As soon as somebody missed, another person replaced him. Finally, Jim Allen said to me, "You go and shoot the ducks." And I got over forty.

Next day, after we had breakfast, we started down toward Icy Cape, inside the ice, working through some places where there was a lot of broken ice. Finally, we crossed the inlet and we stopped at the mounds there at Mitqutailat and picked up a lot of eggs. We filled half of a five-gallon can but didn't pick all of them. We left some for the ducks to raise. We only took half of the eggs every time we picked up eggs, and when we reached the last sand mounds down there, we filled up another five-gallon can.[2]

I let my dogs tow the canoe when there was no ice on the edge of the beach. We went along without a paddle, just riding along.[3] We reached Icy Cape that same day and went around the point and went in. After we had lunch, we started again to Aqiaġuġnat. We stayed there one whole week and dug up seven houses. And then we picked up one grave at Icy Cape, one old one. The bones were all dried up, just a skeleton.

When we finished work there, we moved south through the lagoon and reached Imilik; that's Shaglook's place down there. He used to winter there every year, when I used to stay at Icy Cape. He had a big sod house there. We dug up two houses there, old ones. There were three or four houses there. We found two old ones that were used way back in the early days. We dug those up. There was hardly anything except seal bones and ugruk bones and walrus bones. We found a few artifacts, like a comb and a pick made of bone for digging up roots.

From there we stopped at the mouth of Utuqqaq. We made it to Utuqqaq the same day. It was fair wind sailing along there. We made good time but we got stuck a lot of times right in the middle of the lagoon; it was too shallow some places. We had a hard time going back and forth to find the deeper places where the channel was. We never did find it. It was the same way all the way across. The only place that was deeper was on the edge of the sand spit on the west side. We stopped at Naparuatchiaq, but the houses there were recently made. There were three of them there, but we didn't dig any. When we stopped there I went down to the beach and found a walrus head with tusks on it.

Then we stopped at the place called Sullivik, where the Utuqqaġmiut used to sew their clothing before they went upriver in the late fall, before freeze-up.[4] After we stayed there, we went across and stopped at Tulaaġiaq and looked at those houses. There were three or four of them, but they were not too old, made by people from Point Lay and Icy Cape. Then from there we went into the Utuqqaq River and started working up. Wind was just right and we sailed right up to Aqsraatchiaġvik. We stopped, but we didn't dig there. We went on to Qaanaaq and camped for the night, where the coal mine is.

The next morning we went upriver as far as we could go, traveling all day. Late in the evening we camped again, way below Ittutchiaq. The river was so crooked I let my dogs tow the boat. I just talked to them from the boat, told them where to swim across and go to the other side. Boy, that Larsen was really impressed with my dogs. They were very well trained. I always used them a lot when I go on the coast there, before I had any outboard motor. I let them go across if it's not too wide. Sometimes we missed the main river when we were going up. We had to go back and go around that spot on the other stream. When we found the channel we went along pretty good.

The second day we reached Ittutchiaq and camped above it on that big riffle.[5] When we tried to go upstream on those riffles it took us quite a while. The boat was loaded up, and the dogs couldn't pull it by themselves when we went up those elevations. We had to help them. We usually had a hard time going upriver there. The river was high, and the water was swift. When there was a nice, long gravel stretch, I let the dogs go by themselves. But every place when we went up to elevation,[6] we always helped the dogs, took turns. Helge Larsen and Stanley were always partners when we pulled the canoe. And Norman and I were partners.

Finally, after maybe a week, we reached Kirgavik.[7] That was a long trip. We stopped there at Kirgavik on the sandbar and tried to get some fresh fish. The river was nice and clear; we could see them on the bottom, swimming around there. Finally, we got one or two trout. And we had a good supper that evening, fried them up fresh.

Lots of mosquitoes when we walk. Arraa! There were so many mosquitoes, I had a five-gallon can of seal oil that I took so I could rub my dogs' noses and faces and legs and thin spots, so the mosquitoes wouldn't bother them. That's what I learned from Kakmak, that's what he told me to take. The dogs were never bothered by mosquitoes when you rubbed them with seal oil. So every night when it's nice and calm, I always rubbed them up with seal oil. When you don't rub them, they begin to holler little bit when mosquitoes poke their needles right inside. When the mosquitoes get to them, their noses start to swell up. They always lick the oil every time I rub them with oil on their legs. But that seal oil lasted all the way up to Piŋalu.

It took us nineteen days to get up to Piŋalu. That's the place where Utuqqaġmiut used to congregate many years ago, after they went upriver. The older people used to tell me they helped each other when they went together, when they were going up. And sometimes they came across warriors from other villages like Point Hope, sometimes Indians and lone warriors looking for people who had killed their relatives. Those lone warriors tried to find out who killed their relatives and they tried to get revenge. But they never tried to shoot unless they knew for sure that was the one that killed their relatives.[8]

When we reach Piŋalu we camped there. Boy, the weather was nice all day, hot. One whole week we stayed there, dug up the old part of the houses that were there. We worked at Piŋalu for just a week. Half the village was undermined by the river and had fallen in. We just found a few houses that weren't washed away. When the river broke up, it undermined the bank and eroded those houses. But we dug up a qargi there. The qargi was whole—big one, a big place where they had ceremonial dances or whatever they had. Boy, that qargi was full of flint chips on the bottom. It had a willow floor, and it had a fire pot too, right in the center.[9]

Nobody ever told me about the ruins. Henry Peetook found them when he went upriver, when he was traveling with dog team from there. When he reached Piŋalu he went a little further, and then he reached the willows there. When he and his brother were making some hot tea and cooking some meat for lunch, Henry walked around there and found those houses. Even Kakmak never told me about it, and old Ootoayuk. They were alive at that time. Later on I found those ruins right back of the willows. Nobody ever touched them, those old houses. They had a wooden frame and bones, whale bones and everything.

When we reach Piŋalu I walked up to the top of the mountain. It was late in the evening when the weather gets cool. On top of the mountain is where the Utuqqaġmiut used to watch for caribou. They had a place there, on top of the hill, to sit down. It looks like a man when you look at it from down below.

The weather was so hot we never worked in the daytime. We worked from twelve to three in the morning and stopped working, digging those few houses there—about three or four, I think. In the daytime when you try to work, boy, there's so many mosquitoes. Even the river was warm, lukewarm from the heat. Sometimes when it got too hot we just went down there to the river, took our clothes off, laid down, just stuck our heads above the water.

Every day we saw wolves—three, sometimes four. They went into the willows just below us, from here to the church, I guess that far [about two hundred yards]. They stayed all day, and when the weather got cool, they started roaming around.

That's where the wolves congregated, a whole bunch of them. They always came in from different directions, sometimes three wolves, sometimes two. And on top of the hill, there's a rock piled up, a cliff there called Titqiaq, right across from Piŋalu. That's where they always stayed in the daytime when it was warm. When it got real warm, they went in the caves underneath there and stayed out of the sun. And when the weather got cool they came down to look for mice and food. They came real close to us, but they never bothered us. I could have got some, but Larsen wouldn't let us shoot them. The skin is too thin, that's what he said.

After we stayed a week we went downstream. That same day we passed Aviŋŋaq and we camped below there, down close to that river that goes south. You saw that when we were coming down, just a little above that big bluff there. That's where we camped the first day. And the second day we started downstream again. The wind was coming up and it turned cloudy while we were traveling. When we got close to the lake, a little lake on the south side, Larsen told me to hunt for ducks or birds so we could have meat when we had suppertime.

I started walking on that side. Lots of mosquitoes all right, but they weren't very bothersome. I just took my revolver, .38, and a single shotgun and looked around those lakes. It was the last part of July. The young ones were already grown up, nice big birds, almost like their mother. I shot a mallard, two geese, and four pintails. I plucked four ducks for our supper and got them ready to cut up.

On the second day down, I saw a caribou, a great big one, and I went over there and shot it. I was happy I shot that caribou so we could have all the meat we wanted. A good thing I saw that caribou; we didn't see any more until we got to the mouth of the Utuqqaq River.

Just below Ittutchiaq on that big, long bank down there, on the end of it, that's where I found an elephant tusk, whole thing on the bottom of the river.[10] I could see the big tusk and I wanted to take it, but Larsen didn't want to stop, so we kept going without picking it up. A few years ago, when we went downriver with that rubber raft, I tried to see that tusk, but the river was all filled in with gravel and getting shallow. It is buried there; I know the place all right.

When we got close to the mouth, just above Qaanaaq, we camped. Larsen wanted to camp right on the gravel, but I told him we were going to have a big rain. Clouds were getting dark everywhere. I told him we better put the boat way up there, carry it and put our tent way up there too. During that night, we had a big rain. Boy, the river was real high. It reached our tent, and the water started to come inside our tent. I woke up and found out and woke everybody up. Our canoe almost drifted away. I jumped up without any clothes on and turned the canoe up and pulled it up on the beach alongside our tent. The water almost reached our sleeping gear. Boy, I woke up just in time. It was miserable. When the rain let up a little bit, we decided to move down. That day we caught up with Blair Anakak and his wife. They were downstream too.

We put them in our boat and took them down to Point Lay. We never had any trouble from there. After we had the big rain we stopped at the mouth of the Utuqqaq, then we tried to go on the land side but it was too shallow, so we went across to the Naparuatchiaq place. Charlie Ned's house was there, and a few houses. We just checked up on one house there, the older one. We dug it up and checked it out, and then we headed down to Point Lay. We stayed about three, four days, I guess, in Point Lay. We went down below Point Lay and dug two houses, between Neakok's place and the Kuukpaagruk River.

So we started back from there. We sailed all the way to Aqiaġuġnat near Icy Cape in one day. The lagoon was high that time, and we didn't stick on the bottom. The wind was strong, but it wasn't really rough. We had a light load and went on all the way to Aqiaġuġnat and stayed there for a day, and then when the wind calmed down we went out through Icy Cape inlet and around the cape.

Then we went in through Akuliaqattat Inlet. On shore we found several graves, just the bones. Larsen took all those. He packed them up and shipped them to Fairbanks college. That's where he took all his stuff. That's what he told me anyway. There was lots of stuff he shipped out. We found a big jade when we dug up at Wainwright, at Qipuqḷaich. It was about one and a half feet long. I don't know what he did with it. It was a good one too. It was in one of those five houses. There was even mountain sheep horns in those houses, ivory, fishnets made out of baleen, and all kinds of artifacts, picks made out of ivory with handles for digging roots and *masu*.[11]

We looked around at Qipuqḷaich and found five houses. We found skeletons of people shot by a bow and arrow. A woman had a flint arrowhead right in the hip bone, right here. Two of the men were shot. Larsen shipped all of those skeletons out.[12]

Not so long ago, about two or three years ago, Larsen went to Barrow and he was surprised to see me. He was showing us some movies that he made at Anaktuvuk Pass with that little old man Kakinya. That was the last time I saw him. When I heard he was dying I felt badly. He would live longer, I guess. I don't know how he died. He was a good man.

I liked Helge Larsen; he was a good man to work with. We never had any argument or anything about the trip. And that's why I liked him. He never complained. He worked just the same as anybody on the trip and he was a strong man at that time. He was a good traveler, a good, healthy guy. When it was time to work, he never let up. And that's how come I liked him real well.

The Alaska Territorial Guard
After that, during World War II, I was working in the Alaska Territorial Guard, that's what they called it. They enlisted us as privates when we first started. Major Marston—Eskimos called him Maktak—came up here all by himself when the Japanese landed at Attu.[13] And he put Jim Allen as captain of the National Guard. Pretty soon, I got onto the drilling and they put Roy and I on bookkeeping. All we did is take care of the paperwork. And we had a big boss in Nome, guy named Otto Geist.[14] He was really strict. He always wanted to have the papers on time. He always gave us hell whenever the paper was late little bit... Otto Geist.

When everything was peaceful, after we were out of the National Guard, Geist always remembered me. I worked with him, and I saw him once in a while. When I went to Fairbanks he always told me to stay with him, but I never did.

A Trip with Otto Geist

One time I made a trip with him to Kuuk River, way up there, looking for amber.[15] We were trying to find some sources of amber, but we didn't find it. We found a lot of amber washed ashore on the beach in the river, but we wanted to find the source. Them old-timers knew it, but I don't know it. David Kayalook and his wife knew it. One time when they were caribou hunting way up there, they were coming through Qitiq and he found amber in the mouth of one of the creeks, a branch of Qitiq River.

When Geist come from Barrow by airplane, he wanted to take me up there. So I went with him and spent almost two weeks up there. He paid me forty dollars a day for going. I couldn't figure out why he was so interested in that. I asked him, but he wouldn't tell me. He wanted to find where the source of that amber is located.

He had a canvas boat, a small one, enough for two people paddling along, a narrow one. We loaded some of our stuff in that boat and towed it all the way up to the fish camp. And when we got there, we camped at Pagniġruaq, right across from Qikiqtasugruk, on the narrow place just a little above Sirraqḷuk at the end of the high bank on the south side. That's where the caribou were crossing, migrating toward the north. There were a whole lot of them. We didn't shoot any on the way up, only one for meat purposes, to eat whenever we felt like eating dried meat, or soup. It was a nice, big, fat one too. I shot that caribou with one shot.

Later on, we went up to the Kaŋich and looked around. The river was too dry; we couldn't go through. But we walked up, further up to those tributaries of Qitiq. Otto didn't like to walk far; he was old. Most of the time he stayed in the tent and did writing.

We found quite a few ambers on the beach, washed ashore. But we never found any big ones. We got a sack full of ambers that washed ashore between the rocks. But we never found the source.

We did some hunting that trip. He was collecting birds for the museum at the same time. We got some loons and hawks. I did the shooting. When he shot, he never hit anything. Once in a while he knocked down a bird, but sometimes he always missed. I got two hawks for him and one big loon, yellow-billed loon, and some curlews. There were some curlews around that flat there. We saw them once in a while when they were feeding, and that's where I got them.

On the way home, we saw a bunch of caribou right at the Aksragaġvik up there beyond first coal mine, right on the edge of the bank. All those caribou I shot with one shot each. One of the college boys from Fairbanks was with us and he was following me around every time we went someplace. And he told me I was a pretty good shot, just like a professional. I had a lot of fun with that young kid. He thought the world of me when we were up there.

It was late in the evening, about seven o'clock I guess, and the wind was picking up. The days were short, getting dim too, and we started straight toward Qaġmak Point, across there. We went out there and tried to get to Wainwright, but it was too rough. Boy, the big waves were coming in from offshore, southwest wind, so we had to go back to the end of the bank and we camped on the beach there.

When we tried again, the breakers were still high, but we made it. We just went outside the breakers, going real slow. It was still rough on the outside with high breaking waves, but when they smoothed down you could go in easy. I was floating around out there until a big wave went ashore and flattened out. Then I went full speed with my outboard motor and all of a sudden slowed it down and stopped it and jumped out. We didn't get wet. We had that little canvas boat, too. I told that college boy to pull it out as soon as we stopped. And we made it in without any swamping. Otto spent the whole day at our place, and then an airplane came to pick him up. That was the end of my trip with Otto Geist.

Documenting Land for the
Arctic Slope Regional Corporation

When the regional corporations started to organize, one year they sent for us elderly people.[16] Me and Weir Negovanna and Samuel Agnasagga went up there to Barrow, I think Oliver James too. And we marked all the sites that people used in the early days, selected them on the map so everybody could know where they are. All the fishing places in Utuqqaq and Avvaq and Kuuk and Kuugruaq, those are the ones we were selecting, all the way to Point Lay. We worked with Arctic Slope Regional Corporation personnel on that for maybe two or three days, then we went home.

Samuel Agnasagga and his brother Patrick Tukrook were doing the same thing around Point Lay area, and also Warren Neakok. After we selected all the places, the people that worked for Arctic Slope Regional Corporation put them on the map. And after they finished the map and put down all the names, they started using the map from then on.

We also worked with Flossie Hopson and traveled in the area of Utuqqaq with Bill Schneider and Samuel Agnasagga. We floated downstream with a rubber boat, down to the mouth of the Utuqqaq River. And we came home by airplane from the mouth to Wainwright. Flossie was the one doing the most work on selecting sites in Kuuk area, in Utuqqaq, Nuqullik, back of Icy Cape and on the coast.[17]

Waldo Bodfish
at the 1983 Elder's Conference.
(North Slope Borough, Iñupiat
History, Language and Culture
Commission.)

Mattie Bodfish
at the 1983 Elder's Conference.
(North Slope Borough, Iñupiat
History, Language and Culture
Commission.)

12

Looking Back

When I look back at my life after I live through it, I don't have any regrets. Me and Mattie raised our children as best we know how and taught them to be good American citizens, and I have no regrets. They're all grown up now. I was fortunate to be a father following the Eskimo way of life and teaching them the culture and how to live. I have no regrets at all. When they got older a lot of them didn't follow the rules I gave them. When they started to live by themselves, they do anything.

When I look back, it seems like a short life, but it's quite a long life all right. We didn't starve. Sometimes we had a hard time feeding our children. Like one year there was no White man food, when the store was out of everything. But we pulled through, living on Eskimo food. That's the way we used to live in the early days when I was raised up, when you bought groceries from the ship with furs and reindeer meat. When we used all those up, we lived like any typical Eskimo, without White man food until the ship came.

The happiest time I had was when I was hunting; that's the happiest time I ever had. When I got everything I need, I don't worry about meat. That's the happiest time of our lives, in all those years, when I was hunting.

We were all healthy all the time. We never got sick or anything. When the migration of animals came, we had all the food we needed as long as we had good hunters. Around the reindeer camp, we had everything we needed in meat products. And that is the way all the Eskimo lived up here at that time, and I don't regret anything. I learn to live like any Eskimo when I was a young man. And I got through all the days of my life without any regrets. So I guess that's about it.

The Collaboration

The collaborators:
James Mumigana Nageak,
Leona Kisautaq Okakok,
and William Schneider.
(Photograph by Richard
Veazey, Rasmuson
Library.)

13

The Historical Context

William Schneider

A chapter of this sort typically appears at the beginning of books, to provide a framework for the reader to understand the narrator and the stories that follow. I have instead placed it here, following Waldo's stories, because I want readers to encounter Waldo's words, emphasis, and meanings first, and only afterward to consider the narrative in light of the commentary provided here. When Waldo tells his stories, it's easy to imagine his experiences, to feel the cold of his first whaling camp, to recognize his growing confidence as a herder, and, when he recalls the harder times, to appreciate his struggle to market reindeer products and to keep the herders supplied. His stories establish a framework of their own, regardless of their place among historical events.

In this chapter, though, I discuss Waldo's experiences and observations against the backdrop of historical themes such as exploration, commercial whaling, trading, and reindeer herding. The historical setting also includes the people who influenced Waldo's life. The second part of the chapter highlights these individuals and the way they are presented by Waldo in his stories. While my general approach in this chapter is to use Waldo's experiences as a springboard for discussion, I will begin by briefly recounting the historic events that precipitated the arrival of commercial whalers.

The Explorers

Captain James Cook, the famous British naval explorer, sailed north along the Alaskan coast in 1778. He was in search of an ocean passage across North America, a shortcut to the riches of the Far East. Cook was turned back by the ice at Icy Cape, a place that would play a prominent part in future expeditions and, years later, in Waldo's life.

The Russian government, aware of the British efforts and eager to maintain a presence if not control of the entire Alaskan coastline, sponsored several expeditions north through the Bering Sea. In July 1820 Russian navigators Mikhail Vasiliev and Gleb Shishmarev managed to travel thirty-five miles north of Icy Cape before they, too, were turned back by the ice (VanStone 1977:5).

While the Russians were rather modest in their Arctic exploration, the British admiralty was committed to navigating the Northwest Passage. Sir John Franklin, a British explorer, played a major role and eventually lost his life in that effort. In his second voyage (1825–1827), Franklin traveled overland from the east coast of North America to the mouth of the Mac-Kenzie River in northwestern Canada. He then headed west by boat along the coast hoping to reach Icy Cape. His party was to meet Captain Frederick Beechey, who sailed along the coast in the *Blossom,* approaching Icy Cape from the west. The *Blossom* rounded the cape and proceeded east to Cape (Point) Franklin, then returned to Icy Cape, where Thomas Elson was dispatched in a small boat to travel east to look for Franklin and explore the coast. Elson reached Point Barrow and turned back before making contact with Franklin (Beechey [1831] 1968:425). Franklin had turned back at Return Reef, two hundred miles east of Barrow. The combined effort left only two hundred miles of coastline unexplored, a stretch that Thomas Simpson traversed on foot and by canoe in the summer of 1837, thereby giving Great Britain the honors for completing exploration of the Arctic Coast of North America (see Simpson 1843).

But some of the most interesting observations were yet to be made. Of particular note is the Russian expedition led by Second Lieutenant A. F. Kashevarov in 1838. Traveling in Native craft, Kashevarov made his way north along the coast of the Chukchi Sea. His journal provides ethnographic descriptions of people living along the coast, their territorial boundaries, and their settlements. Like some of his Russian contemporaries, he paid particular attention to ethnographic detail and demonstrated a sensitivity to local people and practices, perhaps because of his own background. Kashevarov was a Creole, of mixed Russian and Aleut or Eskimo descent. He was trained in St. Petersburg to be a naval officer, and at the time of this expedition he had a solid reputation as a navigator (VanStone 1977:9).

Unlike the earlier British explorers, Kashevarov traveled with an interpreter. Some of the places he documented are mentioned in Waldo's story: Icy Cape, Qilamittaġvik, Ataniq, and Piŋusugruk. His description of the Utuqqaq people provides a historically early—perhaps the earliest—picture of their adaptation to inland and coastal resources (VanStone 1977:25). For elders on the North Slope, this written record merely reinforces what they have heard in the oral tradition, but for those of us oriented toward written records, having the names and descriptions in a document over 150 years old adds exciting confirmation to the antiquity.

Interest in the Arctic was not limited to the British and Russians. John Bockstoce records how American whalers ventured north into Bering Strait:

> In 1848 an American whaling captain, prompted by
> Beechey's report of large numbers of whales in the Arctic
> Ocean, reached Bering Strait and quickly took a large
> catch. The enormous success enjoyed by a few ships in
> the next year quickly drew others, and within a few years
> as many as 150 ships were passing into the Arctic Ocean
> annually. (Bockstoce 1977:9)

The whaling captain was Thomas Roys and the ship was the
Superior.

> Despite the continuing apprehension of his officers and
> men, Roys drove the ship another 250 miles north before
> turning back. He took whales all the way. His tryworks
> were never cool so fast did he catch whales and melt oil
> from their blubber. (Bockstoce 1986:24)

A whaling voyage could last two, three, or four years, and
the crew might be bound for the Pacific Ocean, the Indian
Ocean, the Northwest Coast, and after 1848, the Arctic Ocean.
For the next half century, the Arctic whaling grounds were a
primary destination of American whalers, many of whom came
from New England and Long Island ports such as New London, Stonington, Fairhaven, Warren, New Bedford, Nantucket,
and Sag Harbor.

Captain Hartson Bodfish

Captain Bodfish grew up on Martha's Vineyard in the heart of
the East Coast whaling community, a short boat trip from New
Bedford, the most important of the eastern whaling ports.
When the transcontinental railroad was completed, the center
for the Pacific whaling industry shifted to San Francisco (see
Bockstoce 1986:172, 174). Oil and whalebone were shipped by
rail to markets in the east. Bodfish witnessed firsthand the

move to the west but, like some other whalers, he maintained his close ties in the east. In his biography he describes traveling east to visit his family in 1892, arriving in time for Thanksgiving. That same winter he married Clara D. Howes. He relates how they traveled to the 1893 World's Fair in Chicago and then went on to Fresno, where they parted company. He left to sail north and she apparently returned to Martha's Vineyard (Bodfish 1936:86–87). Over the years Bodfish continued to travel east between whaling voyages; his obituary reports forty-four continental crossings by rail (*New York Times,* February 2, 1945, p. 19, col. 4). Reflecting on his first voyage as captain of the *Beluga* in 1899, he wrote

> I made my usual between seasons visit to my home and family, but there was not much time for a man to stop ashore if he was to pursue the whaling business successfully. I dare say that in this respect I fared much better than many of the sperm whalers, but for all that the winters at home passed swiftly. (Bodfish 1936:174)

When the *Beluga* sailed in 1900, Captain Bodfish planned to winter in the Arctic. It was his second trip as captain, and it is likely that Waldo was conceived on this trip. It was not unusual for the whalers to father children with Iñupiat women. Some of the men left when it was time for their ship to sail; others stayed in the North. Quite a few names on the North Slope can be traced back to relations established during the whaling period: Bodfish, Leavitt, Hopson, and Brower. Whalers who became shore-based traders often married Native women, had children, and lived the rest of their lives in the Arctic. Prominent in this respect were Charlie Brower and Fred Hopson at Barrow, Jim Allen at Wainwright, and Tom Gordon at Barter Island.

Captain Bodfish never mentions his Eskimo family in his

autobiography, but family matters in general play a small part in his story. Perhaps the relative isolation of the Alaskan Arctic before World War II insulated the captain from the scrutiny of New Englanders, or perhaps such matters did not attract widespread public attention. In Alaska, however, the situation was quite different, because in Iñupiat society, when two people have sexual relations they form a definite kinship bond, a positive relationship with rights and responsibilities for the couple and the offspring.

I suspect that Lucy Kongona and Hartson Bodfish realized their cultural differences and did what they needed to do: Hartson sailed south but maintained a level of support, while Lucy left the ship at Port Clarence near Teller and raised her child as an Iñupiaq, with knowledge of his father and the world of the whalers and traders, but with the skills, customs, and support that he would need to survive as an Iñupiaq.[1]

The Decline of Commercial Whaling
The *Beluga* sailed south from the Arctic in the fall of 1901, with twelve and a half whales to show for nineteen months at sea. At age thirty-nine, Captain Hartson Bodfish was one of the most successful of the whalers, and in his twenty-one years at sea he had seen significant changes in the industry: the shift from the East Coast to the West Coast, the advent of steam whaling, and the practice of wintering over in the Arctic ice. But by 1901, whales were harder to find than they had been during the boom of 1850, and petroleum had replaced whale oil. Soon synthetics would replace the strong, flexible products derived from baleen or whalebone. Because of the growing interest in the fur trade, trade goods had become a standard part of ships' supplies, and the industry that Bodfish had been so much a part of was struggling to survive (see *New York Times,* February 2, 1945, p. 19, col. 4; Bodfish 1936:190; Bockstoce 1986:166, 327, 335).

Teller in 1901

When Lucy left the *Beluga* in the fall of 1901, Port Clarence and nearby Teller were probably among the busiest places in Alaska, supported not by whaling but by two growing industries: gold mining and reindeer herding. Nome, with its gold discoveries, attracted international attention, while Teller, with its safe harbor, became a reindeer herding center. There was some gold mining in the Teller area, particularly during the boom of 1900, and there was a recording office and a commissioner, but production there never did compete with the Nome diggings (Collier et al. 1908:24, 271).

Reindeer Herding

Teller is best known as the center of Sheldon Jackson's reindeer herding program. The original purpose of the reindeer program was to provide meat to the Eskimos. Jackson saw that the whalers were depleting the whales, and he knew that the caribou were scarce (see chapter 1, note 15). He sincerely believed that the Eskimo people were starving. In his capacity as Special Agent of Education for Alaska, he traveled along the coast on the U.S. Revenue Cutter Service ships, and he talked about his hopes of building a solid economic base. Jackson is usually given credit for the plan to import reindeer from Siberia, but credit also goes to Captain Michael A. Healy of the Revenue Cutter Service.[2] Healy agreed to assist in the transfer of reindeer from Siberia to Alaska, and he was responsible for bringing the deer to Teller.

One of the first Eskimo reindeer herders was Waldo's uncle, Riley Ahlook. Waldo's stepfather, Andrew, was apprenticed to Riley. Riley's experiences extended back to Sheldon Jackson's reindeer herding program at Teller, where he learned to herd from the Saami (Lapp) herders. The reindeer reports trace his success in the program and the increased responsibilities he assumed. Riley was also reported to be part of the famous reindeer drive to Barrow.

In the fall of 1897, whaling ships were caught in the ice near Barrow and were frozen in for the winter. The men were taken to Barrow, and news of their dilemma was sent out. When President William McKinley learned of the situation, he appropriated funds for the military to purchase reindeer and drive them north to feed the whalers. Riley Ahlook was chosen to go on that drive, and he helped establish the first herd at Barrow.[3]

When the herders arrived at Barrow, they found that the men had been well provided for by Charlie Brower, the trader, and by Iñupiat hunters who had been successful in finding caribou far in the Interior. Disaster had been averted and Barrow had the beginning of a reindeer herd.

Although Riley did some herding in Barrow, he spent many of his herding years at Icy Cape. During his tenure, the emphasis was on close herding, staying with the reindeer day and night, and on earning personal deer for each year of herding. In this way, the deer got used to people and to handling. This was the old way; it required a lot of walking and a great deal of time out on the tundra away from the village.

In the first forty years of his life, Waldo grew up with the herds. He traveled to Barrow and Icy Cape, where his stepfather tended reindeer, and he learned the daily life of the herders. His first hunting experience was for geese and ptarmigan that fed on the lee side of the herds.

Waldo's story chronicles major changes in the reindeer industry: the shift from close herding to open herding, the transition from individual ownership to company herds, the rise and subsequent decline in herd size, the difficult search for markets, and the growing discontent of the herders. The most significant policy change was the decision to combine individual herds into community or company herds. This meant that the main time for handling deer was at the annual roundup. After a long period on their own, the reindeer were hard to control, and separating each village's herd was a major part of the roundup. Representatives from surrounding villages were present to collect their deer. The herds were counted, fawns marked, bulls castrated, and deer slaughtered for local use and for sale.[4]

For several years while Waldo was herd assistant, he shipped reindeer skins and carcasses on the USS *Boxer,* a Department of Interior ship, predecessor to the *North Star* ships of the Bureau of Indian Affairs. He found that it was hard to develop markets to sell the reindeer products. There were some local buyers, but selling reindeer meat outside Alaska involved far more work than he could do from Wainwright. As the Lomens had learned in the Nome area, selling reindeer outside Alaska meant fighting with the beef industry and cultivating people's tastes for reindeer meat.[5] Although he took pride in his ability to provide for the herders, Waldo found it hard to make enough money on reindeer to keep the herders in supplies. Keeping good herders was a continual concern.[6] The open herding policy and the combining of individual herds into company herds had not been wise. The transfer from tangible ownership of deer to paper stock shares made little sense to many herders (Rainey 1941:12). It was a difficult situation. By the time Waldo took the Weather Bureau job, there wasn't much of a future for reindeer herding in Wainwright.

World War II and Radio Communication
Waldo and Mattie were fishing on the Kuuk River when word came that the schoolteacher wanted Waldo to train for the Weather Bureau. It was during World War II, and the Japanese had reached the Aleutian Islands. Few Americans realize that Alaska, like Hawaii, was a war zone during the latter part of World War II. In many parts of Alaska, particularly in the Aleutians, in the cities, and along the transportation routes, there was a major military buildup. Many rural areas such as the North Slope remained isolated and were spared a military presence, but reports of the war and military buildup in other parts of the territory fueled feelings of fear and vulnerability to attack.

For Waldo, the Weather Bureau job was a window to the

war and to the people who traveled the coast. It also provided a connection to medical help in Kotzebue and Barrow. In Wainwright, as in other Native communities, the radio diminished the isolation and connected the weathermen to the western world in a direct and immediate way. They were a link in a communications system that extended hundreds of miles from rural villages to towns and big cities. For airplane pilots and ship captains, the weather reports helped fill a gap in the coastline, providing a point of reference for plotting the movement of storms and bad weather. This was a big help for aviators. Before radio operators, when pioneer pilots took off, they often didn't know what weather conditions they would encounter.

Pioneer Aviators

Waldo met some of the pioneer aviators, and he saw many stages of northern aviation, from Eielson's and Wilkins's preparations for their 1928 flight over the pole to modern air taxi service. Eielson and Wilkins attracted attention locally and internationally. The Eielson-Wilkens flight was as important as some of the Russian and British explorations of the eighteenth and nineteenth centuries because it prompted the consideration of new international travel routes. While Eielson realized the importance of his flight, he was modest about the achievement. When asked about the hardships, he said, "It seems like a mockery to compare our trips in a well warmed cabin airplane with the hardships other explorers have endured" (Potter 1945:51). The legacy of these pioneer aviators is evidenced today in the transpolar flights from Anchorage to England and Scandinavia.[7] It is also seen in the growth of air services to the villages.

As bush pilots began to fly the coast, Waldo's and Mattie's house became a familiar and comfortable stopover for pilots resting or waiting on the weather. For many years there were but a handful of pilots who worked the coast. Today there are several flights a day and many air taxi operators.

Traders as a Link to the Outside

Wainwright is no longer the isolated place that it was when Waldo and his cousin Henry Peetook were young boys. They waited at Icy Cape for the trading ships to come up with supplies. For the rest of the year they were isolated from the outside and depended on their traditional Native food. The Native transition to western trade goods began in the days of the commercial whalers, who found that there was a market for white fox fur, and balanced the declining value of whaling with the increased profits to be made by trading for fur (see Pedersen 1944). There was a transition period of sorts, but as trading became the focus of trips north, the race was on to see which companies could get their ships to the Arctic first in the spring to trade for the fur that the Iñupiat trappers had gotten all winter. One of the most famous of the traders was C. T. Pedersen. He is remembered by many elders for his skill in piloting through the ice and arriving before the other ships.

In addition to the trading ships, there were also a few shore-based traders, some representing H. Liebes and Company, some independent. The more prominent traders were Charlie Brower at Barrow, Jim Allen at Wainwright, and Tom Gordon at Barter Island.

These traders played a role in moderating the isolation of northern settlements. Besides providing trade goods, they also conveyed and interpreted news that they received in the mail or from the ships. Waldo's friendship with Jim Allen offered him opportunities to meet new people, "prominent people," to contract coal deliveries, to make trips to Barrow, and to run the store while Jim was away. These opportunities were not available to many others.

Waldo's Iñupiat Teachers

Waldo's relationship with Jim Allen, like the Weather Bureau job, was a window to the world outside Wainwright. But Waldo was also fortunate to have Iñupiat people take a special interest in him and provide him with a window to the Iñupiat world. Waldo's Iñupiat teachers are particularly important because they helped him grow up with the Iñupiat values and understandings that he needed to survive. Waldo's stepfather died during the winter, and the major responsibilities for the family fell onto Waldo's shoulders. Waldo was a young man, competent as a herder, but he had little experience providing for a family. What he did have was a sense of confidence and practical skills, which he had learned from his Iñupiat teachers. He had watched closely and listened carefully to what was shared.

When he was at the Brevig Mission school, Waldo's grandmother played a part in his upbringing. He fondly remembers how she sewed for him and how he packed supplies for her. He learned that she was living off the land, that she could gather and hunt. She gave what she made, and that was special for Waldo. Another important woman in Waldo's upbringing was Angoyuk, the old woman at Icy Cape to whom Waldo gave his first seal, and who reciprocated with a bird net and other forms of support, tangible signs that Waldo had become a hunter and provider. The bond of sharing continued as long as she lived.

Several older men played a prominent part at different times in Waldo's education. His uncle Fred taught him to herd and was like an older brother and "a real pal." When Fred married, Waldo stayed with him and his wife until Waldo was a young man. At Icy Cape, when Waldo was a teenager, he met Shaglook, who took a special interest in him. Shaglook's stories were a source of information about the Messenger Feast and trading with the ships. Waldo respected Shaglook for his hunting and trapping skills and his ability to make a living off the land while helping others.

When Waldo's mother remarried, she married Walluk, a competent hunter. Waldo's description of learning to hunt seals at the breathing hole shows the respect he had for this man and his knowledge of hunting on the ice. Later, when Waldo had mastered hunting and trapping himself, he took old Ootoa-yuk out because the old man had just lost his wife and was lonely. Waldo thought he was helping him adjust, but he found that Ootoayuk was ready to teach him about the Eskimo laws of respect for animals and about his hunting knowledge. Waldo learned about the traditional taboos, and he came to appreciate Ootoayuk's experience and understanding.

Each of these individuals had a positive influence on Waldo at a different time in his life. They taught particular things, and Waldo learned from them. He shows his appreciation by the way he describes them in his narrative: Walluk is a good hunter and provider, Ootoayuk is a fine traveling companion who taught him Eskimo ways, his grandmother is a good sewer who made him caribou socks and squirrel and muskrat parkas, and Angoyuk is the woman who helped him celebrate becoming a hunter. Shaglook is remembered for his generosity, for teaching Waldo how to build snow houses, and Waldo portrays him as a smart, good hunter all around. Finally, Waldo describes the way his uncle Fred taught him to herd and helped him to become a man.

Each of these people is a thread in the fabric of Waldo's personal history. By their examples they enriched Waldo's life and gave him confidence to live on the land. He tells us about their contributions and points out how he learned from them, because they were important in his development.

Learning through personal experience also extends to this book and to my relationship with Waldo. By emphasizing old places on the land, he builds on our experiences together and expands on what he has taught me during our trips to many of the sites.[8] In the next chapter I describe our relationship—how it developed and how it influenced this work.

14

The Collaborative Process

William Schneider

Since 1976, I have worked with Waldo many times. We have traveled extensively to the old places, and we have recorded many hours of his stories in his house. This chapter chronicles our work together and explains how he taught me Iñupiaq history and how I compiled and shaped that information into this book.

Over the years Waldo and Mattie have generously provided their house as a comfortable gathering place for aspiring and accomplished students. Helge Larsen, Otto Geist, Fred Milan, Richard Nelson, and John Burns had been there before me, and others, including Dale Slaughter, Barbara Bodenhorn, and David Libbey, would be there after me.[1] Waldo and Mattie have shared their home and their knowledge with each of us.

Traveling with Waldo, 1976

I arrived at Waldo and Mattie's in the summer of 1976, having been sent by the Cooperative Park Studies Unit of the National Park Service to assist the North Slope Borough in documenting historic sites in the Wainwright area. I was accompanied by Flossie Hopson Andersen and Evelyn Tuzroyluk from the North Slope Borough Planning Department.[2] Flossie was the driving force behind the Borough's program to document historic sites, and her work with elders like Waldo served as the basis for my research in Wainwright.

Waldo and I traveled up the Kuuk River to the old places where the Kuuġmiut (people of the Kuuk River) had lived and where today their descendents continue to hunt and fish. I was excited when I saw those sites, because they represented a type of interior/coastal adaptation which had not been fully described and which could shed new light on Iñupiaq adaptation (see chapter 11, note 4). As Waldo and other elders talked about the old places, I recognized there was sufficient information to piece together the role that these places played in the seasonal rounds of their ancestors. For instance, based on Waldo's accounts on that first trip, I knew that families left the coast and headed upriver in the fall, sailing when the wind was favorable, sometimes using their dogs to tow the boats, and paddling when necessary.

It was a two-day trip up to Uyaġaaġruk, but it was a good camping place where the elders, women, and children would be assured a steady supply of fish while the young men made their way further inland to hunt caribou, which were rich and fat after a summer of grazing on the tundra. Caribou fur, when harvested in the fall, is ideal for making warm clothing. At freeze-up, the hunters returned and families settled at favorite fishing sites, deep water spots called *qaglut,* where the fish congregated in the late fall. Fall fishing and hunting provided the Kuuġmiut with the food they needed for a winter of trapping.

For those families that stayed inland, the advent of spring and the return of sunlight meant it was time to move to the coast for whaling. Prominent points of land like Piŋusugruk and Icy Cape were likely spots for leads to develop in the ice. Whaling crews went there to hunt for bowhead. Then they might stay on the coast to hunt waterfowl, walrus, ugruk, and ringed seal, in that order. Then the cycle started again.

In late August, which is late fall on the North Slope, Waldo, Henry Peetook (Waldo's cousin), and I traveled east on the coast to Ataniq, a natural flyway for waterfowl. The name Ataniq means "isthmus or spit that connects two land masses." I tried to imagine life at Ataniq in the early years of this century, and now I try to imagine how it was when Kashevarov saw it. I learned how the White whaler, John Kelley, had wintered over near here and had experimented with Eskimo-style whaling in the spring (Bockstoce 1986:238; Cassell 1989:21–26). Waldo told me that many ships were lost along this stretch of coast during the commercial whaling period. The shipwrecks were a ready source of wood and brass nails, which people re-used in making houses and sleds. I wonder now if one of these wrecks led to the disaster of 1871 in which so many Siḷaliñar-miut (Siḷaliñigmiut) died from poisoning (see chapter 1, note 4).

While we were camped at Ataniq, a fall snowstorm blew up and we moved from the breezy wall tent to the comfort of Weir Negovanna's sod house with its warm coal stove. There was plenty of time to listen to old stories as we waited out the storm. On that trip, Waldo told how Kakmak and Walluk once killed fifteen bears in one day and how Wesley Ekak once killed eight in a day at Ataniq. I didn't know then that Waldo's mother had lived at this site, and that Walluk, the polar bear hunter, was Waldo's stepfather. And I didn't yet know about hunting seals at breathing holes, or about the trips that Waldo had made to Ataniq to haul supplies. Now, having heard Waldo's life history stories, I can imagine what life was like there for Walluk and Lucy. I can visualize their trips to the freshwater lake for drinking water, and I wonder whether Lucy cooked on one of the coal stoves which now lies discarded on the tundra.

Waldo answered my continuous stream of questions and

pointed out the outlines of old houses. That summer I saw more features and artifacts, including ivory and bone tools eroding from the banks, than most prehistoric archaeologists see in ten years of research.

Subsequent Trips, 1977

During the next summer, 1977, Wainwright was an active place. The North Slope Borough's Capital Improvement Program was in full swing. Crates of house parts were stacked up on the beach, waiting to be opened. Workers pounded nails from eight in the morning till five at night. New village housing, a firehouse, and a school were under construction. The village was expanding, and I recall that even the shipping crates became part of the construction. Many of them had been adapted for use as storage sheds next to the new houses.

A few years later, when I had the opportunity to go back up the Kuuk River, I remember seeing shipping crates that had become siding for cabins out at the sites. I recall my surprise as we approached Uyaġaaġruk; against the low relief of tundra the new cabins made the site look more like a village than a camp.

The village was geared up for work. Days were filled with construction, evenings and weekends were spent hunting. Friday nights were quite a scene, as families packed up and left to go upriver. I remember trying to conduct a survey of hunting and fishing patterns. I had thought that evenings would be a good time to talk to hunters, but on several nights when I visited households, the men were out hunting walrus. After putting in a full day's work building houses, they left right after supper to hunt, returning in the early morning hours.

Waldo and I also worked hard that summer. The federal government was preparing a plan to open the National Petroleum Reserve for oil development. The National Park Service had been charged with determining the historical and cultural resources in the reserve.[3] There was little written information on historic sites, and the timetable provided little opportunity for field research; the job was immense. Fortunately, there was sufficient money to hire researchers to work in each village.

I returned to Wainwright, accompanied by Pam Ivie, an archaeologist, and Waldo's home became headquarters for our expeditions.

That second summer we made three trips—down the Utuqqaq River, down the coast toward Icy Cape, and up the Kuuk River to Ivisauraq. Waldo's family helped make those trips a success. Waldo, Jr., and Eddie served as expert boatmen, and Mattie always made us feel comfortable. We were joined on the Utuqqaq by Samuel Agnasagga, who was one of the last of the Utuqqaġmiut, one of the last people to live on the Utuqqaq River and follow a pattern of inland fishing and hunting, and then spring whaling at Icy Cape.

On the Utuqqaq River trip, Waldo told us about Helge Larsen and their trip up the river in 1945. Often he reminded us of the mosquitoes and hot weather that had plagued them, and the "elevation" of the stream where they had to get out and help the dogs pull the boat through the swift current. How much easier we had it, flying up to the upper Utuqqaq and beginning our trip headed downstream.

But it wasn't an easy trip. The water level was low and we had to tow the raft through shallow places. On that trip, I learned that two weeks was a long time to travel with six people in a remote area. I had misjudged the amount of pilot biscuits and meat we would need, and when we ran out it seemed like we younger people tended to get irritable.[4] Waldo and Samuel were calm and their pleasant dispositions helped to set a good tone. I have often wondered how many times in the past Iñupiat elders have taught patience and cooperation, important survival skills.

The best trip that summer was the coastal trip. After hearing Waldo's life story, I am more aware of the meaning of the sites, such as Narvaqpak, the place where Waldo buried his stepfather, two or three miles to the southwest of Nivaat. Their old sod house—a small wood frame with sod on the outside and a three-by-four-foot skylight in the roof—was still standing. At the time of our visit, all I knew was that Waldo and his parents had stayed there. I didn't notice Waldo walking back to the place where he had buried his father.

We continued down the coast and finally reached the site of Aqiaġuġnat, where old Shaglook had lived. I learned a great deal about that old man and his wife from Waldo, and it was exciting to see his wooden frame house, made from milled lumber with standard window casings. I wonder now if the lumber and windows had been brought up on the *Karluk*. Despite the remains from the abandoned DEW Line, and from Coast and Geodetic Survey activities and oil exploration, I could still imagine that old-timer and his wife, Mayaroak, waiting for the ships to come so they could trade their furs for boxes of ammunition and sacks of flour.

Just across from Aqiaġuġnat is Avvaq Inlet. There we found the remains of a prehistoric site—flint chips and butchered bones scattered on the tundra. The work of prehistoric hunters dominated my attention, and I missed Waldo's descriptions of the natural features used to help corral the reindeer. I didn't realize then that Avvaq Inlet had played such an important part in reindeer herding.

On the final trip that summer, we went up to the old Ivisauraq River camp, thus completing a full season of recording historic sites. There was a real urgency to our work; we thought that oil exploration and development in the reserve was imminent, and we wanted to describe as many of the old places as we could. That winter we wrote up the final results of our research and hoped that the old sites would be considered in the course of exploration plans. In the years since, there has been some exploration, but no full-scale development. The basic documentation of historic sites has continued, and now hundreds of sites have been documented, a tribute to the elders who have shared their knowledge, and to the Planning Department of the North Slope Borough, which has continued to support this work.

As I look back at those two years, I recall learning how these places were used, how decisions were made about moving to other sites, and how each place fit into the seasonal round of activities, but I didn't ask or think about how they fit into Waldo's experiences. That information came out later, as we worked on Waldo's life history.

After our two years of concentrated work together, I went off to other projects, and Waldo and Mattie went up to Sirragruich, where they assisted Dale Slaughter in excavating an old site on the coast not far from Ataniq (Slaughter 1979; Slaughter 1982). I saw Waldo and Mattie several times during the next couple of years.

Returning to Wainwright, 1985

At a Scottish festival and bagpipe session held at the Eagle's Hall in Fairbanks, Edna Ahgeak MacLean and I were sitting next to each other.[5] From our conversation emerged the idea to create a life history project. Edna wrote a proposal, in Iñupiaq, to the North Slope Borough Commission on History, Language, and Culture, and in 1985 they provided funds for Edna to supervise and conduct life history research with elders.

I was excited because I was completing a life history of an Athabaskan man, Moses Cruikshank, and Edna's project gave me a chance to apply the same research approach with an Iñupiaq elder. I knew the richness of Waldo's experience, and his personal sense of history made him a natural choice for a life history project.

At the first recording session, I had a list of some of the things I wanted to ask Waldo. We knew each other well, but we were about to begin a new type of work together, a collaborative venture, the shaping of his life history. There would be two recording trips, a review trip, and lots of letters and phone calls to cross-check details. And for me there would be surprises: the wonderfully personal account of Waldo's killing his first seal, the eagerness he felt about learning adult skills, the sadness he felt when he buried his stepfather, and his pride in learning to "herd like any man." I prodded for more detail, sometimes with good results, as in the chronology of the changes in reindeer herding, sometimes with few results, as in my inquiries about teaching his children. This is typical of the way the oral biography process goes: both the narrator and the interviewer shape the final product.

I asked Waldo to speak in English. His response came in a tone I can still recall. He said "O-o-kay," a reluctant accommodation. I wanted the narratives in English because I was concerned about the difficulties in getting an accurate and timely translation. I also wanted to know what Waldo was saying as we recorded so that I could tell what he covered and could follow up with questions or change the subject when the narrative got bogged down or wandered. I didn't want to relinquish all responsibility to Waldo. I had a general outline of topics that I wanted Waldo to address, things that he had talked about before and that were of historical interest. I also wanted to be sure that he discussed the different stages of his life and that he gave explanations for the changes that occurred over his lifetime. Good stories are important, but a life history has to reflect the narrator's life stages and transitions. I didn't know what Waldo's transitions were at first; I had to listen and then ask questions, and finally the themes emerged. The chapter headings and subtitles reflect these themes, which are generally the stages of Waldo's adaptation to life on the North Slope.

Waldo's primary language is Iñupiaq, and I put him at a slight disadvantage by requesting that he speak in English, although, as his stories attest, he is certainly fluent in English. I don't regret the decision, but as the project evolved, I was grateful for the special assistance of Leona Okakok and James

Nageak, two Iñupiaq language experts. Their contributions were important and are discussed later in this chapter.

Editing the Transcripts

Once the transcribing was completed, I listened to all the tapes with transcripts in hand to review for omissions and errors. I then sent the corrected transcripts to Waldo for his review. Waldo made corrections, primarily changes in spellings, but he also added details for clarification.

The next step was to shape the narrative from the transcripts. I first sorted the discussion into topical and roughly chronological order, cutting and pasting together portions of the transcripts. I edited this compilation to produce a readable narrative, although plenty of rough spots and false starts remained. I then edited this product further to produce what I call an *archival manuscript*[6]—one clearly understandable but quite long and too rambling and detailed for a general audience. The primary editing audience up to this point was Waldo and his family. Then, with a general reading audience in mind, I edited the archival manuscript to produce the first draft of what you see published here.

I deleted detail where I thought it slowed the story, but I cut sections only after considering whether they were integral to the story. For example, if Waldo told two identical or similar accounts, I considered whether to include both. Sometimes I kept the best one, as in chapter 4, when Waldo provided two accounts about swimming across rivers in pursuit of reindeer. I cut the second one because it did not provide new information and it wasn't as interesting to read.

Usually I deleted repetitive information or Waldo's extended accounting of who was present at a particular time or place. This information may be important to some people, so it is retained in the archival copy, but it is probably not vital to the general reader.

My major considerations in editing the final narrative were to preserve Waldo's style and meaning and to facilitate the presentation of his story in written form for a broad audience of students and scholars of the North. I made several types of changes to preserve the storytelling style for audiences who do not know Waldo. The most obvious change was to add words to complete a thought, and in rare cases, to facilitate a transfer from one subject to another. For instance, a sentence from chapter 5 reads, "Later, after we turned them loose—*it was* over five years I guess—the deer were getting smaller..." (italics added). In this case, I added the words "it was" to clarify Waldo's meaning. I retained his wording "the deer were getting smaller" (fewer in number) because the phrase illustrates Waldo's particular use of English and the meaning is fairly clear from the context. Another example from chapter 5 reads, "Even the White people that live around the Fairbanks and Anchorage areas, *they order them.*" In this case, I added "they order them" to complete the thought. In chapter 11 the discussion of traveling with Otto Geist ends with the sentence, "That was the end of my trip with Otto Geist." I added the sentence to complete the paragraph and provide a transition to the next paragraph, in which Waldo begins to talk about the historic site documentation for the land claims.

In some places I reorganized Waldo's words, moving text around to present a logical order that more clearly reflects the meaning expressed in the story. This may seem radical, but readers should keep in mind that the narrative is derived from many different recordings; it is a composite. An example of this type of editing appears in the first paragraph of Waldo's narrative, where he says "I am an Eskimo. I don't want to change my nationality..." That quote comes from the last recording we made when I asked Waldo to reflect on his life and provide a conclusion to his story. When I began to cut and paste the story together it seemed to me an excellent way to begin the narrative. Waldo did not object.

The chapters of Waldo's narrative reflect a natural chronology of events from his childhood to the present. While the story is chronological, it is also organized around themes such as working with Jim Allen, herding reindeer, or documenting the old places. Sometimes the relational organization supercedes the chronology. For instance, Waldo's relationship with Jim Allen goes way back in time but it is presented in the context of the period when Waldo was working for the Weather Bureau. That's when he worked the most for Jim Allen.

Another editing consideration involved the use of nonstandard English, which in some cases can be awkward for the reader, and at other times can express a concept eloquently. A sentence from an early version of chapter 1 reads "Before that, when I was small, they sometime, they, when the animal was scarce they have a hard time feeding us, our folks." I edited the sentence for clarity and it now reads "Before that, when I was small, sometimes our folks had a hard time feeding us when the animals were scarce."

Sometimes problems arose because of the differences between English and Iñupiaq. When speaking of his family, Waldo said, "And my mother's parents was Esowana, her father, and Akutugreak, he's the mother of my mother." Iñupiaq speakers don't feel the need to differentiate between male and female through pronoun use. The word order in Iñupiaq is also different, and this can cause problems when a native speaker of Iñupiaq speaks in English. In the final version the sentence reads "My mother's father was Esowana and her mother was Akutugreak."

There were also examples of refreshing new uses of English: in chapter 1 Waldo says, "That's the best food I ever eat when I was a young boy"; in chapter 2, "His folks were living in Cape Prince of Wales, but they always went to Nome sometimes to work there…" (see chapter 3, note 27). Specialized uses of English can be very effective in conveying cultural concepts, such as the Iñupiaq idea of how a young child becomes aware of people and events. This is sometimes expressed by the statement "when I first became aware." In chapter 1 Waldo speaks of "That time I *began to know people,*" or "*from there* I learn; I was old enough, a little bit...."

In the Iñupiaq language, tense is conveyed by context, not by a verb form. When Waldo speaks in English, he doesn't always use past tense to indicate that the event he is describing took place in the past. In editing his narrative, I have used past tense when it is grammatically appropriate, except for a few cases where present tense is used to convey a feeling that the activity is or was ongoing. This editing does not reflect a cultural pattern but does help to set a culturally appropriate tone to the written narrative. Some examples may help. In chapter 7, when describing how to prepare a cache of caribou meat, Waldo says "...you *knead* it, *put* tussocks all around it until you *reach* where you started," indicating how it *was* and *is* done. Sometimes the present tense indicates conditions that can and do recur. For example, in chapter 1 Waldo says, "Jim was telling me that when it *turns* real foggy just before freeze-up in late fall, my father used to sneak out and get a whale before anybody went out."

Having explained how I recorded and shaped Waldo's story, I'd like to point out that other biographers might have written differently about Waldo. They certainly would have asked different questions, and Waldo would have told them different things. For example, when Richard Nelson reviewed the manuscript he was surprised that there weren't more hunting stories (see appendix D for Nelson's remarks). This reflects the different relationships that Waldo has with each of us. Several of my colleagues have been interested in Waldo's father, Captain Hartson Bodfish, and the commercial whaling part of the story. I tried not to overemphasize this aspect of Waldo's life but to give it as much exposure as I sensed it deserved in relation to other aspects of his life. I never asked Waldo how much to put in, but I did ask him about his father and used most of his stories in the narrative, so I feel comfortable with the emphasis. I chose not to include additional information on reindeer herding and travels with the reindeer even though it was available. I estimate that eighty percent of the transcript material was used in this manuscript.

Presenting Waldo's Story
The biggest challenge in producing oral biographies is to determine how to balance the narrator's telling of his or her story and the readers' needs for historical and cultural context. In traditional biographies a writer builds a narrative around an individual's life, but in oral biographies an individual narrates his or her own life story. In the former case, the writer builds context for a broad audience throughout the manuscript. In the latter case, the narrator provides the recorder/compiler with details based on his or her perception of what the recorder needs to know to understand. The amount of detail is often insufficient for a wider audience unfamiliar with the narrator or the narrator's culture. In oral biographies the issue of explanation is particularly difficult because in working with the narrator's stories, the writer must highlight the description in ways that support rather than overshadow the narrator's telling. It must remain the narrator's book. I have placed my comments as compiler, anthropologist, and writer at the end of the manuscript to ensure that the book retains a strong sense of the narrator's voice[7].

In approximately twenty-five hours of tape, a biographer cannot possibly capture an entire lifetime of experiences. One hopes to get the most important parts and to portray the information in a way that approximates the style of the narrator. Oral biographies are like portraits: readers can recognize the subject immediately, and as they continue to read they can see how the biographer has captured many aspects of the subject's character. A good biography leaves readers not only with an outline of the subject's lifetime of experiences, but also with a strong sense of the style and manner of the person. Readers come to know some of the person's feelings, interests, aspirations, and inclinations, but the story, like a portrait, is not a mirror image. Certain features have been emphasized over others because writers, like artists, have a style and manner of working. The topics discussed and the meanings conveyed are influenced by the relationship between the biographer and the narrator. In this biography our travels influenced the way Waldo described his life and the detailed descriptions about movement from one place to another. In fact, many times he assumed I knew more than I really did about the places, and I had to ask for more explanation.

Reviewing the Manuscript

In addition to Waldo's review of earlier drafts and reviews by professional anthropologists, the manuscript received another important review of the editing and interpretation. Leona Okakok, deputy director of administration in the Planning Department of the North Slope Borough, and past liaison for the North Slope Borough Commission on Iñupiat History, Language, and Culture, reviewed the manuscript. She is an expert translator, and, as chapter 15 and her notes indicate, she is an expert in Iñupiaq history and culture. In chapter 15 Okakok describes how she reviewed and documented the language and cultural considerations.

In May 1989, I went to Wainwright to review the manuscript with Waldo. James Nageak, an instructor of Iñupiaq language at the University of Alaska Fairbanks, accompanied me. The recording and transcript of that interview reflect Nageak's style of interviewing. In his dialog with Waldo, Nageak reinforces, reiterates, affirms, and in some cases even assumes (based on personal experience). The richness of Waldo's responses to James reflects how comfortable he was with that style, which resembles Iñupiaq storytelling, in which confirmation and affirmation are essential. Nageak's interview also reflects the difference between Waldo's style when he speaks to someone intimately familiar with hunting and his style of speaking to someone who has limited experience. In Nageak's interview, Waldo didn't feel a need to explain what they both know. For instance, the whale hunting story that Nageak has transcribed and translated in appendix G shows how important it is to go beyond the literal translation, to explain for audiences unfamiliar with the topic or the narrator. I include it as an example of how the interview is shaped by the narrator's perceptions of the listener's background and how translation must go beyond the actual words to the concepts expressed. For instance, in this particular case, Nageak had to explain to me how the ice was moving and what the whale was doing. His translation for me included more than just the literal meaning of Waldo's words.

It is important to end this discussion by reiterating the point that every life history bears the marks of the narrator, the compiler, and their experiences together. I am pleased to know Waldo Bodfish and to present this small window on his life.

Plywood siding made
from shipping crates,
David Kagak's house at Kaŋich.
(Photograph by William Schneider.)

The site of Uyagaagruk
on the Kuuk River.
(Photograph by
William Schneider.)

Waldo and Mattie Bodfish on their way to church, summer, 1988. (Photograph by William Schneider.)

Waldo and Mattie Bodfish with their great grandchildren, Bradley Bodfish and Bernadette Fischer with Waldo, and Martha Bodfish on Mattie's lap. These are the children of Darlene Bodfish, Margie Fischer, and Grace Bodfish, all daughters of Nimrod and Emma Bodfish. Nimrod is Waldo and Mattie's son. (Photograph from Margie Fischer.)

Waldo Bodfish, Sr. in his home.
(Photograph by Dave Libbey.)

15

Language and Cultural Considerations

Leona Okakok

The first mandate stated in the formation of the North Slope Borough's Commission on Iñupiat History, Language, and Culture (IHLC) requires the Commission "to develop a complete historical record of the land, people and villages of the North Slope." One of the ways the Commission has chosen to carry out this mandate is by taping oral accounts of history as told by the elders. Life histories, such as this book, are a natural by-product of this process, since the elders tell much about themselves while giving their accounts.

When Edna Ahgeak MacLean submitted her proposal in 1985 for life history research, the Commission fully supported the concept and provided funds for the project. The interviews for Waldo's life history and five others were completed in early 1987, and the transcripts are on file at the IHLC offices.

I was asked to assist with Waldo's life history because of my language skills and my knowledge of the sources. Together Bill Schneider and I read the whole manuscript, chapter by chapter. I found that it contained certain English words and phrases that mean one thing to an Iñupiaq speaker, but that would probably be understood in an entirely different way by English readers. This prompted us to include notes by an Iñupiaq speaker, me.

Since I am fluent in both English and my own native Iñupiaq Eskimo dialect, it was easy for me to identify areas that needed clarification. It was much harder to provide the clarification.

The Process

We did the easy job first. Bill and I read the manuscript and identified areas where further clarification might be needed. We discussed the meanings, and Bill, who does not speak Iñupiaq, served as my test. When we agreed on the meaning of the English, we left the text alone, since in these instances an English-speaking Iñupiaq's understanding of the words or phrase coincided with the common English meaning.

When we did not agree on the English meaning, I gave an explanation in a note. Examples include such expressions as "proud" as used in the statement "I was really proud of that old woman when she gave me that ptarmigan net" (see chapter 3), or "always sometimes" as used in the statement "His folks were living in Cape Prince of Wales, but they always went to Nome sometimes to work there before the ship comes from Seattle" (see chapter 2).

Identifying Sources for the Notes

As I stated earlier, deciding to clarify a point through a note was easy. The hard part was stating how I knew clarification was needed and then identifying appropriate sources to document the clarification. I began searching for sources at the IHLC offices in Barrow.

Iñupiaq words or phrases could be checked against the Iñupiaq dictionary (MacLean forthcoming), genealogical information could be compared to the files at the IHLC office, and

items of common knowledge could be checked with local people and elders.

The notes that took more time to explain dealt with the following topics: English words and phrases that have a specialized meaning to Iñupiaq speakers, English translations of hard-
to-translate Iñupiaq words, and practices which are common
local knowledge but relatively unknown to the outside world.
Below are examples of each type.

Specialized meanings.   I prefer to capitalize English words
and phrases which have acquired specialized meaning to
Iñupiaq speakers. In this way the reader and I know that this
common English word is being used apart from its usual meaning. The word *Outside* is an example. To many Alaskans it
means "the contiguous United States," so whenever it appears
in that usage it is capitalized.

Difficult translations.   There are English words and phrases,
such as *let me,* which mean something different to Iñupiaq
speakers. The problem stems from the short translation of the
Iñupiaq postbase *-pkaq,* whose meaning encompasses both the
concepts of "allow" and "cause to."

Example
Aakagma aatchipkaqtaŋani.

Translations
My mother allowed me to take some things over to them.
(As in "Since I insisted I had to, my mother finally allowed
me to take some things over to them.")

My mother made me take some things over to them.
(As in "I was lazy about doing it, but my mother made me
get out there and take some things over to them.")

Because of the negative connotation of the second translation, most English-speaking Iñupiat prefer to say "let me" in any instance of use. English speakers don't use the words "let me" to encompass such a broad spectrum of meaning, but this adaptation of an English phrase by English-speaking Iñupiat suits a specific purpose. It enables them to convey a range of meanings which are comfortably handled by *aakagma aatchipkaqtaŋani*. In fact, it has become so much a part of our speech that when Native Iñupiaq speakers hear the words "let me" in ordinary English conversation, they will most likely understand it the way they learned it—as encompassing both concepts.

Regional common knowledge.   Some practices or concepts are common to a group of people but are relatively unknown outside the community. Among our people, these are things such as extended family relationships, naming of children, and networks for sharing resources. When Waldo mentions these concepts, I have included an explanatory note based on my own background as well as the following sources of information.

Elders' conferences.   The IHLC Commission, realizing that much of the traditional knowledge was fast disappearing, decided to bring together elders from all villages of the Slope to record their knowledge regarding Iñupiat life. The first Elders' Conference was held in May 1978. Since then, after a few annual conferences, they have become a biennial event.

For the first couple of years, the agenda was determined by the IHLC Commission, IHLC staff, and others who needed information which could only be gathered from elders. Then elders expressed their desire to talk about things which they strongly felt needed to be passed on to the younger generation, but which no one ever thought to ask them about.

From then on, every conference became flexible enough to allow the elders a chance to form their own agenda for part of the conference. In this way the staff was able to get the information needed for our purposes, yet we also gave the elders a chance to speak on topics of their choice.

Much information has been gathered to date on various topics. Elders have discussed cultural ceremonies and events, health, history, houses and shelters, hunting and game preparation, legends, the natural environment, recreation and entertainment, the supernatural and taboos, traditional law, and contemporary issues. Proceedings of some of the Elders' Conferences have been published (see Kisautaq 1981). A great deal more will be published in the future. For now, this material is stored in the Commission files and is accessible to researchers and the interested public. In this book, I have drawn on the Elders' Conferences to explain Waldo's references to such things as naming practices, traditional law, and old houses.

Traditional Land Use Inventory. Our office has worked very hard these last few years to provide an accurate listing of place-names to serve as a reference for anyone wanting information on sites within the North Slope Borough. This resource, the Traditional Land Use Inventory (TLUI), was compiled primarily through the efforts of Flossie Hopson Andersen. This is one of the most useful inventories within our division, and we are continually working to make sure it is accurate and more complete. We expect this effort will continue for some time.

In 1976, when Flossie was the head of the division, she went from village to village, arranging meetings and gathering traditional land use information from the elders. In years past, the elders traveled throughout these areas and depended on the subsistence resources available at the sites. They know the names and the history of the sites, and their knowledge serves as the basis for the inventory.

Each site within each village territory was documented as to location, historical use, current use, history, burial sites, and resources. This information was then translated and transcribed from audio tapes. Once in written form, it was then organized into the Iñupiat History, Language and Culture Commission's TLUI format, which includes site descriptions and location maps. We have often cited these TLUIs when information is requested regarding possible damages which might result from oil exploration and other development within areas at or near our villages. Much work is being done to ensure that site names in the TLUIs are correctly spelled. Site lists provided in the TLUIs are the standard for correct spelling of Iñupiaq place-names, and the Wainwright TLUI has been followed closely in this book.

The IHLC has also provided funds for documenting cultural resources at the sites listed on the TLUIs. The work has been conducted by anthropologists working with village elders and other local resource specialists. This type of academic documentation, though more readily accepted by state and federal agencies for purposes of identifying resources and for historical data, is produced only at the end of a slow and expensive process. In this book, Bill Schneider has referenced North Slope Borough contract work done in Wainwright, Point Lay, and the Barrow-Atqasuk areas.

Elders.   Our most useful resource, by far, is our elders. They are natural teachers, truly committed to passing along the culture to the young people, and they are always willing to sit down and patiently explain whatever it is we need to know. When I was working on a translation project while living in California, I had to call up a certain elder quite often to get the definition of a word with which I was unfamiliar. I was never rudely cut off, ever, although, with the frustration of distance and the sometimes not-so-clear connections, I was often ready to quit. Without the elders and their commitment, the IHLC Commission would never have been able to do its job adequately.

In the case of this book, I have consulted Waldo and my father, Samuel Simmonds, and several other elders about the meanings of words, double-checking the pronunciation of site names, and verifying family and given names.

Spelling Decisions

It has become standard procedure in our office to go through our manuscripts prior to publication to correct the spellings of Iñupiaq words, names, and place-names. I agreed to do this with Waldo's life history as well.

In this text, Iñupiaq place-names and personal names are printed in roman type. Other Iñupiaq words are printed in italic type the first time they appear; thereafter, they are printed in roman type. Pronunciation guides and a glossary of personal names appear in appendices A, B, and C, and a list of place-names appears in appendix E.

The Iñupiaq spellings are given in the singular or plural form according to the context and meaning. One of the words that appears often is Iñupiat and its singular form, Iñupiaq. Iñupiat has been often translated as "real people." In this usage, the postbase *-piaq,* which is the singular of *-piat,* means "more customary" or "older, or more common" as in *iglupiaq,* which we use to refer to older styles of houses, or *atigipiaq,* which means an older style of fur parka with no zipper. So Iñupiat, upon closer analysis, is "the people we are most familiar with, most common to us." In this book, Iñupiaq is used to designate the language of North Slope Iñupiat people.

Unfortunately, a full, unabridged dictionary of our language has not yet been published, although Edna Ahgeak MacLean's work, the most up-to-date and complete source, is near completion. This is the source I relied on for spellings in the text and the notes of this book. Because it is still in a working stage, readers are cautioned that entries and explanations in the published dictionary may differ slightly from what appears in this book.

A companion to this unabridged dictionary is the *Iñupiaq*

Postbase Dictionary, also being researched and compiled by Edna Ahgeak MacLean. Note entries of postbase definitions are taken from this source. A postbase is a morpheme that is attached to a stem (a noun or verb) to expand the meaning of a word. One of the more common postbases in Iñupiaq is *-miut,* which means "inhabitants of," as in Utuqqaġmiut, "inhabitants of the Utuqqaq River."

Before deciding to change any spellings in the manuscript, I needed to consider several things. First, I had to be sure that the spellings conformed to our current orthography, or were cross-referenced to the current orthography. This often meant listening to the recording to hear how the words were pronounced. For example, in the section where Waldo lists his mother's siblings and their spouses, I was able to verify the pronunciation from the taped interview segments, and I then compiled the name pronunciation guide, spelling the names in the current orthography to indicate the correct pronunciation.

In addition to the current orthography, which we consider to be the most accurate, there are earlier orthographies which have been developed and used since the turn of the century by missionaries and anthropologists. These needed to be considered, and in the case of personal names, followed. These older orthographies used letters from the English alphabet to approximate Iñupiaq sounds, and they gave us the spellings for our family names and place-names, spellings which are still widely used and recognized today. Most elders, like Waldo, understandably prefer the older spellings to the current ones, since they are most familiar with them. The problem with the older orthographies, though, is that they did not adequately represent all of the sounds of the Iñupiaq language.

The latest orthography was developed at a meeting at the University of Alaska Fairbanks in 1971. The changes made at that meeting helped clarify a number of language issues, such as the distinction between the velar and uvular sounds in our language (the distinction between the "k" and "q" sounds).

Younger people have learned the new system well. Because it was developed specifically to accommodate the writing of sounds which had been overlooked by previous orthographies, it helps young speakers—who are unfamiliar with the old words—become proficient in pronouncing these words.

Unfortunately, the new orthography confused a lot of older people who did not write in our language often enough to become literate in the new system, but who had heard enough about the changes to know they should include such letters as *q, ġ, ł,* etc.

As a result, many people mixed orthographies, spelling names with the letters *e* and *o* from the old orthography, as well as the *q* and *ł* from the new. Or they spelled the same name two or three different ways within the same text.

With Waldo's manuscript, I chose to address this problem by re-spelling the mixed-orthography names within the text using the old system, then providing Appendix B as a reference to the correct pronunciation.

There are reasons for keeping the traditional spelling (i.e., without diacritical marks) of the names, especially family names. First, people strongly resist any change in the spellings of their names. Although I would prefer that all names be correctly spelled using the current orthography, I recognize and respect the elders' preference for the old spelling. Even if the old spelling is awkward, the pronunciation of names, especially family names, is easily verified by consulting family members.

Additionally, even when our Iñupiaq names are correctly spelled using the current Iñupiaq orthography, the current legal system and other governmental agencies resist the use of non-standard orthographies. This perpetuates not only misspellings, but variations of misspellings by substituting "regular" letters for our "nonstandard" letters. For instance, a child's Iñupiaq name is often entered correctly on the birth certificate;

however, the Vital Statistics Department,whose computers cannot render Iñupiaq letters, spells the name without the essential diacritical marks and special characters, thereby rendering the name unpronounceable or changing its meaning entirely.

For these reasons, I prefer to minimize confusion and to use the old spelling for family names and given names in this book. Appendix B is the key to both correct pronunciation and current spelling.

Conclusion

I've enjoyed collaborating with Bill Schneider and the IHLC Commission on Waldo Bodfish's life history, and I'm pleased that we were able to include James Nageak in this work. We derived much satisfaction from our efforts, and we hope this process will become a standard for people working on projects which require a lot of cross-cultural communication. We have learned a great deal from working with each other.

Appendix A

Iñupiaq Pronunciation

Lawrence D. Kaplan

Iñupiaq sounds are pronounced according to the standard values of the International Phonetic Alphabet, with the following exceptions:

ġ	voiced uvular fricative
qh	voiceless uvular fricative
kh	voiceless velar fricative
ḷ	voiceless *l*
ḷ̣	voiceless palatalized *l*
ḷ	palatalized *l*
r	voiced retroflex
sr	voiceless retroflex

Long vowels and long consonants are written double.

Appendix B

Pronunciation Guide for Iñupiaq Personal Names

Spelling	Pronunciation	Spelling	Pronunciation
/A/		Ahklogak	Aqłuġaq or
Aaklu	Aaġlu		Aqłuŋaq
Agnagolook	Aġnaġluk	Aishanna	Aisaana
Agnasagga	Aġnasagaq	Akamalutuk	Aqamalutaq
Aguvluk	Agavlak	Akligok	Agliġuq
Ahalik	Aaqhaaliq	Akpik	Aqpik
Ahgeak	Agiaq	Akpiksrak	Aqpiksraq
Ahgoruk	Aaġuraq	Akudrigik	Aqargiq
Ahloak	Aaġluaq	Akuklook	Akuġluk
Ahlook	Aaluk	Akutugreak	Akutuksriaq
Ahneovak	Aniuvak	Amikak	Amiqqaq
Ahngaorak	Aaŋauraq	Anakak	Annaqaq
Ahngogasuk	Aŋugasak	Anakaurak	Annaqauraq
Ahngulook	Aŋulluk	Anaktook	Annaqtuuq
Ahvakana	Avaqqana	Anashugak	Annasugaq
Ahjuvik	Ayyuvik	Aneuvak	Aniuvak

Spelling	Pronunciation	Spelling	Pronunciation
Angalik	Aŋalik	Kaiyakpak	Qaiyaaqpak
Angoyuk	Aanġuyuk	Kakinya	Kakiññaaq
Angashuk	Aŋasak	Kakmak	Qaġmak
Anguruk	Aŋurruk	Kalayauk	Qalayauq
Anukti	Aŋuqti	Kanayuk	Kanayuq
Ardgailuk	Argailaq	Katuak	Katuaq
Aseaginna	Asiaġiña	Kayalook	Qayaaluk
Atkilak	Atqiḷaq	Kayutak	Qayuutaq
Attungowruk	Ataŋauraq	Kelignik	Qiḷiġniq
Audlakroak	Aullaqsruaq	Keogak	Qiugaq
Aveoganna	Aviugana	Kiasik	Kiasik
Ayalgook	Ayałhuq	Kignak	Qiġñak
		Kimachook	Qimatchuq
/E/		Kimilook	Qimiġḷuk
Egnavina	Igñaviña	Koguyuk	Quŋuyuk
Egowa	Igaugaq	Kongona	Qunguna
Ehlook	Iiłuk	Koochik	Kuutchiq
Ekak	Ikaaq	Koonik	Quuniq
Ekosik	Ikusik	Kootoalook	Quuttualuk
Ekowanna	Ikugana	Koyukuk	Koyukuk
Eluktuna	Iluqtuna	Kunaknauruk	Kunagnauraq
Engnavina	Iŋñaviña	Kunnaana	Kunnaana
Enyoaveoruk	Iñuaġviuraq	Kupaak	Kupaaq
Esowana	Isaugana	Kusik	Kusiq
		Kutuk	Quuttuq
/I/			
Ilannik	Iḷaaniq	**/M/**	
Illiak	Iliaq	Masak	Maasak
Innuksuk	Iñuksuk	Mayak	Mayak
Ipalook	Ipaaluk	Mayaroak	Mayagruaq
		Mayokok	Mayuuqquq
/K/		Mitiq	Mitiq
Kagak	Qaġġaq	Mukpik	Maqpik

Spelling	Pronunciation	Spelling	Pronunciation
/N/		Patkotak	Patkutaq
Nakaak	Nakaaq	Patunak	Patugnaq
Nanginaak	Naŋinaaq	Peetook	Pituk
Nashaknik	Nasaġniq	Pigaaluk	Pigaaluk
Nashoalook	Nasualuk	Poongaroak	Punŋaruaq
Nayakik	Nayaakkiq	Pootkakroak	Putqagruaq
Neakok	Niaquq		
Negovanna	Niġuvana	**/S/**	
Nikkaktoak	Niqqaktuaq	Sakeagak	Sakiagaq
Niugalak	Niugallak	Samarona	Samaruna
Nuleak	Nuliaq	Samarualook	Samarualuk
Numnik	Namniq	Segevan	Siġvan
Nusunginya	Nusaŋiña	Shaglook	Sagluaq
Nutaak	Nutaaq	Shoudla	Saullaaq
		Sikrikak	Siksrikkaaq
/O/		Siuchiarook	Siutchiaġruaq
Oenik	Uiññiq	Sikvauyugak	Siġvauyuŋaq
Okeleak	Uqiḷḷiaq	Sovalik	Suvaḷiq
Okresak	Uqrisaq	Sublugak	
Olemaun	Ulimaun	Susook	Suusuk
Oneuk	Uniiyaq		
Ootoayuk	Utuayuk	**/T/**	
Ooyogoak	Uyuġuaq	Tagarook	Taagruk
		Tagilook	Taagiiḷuk
/P/		Tagotak	Taquttaq
Pameok	Pamiuq	Takpak	Taaqpak
Panigeo	Panigiuq	Tazruk	Tarruq
Panik	Panik	Tigilook	Tiġigluk
Paniklook	Panigḷuk	Tingook	Tiŋuk
Papiklook	Papigluk	Tivook	
Panikpak	Panikpak	Tookak	Tuukkaq
Patik	Patik	Tookaloona	Tuqaluna

Spelling   **Pronunciation**

Spelling	Pronunciation
Toorak	Tuurraq
Toovak	Tuvaaq
Tuginna	Tuġiña
Tukumik	Tukummiq
Tukrook	Taksruk
Turinya	Tuġiña

/U/

Upicksoun	Ukpiqsaun
Utkusik	Utkusik

/W/

Walluk	Ualuk

Appendix C

Glossary of Personal Names

Aaklu   gave two dogs to Waldo when Waldo was building his dog team.

Agnagolook   an Iñupiaq woman who traveled with Knud Rasmussen when he came to Alaska.

Old Agnasagga (Amos Agnasagga)   father of Samuel Agnasagga, Patrick Tukrook, and Michael Kayutak. He sold a canoe to Andrew Ahneovak in Wainwright so that Andrew could take his family to the Icy Cape area.

Samuel Agnasagga   son of Amos Agnasagga, brother of Michael Kayutak and Patrick Tukrook. Now he is an elder in Wainwright. He spent many years in the Icy Cape, Utuqqaq, and Point Lay areas. At the time of the land claims, he advised the Arctic Slope Regional Corporation on important lands in the Point Lay area.

Charlie Aguvluk   husband of Grace Kelignik. He was one of the men who went to Icy Cape from Wainwright to check on Waldo when he got caught in the big storm.

Roger Ahalik   one of the last mail carriers to travel by dog team. His brother, Joe Sikvauyugak, was also a mail carrier.

Ahgoruk   father of Carrie Anakaurak, Joe Aveoganna's wife.

Ahloak   lived at Icy Cape when Waldo was a boy.

John Peter Ahlook   namesake and good friend of Riley Ahlook. John Peter was known for his skills as a Native healer, a person who could make others well by feeling their bodies. He helped Waldo once when Waldo was sick.

Riley Ahlook   Waldo's uncle, brother of Lucy Kongona. He was the second oldest of the children and was one of the first reindeer herders.

Andrew Ahneovak   Waldo's first stepfather. He was from the Teller area and was a reindeer herding apprentice to Riley Ahlook.

Ahngogasuk   a member of Waldo's whaling crew.

Ahngulook   Waldo's grandmother, mother of Andrew Ahneovak. She lived in the Teller area when Waldo knew her.

Lloyd Ahvakana   son of Floyd Ahvakana and Laura Eunilook. When Waldo and Mattie returned from Barrow in 1925, after they were married, they stopped at Peard Bay where Lloyd's father's folks were camped.

Samantha Ahvakana   helped raise Mattie Bodfish.

Freddie Aishanna   son of Mark Kutuk. Waldo came to know Freddie when Waldo was a boy herding at Icy Cape.

Akamalutuk   wife of Kupaak, mother of Kakmak, grandmother of Frank Long.

Alice Akligok   Waldo's aunt, sister of Lucy Kongona, mother of Henry Peetook, wife of Thomas Tazruk.

Bob Akpik   father of Walter and Simeon Akpik. He was living on the Meade River, near present-day Atqasuk, when Waldo and Wilson conducted the 1940 census.

Simeon Akpik   son of Bob Akpik. He is from the Meade River area.

Grouse Akudrigik   went to check on Waldo when he was

stormbound at Icy Cape. Grouse's daughter was married to Riley Ahlook's son, Woodrow Wilson Kalayauk.

Akuklook   brother of Mattie Masak, who married Peter Panik, father of David Panik. He was staying at Milliktagvik when Waldo returned from Barrow with reindeer that had strayed.

Akutugreak   Waldo's grandmother, mother of Lucy Kongona.

Rose Akutugreak   daughter of Riley Ahlook, wife of James Angashuk.

Alice Allen   daughter of Jim Allen and Eleanor Upicksoun.

Jim Allen   husband of Eleanor Upicksoun, father of Alice (Allen) Killbear and Katherine (Kate Allen) Mount, and adoptive father of Amy Bodfish (#1),who was the daughter of Waldo and Mattie. Jim was the trader in Wainwright.

Kate Allen   daughter of Jim Allen and Eleanor Upicksoun. After Jim Allen died, Kate sold his old house to Waldo.

Amikak   a native healer, a "feeler" at Barrow.

Blair Anakak   was on the Utuqqaq River when Waldo was there with Helge Larsen.

Jack Anakak   chief herder in the Wainwright area before Waldo was appointed to that position.

Carrie Anakaurak   wife of Joe Aveoganna.

Edwin Anaktook   from east of Barrow. He came down the coast to herd reindeer. Waldo was apprenticed to Edwin for four years.

Fred Anashugak   brother of Lucy Kongona, husband of Cora Ayalgook. He helped to raise Waldo.

Flossie Hopson Andersen   daughter of Eben and Rebecca Hopson. She worked for the North Slope Borough and developed the Traditional Land Use Inventory for the villages on the North Slope.

Angalik   wife of Attungowruk. She was an old woman at Icy Cape when Waldo was a boy.

James Angashuk   husband of Rose Akutugreak, Riley Ahlook's daughter. Also known as Oliver James, he helped the Arctic Slope Regional Corporation identify important lands in the Wainwright area at the time of the land claims.

Angoyuk   mother of Johnson Tuginna and Neakok Knox. She was an old woman from Icy Cape. Waldo gave his first seal to her.

Anukti   a man from Icy Cape.

Charlie Ardgailuk   father-in-law of Edwin Anaktook. He was an old-timer who was at the whaling camp with Waldo when they had trouble with the ice breaking up.

Aseaginna   Waldo's uncle, brother of Andrew Ahneovak.

Atkilak   wife of Siuchiarook.

Attungowruk   brother of Walluk.

Peter Audlakroak   son of Samantha Ahvakana, husband of Mary Patik.

Roy Audlakroak   son of Mark Kutuk.

Joe Aveoganna   husband of Carrie Anakaurak. He was the last person to be in charge of the reindeer herds in the Wainwright area.

Cora Ayalgook   daughter of Mark Kutuk, wife of Fred Anashugak.

John Backland, Sr.   a ship captain and trader on the Arctic Coast.

Tom Berryman   a storekeeper in the Kotzebue area who did some trading along the Arctic Coast.

Frank Bester   member of Waldo's whaling crew.

Amy Bodfish (#1)   daughter of Waldo and Mattie. Jim Allen and Eleanor Upicksoun adopted her, but she died when she was young.

Amy Bodfish (#2)   daughter of Waldo and Mattie.

Barry Bodfish   son of Waldo and Mattie.

Betty Bodfish   daughter of Waldo and Mattie.

David Bodfish   son of Waldo and Mattie.

Dempsey Bodfish   son of Waldo and Mattie.

Eddie Bodfish   son of Waldo and Mattie.

Hartson Bodfish Waldo's father, a commercial whaling captain.

Homer Bodfish son of Waldo and Mattie.

Marietta Bodfish daughter of Waldo and Mattie.

Mattie Bodfish wife of Waldo, daughter of Joseph Papiklook and Mary Oenik. She was adopted by Joseph's brother, Daniel, and his wife, Dorothy. Dorothy's mother, Samantha Ahvakana, helped raise Mattie and Nannie Kagak.

Minnie Bodfish daughter of Waldo and Mattie.

Nimrod Bodfish son of Waldo and Mattie.

Waldo Bodfish, Sr. son of Captain Hartson Bodfish and Lucy Kongona.

Waldo Bodfish, Jr. son of Waldo and Mattie.

Wayne Bodfish son of Waldo and Mattie.

Pete Brand trader who traveled on the coast and bought Native products.

T. L. Brevig father of Dagney, Thelma, and Lorene Brevig. He was a Lutheran missionary who devoted many years to mission work on the Seward Peninsula.

Charles Brower came to the Arctic as a commercial whaler and set up a trading station at Barrow. He worked for H. Liebes and Company.

David Brower son of Charles Brower.

Robert Brower son of Charles Brower.

Tom Brower son of Charles Brower.

Joe Bush a captain of the *Boxer.*

Aarnout (Jack) Castel a commercial whaler who traveled on the coast and settled in the Nome area.

John Cross a bush pilot who carried mail on the Arctic Coast.

Fay Delzene a famous dog team racer from Nome.

Albert Driggs a Wainwright man.

Evans Egowa husband of Eunice Ahnagochealook, father of Arnold and Evans Egowa, Loila Itta, and Edith Tegoseak. The Egowa family lived on the Inaru River when Waldo conducted the 1940 census.

Ehlook   lived at Icy Cape when Waldo was herding reindeer.

Ben Eielson   famous Alaskan pilot and polar aviator.

Wesley Ekak   husband of Mary Kimachook. Wesley was an apprentice reindeer herder to Riley Ahlook.

Ekilalook   wife of Takpak, sister of Shoudla

Ekosik   lived with his family at Qaglugruaq on the Meade River when Waldo conducted the 1940 census.

Roxy Ekowanna   was fishing at Qaglugruaq when Waldo did the 1940 census.

Carrie Eleyuk   daughter, by adoption, of Michael Keogak.

Eluktuna   one of the first Iñupiaq reindeer herders.

Engnavina   a mail carrier who traveled by dog team.

Esowana   Waldo's grandfather, father of Lucy Kongona.

Arthur Fields   grandson of Tom Berryman.

Clara Forseland   sister of Wesley Ekak. Clara learned to dance from Lucy Kongona.

Jens Forshaug   unit manager for the reindeer herds on the North Slope when Waldo was herd assistant.

Eva Geary   wife of James Geary. She was a teacher at Icy Cape 1910–1913.

James Geary   husband of Eva Geary. He was a teacher at Icy Cape 1910–1913.

Otto Geist   a paleontologist from the University of Alaska, well known in rural Alaska for collecting specimens. He was also an officer in the army during World War II.

Tom Gordon   a trader at Barter Island.

Norman Grouse   accompanied Waldo and Helge Larsen on the Utuqqaq River trip.

Jack Hadley   husband of Mary Samarona, who was Lucy Kongona's sister. He saved Waldo's life when Waldo was caught in the water at Barrow, and he was one of the men who drifted out on the ice from Barrow and finally reached land near Point Hope.

Dick Hall   a trader who ran the Midnight Sun Trading Company in Wainwright.

Charlie Hanson   ran a trading post at Icy Cape for John Backland. He moved to Wainwright where he also had a store.

Alfred Hopson   a reindeer herd assistant in Barrow and he also worked on the 1940 census.

Ilannik   a family that Waldo knew when he was growing up with the reindeer herders at Icy Cape.

Illiak   a Native healer, a "feeler" at Barrow.

Innuksuk   first wife of Walluk.

Fred Ipalook   a Barrow whaler who got a whale once when Waldo was at Barrow.

Josephine Panningona Itta   lived at Flaxman Island when she was a young girl.

Byron James   a member of Waldo's whaling crew.

Oliver James   see James Angashuk.

Michael Jimmy   see Michael Kayutak.

Tony Joule   traveled with Waldo down the coast from Point Lay on an inspection trip with Jens Forshaug.

James Kagak   husband of Nannie Kagak.

Nannie Kagak   daughter of Mary Patik and Peter Audlakroak, granddaughter of Samantha Ahvakana. She and Mattie Bodfish were raised together after Mattie was adopted by Peter's sister, Dorothy, and her husband, Daniel, brother of Mattie's father, Joseph Papiklook. Nannie and Mattie call each other "sister."

Johnson Kaiyakpak   a fur buyer for Tom Berryman. He was also a mail carrier who traveled by dog team when Waldo was a young boy.

Elijah Kakinya   an old-timer from Anaktuvuk Pass.

Kakmak   son of Kupaak, father of Frank Long, and stepfather of Irene Solomon. He and his family were living at Icy Cape when Waldo was a young boy. Waldo first went whaling with Kakmak.

Robert Kalayauk   husband of Ina Kalayauk. He lived on the Inaru River when Waldo conducted the 1940 census.

Bessie Kanayuk   daughter of Samuel Kanayuk. She married William Penn at the same time that Waldo married Mattie. Waldo knew the Kanayuk family from his days herding at Icy Cape.

Stanley Katuak   accompanied Waldo and Helge Larsen on the trip to the Utuqqaq River.

David Kayalook   found amber at the mouth of one of the tributaries of the Kuuk River.

Michael Jimmy Kayutak   son of old Amos Agnasagga, brother of Samuel Agnasagga and Patrick Tukrook. Michael was Waldo's partner when they were herding reindeer.

Grace Kelignik   wife of Charlie Aguvluk.

Michael Keogak   adoptive father of Carrie Eleyuk, father-in-law of Ernest Kignak. Waldo saw Keogak at Peard Bay when he and Mattie returned from Barrow, where they were married. Keogak was also at Pulayaaq, on the Meade River, when Waldo conducted the 1940 census.

Ernest Kignak   was born inland but was raised in the Barrow area. He traveled the inland rivers as he grew up.

Alice Killbear   daughter of Jim Allen and Eleanor Upicksoun, wife of Harold Killbear.

Harold Killbear   son of Enyoaveoruk Killbear, husband of Alice Killbear. Waldo took him trapping up the Meade River.

Mary Kimachook   sister of Andrew Ahneovak. One of Waldo's sisters was named after her, and Waldo and Mattie named one of their sons after her.

Neakok Knox   son of Angoyuk, grandfather of Warren Neakok of Point Lay.

John Koguyuk   brother of Waldo.

Lucy Kongona   mother of Waldo, wife of Kusiq, wife of Andrew Ahneovak, wife of Walluk.

Harry Koochik   one of the competitors in a reindeer race with Waldo at Wainwright.

Kunaknauruk   a whaler at Point Hope.

Kupaak father of Kakmak. He was an old-timer at the whaling camp when Waldo first went whaling.

Kusiq first husband of Lucy Kongona. Kusiq is also Waldo's Iñupiaq name.

Mark Kutuk father of Freddie Aishanna, Roy Audlakroak, Roseanna Negovanna, and Cora Ayalgook.

Helge Larsen a Danish anthropologist who traveled with Waldo on the Utuqqaq River.

Adam Leavitt son of George Leavitt, Jr., and Mae Masak. Adam was a boy when Waldo went to Barrow to get the reindeer that had gotten mixed with the Barrow herd.

Herbert Leavitt brother of Adam Leavitt. He met Waldo when Waldo went to Barrow to get the reindeer that had gotten mixed with the Barrow herd.

Ernest de K. Leffingwell a geologist who had a house at Flaxman Island.

Lomen family came north at the time of the Nome gold rush. Gudbrand Lomen and his son, Carl, were heavily involved in the reindeer industry and other ventures in the Nome area.

Frank Long son of Kakmak. Frank and Waldo were together when they were young boys at the whaling camp. They were the cook's helpers.

Marvin ("Muktuk") Marston organized military units in many of the coastal villages during World War II.

Mattie Masak wife of Peter Panik, sister of Akuklook.

Mayaroak wife of Shaglook. Also known as Mayak, she was a skilled trader.

Robert Mayokok a childhood friend of Waldo in Nome.

Mitiq a young boy who traveled with Knud Rasmussen. Waldo met him at Icy Cape.

Stanley Morgan a radio operator at Barrow when Waldo was reporting the weather from Wainwright.

Carl Mukpik son of Abraham Ilannik. Carl and Waldo played together when they were young boys at Icy Cape.

Murphy   one of the crew members of the *Baychimo*.

Dorothy Nakaak   stepmother of Mattie, by adoption.

Henry Nashaknik   lived with his family on the Meade River near present-day Atqasuk when Waldo conducted the 1940 census.

Alva Nashoalook   father of Alva Nashoalook, Jr. He was one of the young boys Waldo grew up with at Icy Cape. Later, Alva ran the Native Store at Wainwright that became the Wainwright Reindeer and Trading Company.

Samantha Nashoalook   wife of MacRidge Nayakik. Samantha and MacRidge were married at the same time that Waldo and Mattie were married in Barrow.

Charles Nayakik   father of Moses Nayakik.

MacRidge Nayakik   a reindeer herder at Icy Cape. In the triple marriage Waldo described, MacRidge married Samantha.

Moses Nayakik   son of Charles Nayakik, husband of Marietta Bodfish.

Warren Neakok   son of Eva Papiklook, who is the sister of Mattie Bodfish. At the time of the land claims, Warren helped the Arctic Slope Regional Corporation identify important lands in the Point Lay area.

Charlie Ned   brother of Kusiq.

Roseanna Negovanna   wife of Weir Negovanna, daughter of Mark Kutuk, sister of Cora Ayalgook. She learned to dance from Lucy Kongona.

Weir Negovanna   husband of Roseanna Negovanna. Weir was one of the elders from Wainwright who went to Barrow to advise the Arctic Slope Regional Corporation at the time of the land claims.

Adam Nikkaktoak   brother of Joseph Papiklook, father of Ben Tagarook.

Roy Niugalak   brother of William Niugalak. Waldo knew Roy and William when he was growing up at Icy Cape. Roy and Waldo were the same age.

William Niugalak brother of Roy Niugalak.

Numnik father of Jean Segevan Numnik. He lived with his family at Pulayaaq on the Meade River when Waldo conducted the 1940 census.

Ned Nusunginya a mail carrier who traveled by dog team. He was also a Barrow area whaler.

Mary Oenik mother of Mattie Bodfish.

Okeleak grandfather of Weir Negovanna. Lucy Kongona used to rent a house from Okeleak and his wife.

Okresak one of the older men on the ice with Waldo when the leads made it hard for them to get back to shore.

Oneuk lived with his family at Pulayaaq when Waldo conducted the 1940 census.

Ootoayuk an old man who shared his traditional knowledge with Waldo. After Ootoayuk's wife died, Waldo took him out trapping.

Ooyogoak one of the Native healers from Barrow.

Paine a teacher in Wainwright when Waldo got caught in the storm as he took a load of supplies to Icy Cape.

Sammy Pameok was with Waldo at the whaling camp when they got caught on the moving ice and had trouble getting ashore.

Bert Panigeo husband of Nellie Panigeo. Waldo and Mattie stayed at Bert's house when they went to Barrow to get married. Bert carried mail by dog team when Waldo was a boy.

Nellie Panigeo daughter of Adam Nikkaktoak, who is the brother of Joseph Papiklook, father of Mattie Bodfish.

Peter Panik husband of Mattie Masak, father of David Panik. Waldo got to know the Panik family when he was a teenager herding reindeer at Icy Cape.

Jessie Panikpak husband of Ethel Papiklook.

Ethel Papiklook sister of Mattie Bodfish, wife of Jessie Panikpak. Ethel and Jessie were married at the same time that Waldo and Mattie were married.

Joseph Papiklook   father of Mattie Bodfish.

Mary Patik   wife of Peter Audlakroak, mother of Nannie Kagak. Mary was a Native healer, a "feeler."

Billy Patkotak   husband of Amy Bodfish, son of Paul Patkotak. Billy and Paul were members of Waldo's whaling crew.

Patunak   a Native healer, a "feeler" at Barrow.

C. T. Pedersen   a ship captain and trader known for his skills in piloting through the ice.

Henry Peetook   son of Alice Akligok and Thomas Tazruk.

William Penn   husband of Bessie Kanayuk. William and Bessie were married at the same time that Waldo and Mattie were married.

Pigaaluk   a boy whom Waldo knew at Icy Cape.

Pootkakroak   sailed down the coast from Wainwright with Waldo's family when they were going to the Icy Cape area.

Stewart Rabeau   a medical doctor stationed at Kotzebue.

Froelich Rainey   an anthropologist who worked in Point Hope with Helge Larsen.

Ira Rank   a trader from Nome who came up the coast buying fur and selling goods.

Knud Rasmussen   a Danish and Iñuit explorer and anthropologist who documented Eskimo culture in Greenland, Canada, and Alaska.

Sidney Rood   a reindeer superintendent.

Isaac Samarona   half-brother of Waldo. He was a member of Waldo's whaling crew.

Mary Samarona   sister of Lucy Kongona, wife of Jack Hadley.

Samarualook   Waldo hired his dog team when he went to Point Lay with the Unit Manager.

Sheldon Segevan   worked as a weatherman with Waldo. They also both tended Jim Allen's store.

Shaglook   husband of Mayaroak. He was a wealthy Iñupiaq man from Icy Cape, known for his skills as a trapper and trader. Waldo met him while herding at Icy Cape.

William Shoudla   father of Edna Shoudla.

Sikrikak   relative of Mattie.

Sikvauyugak   one of the mail carriers who traveled by dog team.

Samuel Simmonds   father of Leona Okakok. He is a Presbyterian minister who served in Wainwright, and he was Waldo's pastor.

Sinefelt   a medical doctor who gave typhoid and diphtheria immunizations to people in Wainwright in 1942.

Siuchiarook   husband of Atkilak, brother of Kusiq.

Irene Solomon   stepdaughter of Kakmak.

Pete Sovalik   a member of Waldo's whaling crew.

Pete Strand   a trader who operated along the Arctic Coast. He had a schooner and took supplies from Wainwright to Icy Cape.

Leonard Sublugak   a friend of Waldo's at the Teller Mission School.

Susook   a friend of Waldo's when Waldo traveled with Susook's family from Wainwright to Icy Cape.

Ben Tagarook   son of Adam Nikkaktoak.

Tagilook   had a house in Wainwright when Waldo first saw the place.

Tagotak   Waldo's uncle from Nome.

Takpak   husband of Ekilalook, who is the daughter of William Shoudla. Takpak was a famous Iñupiaq whaler.

Thomas Tazruk   husband of Alice Akligok. Thomas was a reindeer herder.

Dick Thomas   brother of Henry Peetook. He was a member of Waldo's whaling crew.

Tilton   possibly James Tilton, a whaling captain who was reported to have wintered over at Herschel Island.

Tingook   a reindeer herder.

Dwight Tivook   one of Waldo's childhood friends in Nome.

John Tookaloona   an old reindeer herder whose job was to drive the deer into the corrals.

Mickey Toorak   a reindeer herder whom Waldo knew when Waldo was a reindeer boy.

Toovak family   lived on the Meade River when Waldo conducted the 1940 census.

Johnson Tuginna   son of Angoyuk.

Patrick Tukrook   son of Amos Agnasagga, brother of Samuel Agnasagga and Michael Kayutak. Waldo knew him when they were boys at Icy Cape. Patrick helped the Arctic Slope Regional Corporation identify important lands in the Point Lay area.

Frank Tukumik   a member of Waldo's whaling crew.

Arthur Upicksoun   traveled to Barrow with Waldo to get supplies.

Eleanor Upicksoun   wife of Jim Allen, mother of Alice and Kate Allen.

Walluk   third husband of Lucy Kongona. He taught Waldo how to hunt seals at the breathing hole.

Walton   a bear hunter from Michigan whom Waldo took out hunting.

Waugh   a medical doctor who came to Wainwright on a Coast Guard ship.

Richard Webb   a teacher in Wainwright in the 1940s.

Sig Wien   a famous bush pilot who flew mail along the Arctic Coast.

Wiggerson   a cook at Teller Mission.

Emma Willoya   was raised at Teller Mission and helped at the school there. Later she worked with the Nome Skin Sewers.

Paul Wilson   a census taker for the 1940 census. Waldo took him from Wainwright up the Meade River and down to Barrow.

Appendix D

Major Genealogical Relations

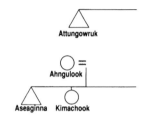

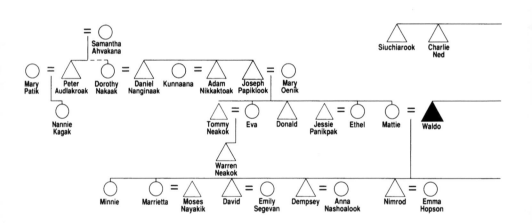

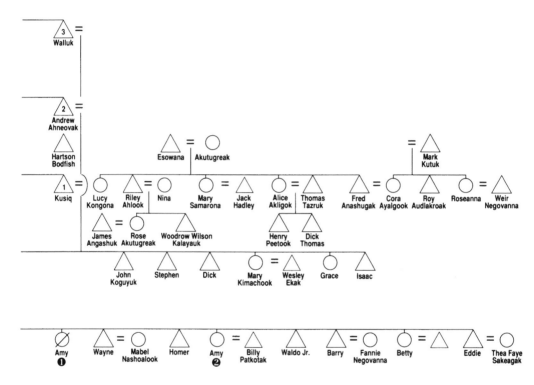

Appendix E

Iñupiaq Place-Names and
U.S.G.S. Spellings

Iñupiaq Spelling	U.S.G.S. Spelling	T.L.U.I.* Number
Aksragaġvik		36
Akuliaqattat	Akoliakatat Pass	95
Akuliaqattat Inlet	Akoliakatot Pass	95
Aluaqpak (Coal Mine #3)	Kilich Point	40
Aqiaġuġnat	Akeonik	106
Aqsraatchiaġvik		112
Ataniq	Atanik	4
Atqasuk	Atkasuk	BA 62
Aulataġruaq River	Alatakrok River	71
Aumalik		44

*T.L.U.I stands for Traditional Land Use Inventory. All T.L.U.I numbers without a prefix refer to the Wainwright inventory. Prefix BA refers to the Barrow-Atkasook (Atqasuk) inventory. PL refers to the Point Lay inventory. PH refers to the Point Hope inventory.

Iñupiaq Spelling	U.S.G.S. Spelling	T.L.U.I. Number
Avalitquq	Avalitkok Creek	57
Avalliq River	Avalik River (Narvaqpak)	56
Aviŋŋaq		142
Avvaq	Avak Inlet	103
Igluqpauraq		34
Imilik		108
Imnaaguq		
Inaru River	Inaru River	
Iñuktuyuk		79
Isuqtuq	Usuktuk River	
Itqiuraq		BA 73
Ittutchiaq		129
Iviaŋŋiik		PH97
Ivisauraq	Ivisaruk River	60
Ivrit		
Kaŋich	Kangik	53
Kaulaaq	Kaolak River	55
Kiŋiŋmiut		
Kirgavik		135
Kuugruaq	Kugrua River	118
Kuuk	Kuk River	
Kuukpaaġruk River	Kukpowruk River	
Kuulugruaq		
Kuutchiaq		PL5
Milliktaġvik	Miliktavik	86
Mitchak		
Mitqutaiḷat		92
Naparuatchiaq		
Narvaqpak		128
Niġisaqtuġvik	Nigisaktuvik River	BA 51
Nivaat	Nevat Point	99
Nuataaq	Noatak	

Iñupiaq Spelling	U.S.G.S. Spelling	T.L.U.I. Number
Nunavaaq	Nunavak Bay	BA 8
Nuqullik	Nokotlek Point	93
Nuvuk	Nuwuk	BA 1
Pagniġruaq	Puknikruk	50
Piŋalu		147
Piŋuksraġruk	Pingorarok Hill	89
Piŋusugruk	Pingasagruk	2
Pitmigiaq		
Pulayaaq		BA 36
Qaanaaq		122
Qagluġruaq		BA 49
Qaġmak Point	Karmuk Point	74
Qaviaraq		
Qayaiqsiġvik	Icy Cape	105
Qiaġruaq		103
Qikiqtasugruk	Kikiktausgruak Island	46
Qiḷamittaġvik	Kilimantavi	82
Qipuqḷaich		26
Qitiq	Ketik River	
Saaŋiaq		
Sanniŋaruq	Shaningarok Creek	
Siñġauraq	Sinarurok River	15
Sirraġruich		7
Sirraqłuk		49
Sullivik	Solivik Islands	109
Tikiġluk	Meade River Village	BA 64
Titqiaq		142
Tuapaktusuk		BA 19
Tulaaġiaq	Tolageak	113
Tunulik River	Tunalik River	104
Tuttilivik		31
Tuttuaġvik		25

Iñupiaq Spelling	U.S.G.S. Spelling	T.L.U.I. Number
Ulǵuniq	Wainwright	19
Umiŋmak	Omikmak Creek	32
Uqsruq River		116
Utuqqaq River	Utukok River	
Uyaǵaaǵruk	Oyagaruk Creek	164

Appendix F

Waldo as a Hunter:
A Note from Richard Nelson

William Schneider

Richard Nelson, after reading a draft of this book, remarked how little Waldo had discussed hunting in the manuscript. In a letter to the University of Alaska Press (August 7, 1989), he wrote

> When I lived in Wainwright Waldo was in his sixties, yet he still hunted caribou on foot, alone, during the fiercest winter gales, when blowing snow reduced visibility to a few yards and obliterated the sound of his footsteps on hard-packed drifts. If he came across bits of skittering tundra vegetation, he would follow them upwind until he found the animals, usually at close range and by complete surprise. And when he either shot caribou or gave up trying, he had to find his way back to the village or face a long, stormy winter night without shelter. To my knowledge, he was the only man who hunted this way rather than waiting for good weather and going after the caribou with a dog team. If Bill thinks it's worthwhile to add a comment about Waldo as a hunter, I would be glad to talk with him about it.

When Dick Nelson and I discussed this later, Dick offered several stories to illustrate the kinds of information that Waldo has shared with him. The following account is taken from Dick's Wainwright notes:

> Several years ago [Waldo Bodfish], one of the most active hunters in Wainwright went inland by snow machine to hunt caribou. He found a bunch and shot three, then went about skinning them. While he was at work, a wind suddenly came up and grew stronger by the minute. When he had finished with two animals he realized that he had better put up the tent he carried and get prepared for a storm. By the time he had the tent ready the wind was blowing fiercely.
>
> The caribou were only a hundred yards away so he decided to pull them up to his tent. He could see just a few feet now through the blowing snow, and when he had gone far enough he found nothing. So he turned back for the tent, but could not find it either. Slowly he groped through the snow that whirled before a southerly gale, turning back and forth in search of the tent that must be so near. The caribou were irrelevant now.
>
> Finally he decided that he was not going to find the tent, so he followed the traditional edict that a lost person should make a shelter and sit tight. Wandering around in the storm would only use precious energy and get him more lost. It was fall and the snow was not deep, so he could only make a little snow block wall to protect his back and sides. Then he packed it with soft snow to keep the wind from eroding it away. This at least gave him a place to sit out of the gale, though a roofed snowhouse would have been much better.
>
> Wet snow whirled around him as night fell, soaking his clothes and mittens. Every twenty minutes or so he got up and walked around to warm up and loosen his stiff

muscles. He also packed more snow against places where the wind was eating at the wall. As the night wore on he thought about his thermos of hot tea, lying somewhere nearby inside the tent.

Morning light finally came, and the awful storm diminished slightly. He found that he could see about six feet along the ground, so he began searching back and forth for the tent. Shortly he came across a streak of blood where he had dragged one of the caribou; he used this to guide him, at last, back to the tent. He crawled inside immediately, drank some hot tea, and fell asleep.

When he awoke he went outside to look around and he found that the weather had improved enough for travel. He saw the tracks from his futile searching the night before—they passed within four feet of the tent, but somehow he had neither seen it nor stumbled over its guy ropes. When he was ready to leave he walked over and looked at the windbreak that had probably saved his life. "I just laughed,'" he said as he concluded the story, "looking at that little space I spent the whole night in." (Nelson 1981:49)

When I started researching Waldo's history, I was aware of Dick's work in Wainwright; in fact, Dick and I discussed the life history project and we agreed that it was important and urgent. We spoke of Waldo's extensive knowledge of many things, and how he loves to share what he knows. However, I don't recall discussing the differences between what Waldo chose to share with each of us, so I decided to interview Dick about his relationship with Waldo. The following is an edited excerpt from that interview.

An Interview with Richard Nelson

"Waldo was really the main person I learned from in terms of intellectual knowledge, traditional knowledge of the past, the kind of knowledge you don't really see when you're out hunting, the kind of thing that's mental. That came to me, of course, from a lot of people—Weir Negovanna comes to mind. But more than anyone else it was from Waldo.

"The routine for me was to visit Waldo as often as seemed appropriate. I probably would have visited Waldo every day, probably would have hung around his house, but I didn't want to overdo it. So I visited him a lot, especially when it seemed like nobody [else] would be home and he would feel like talking. He had a little table by the window, very much like this table we're sitting at here in my house. And we would sit there very much like you and I are doing right now, without turning on the lights. I remember it being dark. And Waldo usually sat by the the window, just like you're doing, and he would just tell me things.

"Waldo had a real clear idea of what I was doing there. I'm sure early on I explained to him what I was interested in, and from his sons he probably heard more, but Waldo just decided that he was gonna teach me stuff. So it didn't really take a lot of effort on my part to focus conversations, although I would always ask him questions. But if Waldo would think of something he thought would relate to my interests, then it would just come out.

"I would go over to his house, and bingo!—he would just start talking about these things. He has an inexhaustible capacity for conversation and for storytelling, and a phenomenal memory. So he would just leap off into subjects. I spent a tremendous number of hours in his house, listening. I never wrote any notes. I would run over to my house afterward, sketch out a list of all the things he had said, and then fill it in.

"One of the very important things for Waldo's way of teaching is that he did it with a lot of stories. I really don't know if this was peculiar to what Waldo was trying to teach me because we never talked about that directly. But basically, I think his preference was to do his teaching through stories. His memory and his attentiveness to the details of things was really stunning, because Waldo would tell me about a particular hunt that might have happened thirty or forty years earlier. I don't know how long ago these things happened. For example, it seems that almost every time he told me a story about hunting caribou he told me how many there were. He would say things like, 'There were sixteen caribou and I got the whole bunch.'" You know, 'I got every one of them.'

"And then he would tell me how he did it, by shooting the leader as they would run in one direction, then shooting the new leader as they ran in the other. But what I remember so vividly is that he would always tell me how many animals there were! That's what kind of memory he has.

"The other thing that probably has stayed with me most vividly about Waldo is his style of telling stories, and the slow, meticulous unfolding of things that came from him. Waldo is not a humble man, really, but that doesn't mean he's proud to a fault. Waldo loved to tell stories about his biggest mistakes, and about times that things went most terribly wrong for him.

"I remember him talking about animals that eluded him, like how he was stalking a seal on top of the ice, just going through everything, getting close to it, doing everything absolutely perfect, and then losing the seal. When he finished a story like that, he would just drift off into this uncontrollable laughter. I remember him; I can picture him with his eyes just wet with tears from laughing at himself for the foolishness he had done or for the way he had been fooled by things outside of himself.

"On the other hand, he would tell a lot of stories that illustrated his pride in himself: about the time that he sneaked up to a bearded seal on the ice and he kept getting closer and closer. Finally he realized he was so close that maybe he could grab it. And so he sneaked up and grabbed that seal and caught it that way, and killed it with his knife. I don't remember all of the details of that story. Waldo would if he was sitting here right now!"

This story is typical of the type of experiences Waldo chose to share with Dick, and it illustrates the difference in emphasis in the relationship Waldo has with Dick as compared to the relationship that Waldo has with me.

Appendix G

An Unusual Whaling Season
An Interview with
Waldo Bodfish, Sr.

James Mumiġana Nageak

I interviewed Waldo Bodfish, Sr., on May 27, 1989. The following transcription of a part of that interview illustrates how Waldo directed the narrative according to his understanding of his listener's background. Waldo knows that my Native language is Iñupiaq and that I am familiar with hunting, so he did not have to explain terms or set a detailed context for me before he started telling his story. I responded to his story by affirming what he said, reiterating certain points, and asking for clarification to make sure I understood.

The first section below is a transcription of the interview as it was conducted in Iñupiaq. My comments appear in parentheses. The second section is a literal English translation, with the meanings of certain Iñupiaq words appearing in brackets. Following the literal translation is my interpretive translation of the story, along with some background information.

An Interview with Waldo in Iñupiaq

Aġvakama suqqalikpagmik, sikumi auŋaiḷaami, innatun maptutigiruami sikumi, [argagmiñik urriqaruq] aġviġum puiraŋani, tuqutiġikput satkuvlugu. (Sikumi.) Sikumi, imaiḷaami. (Ii.) Tuvvam, tuvaq samma *mile*-kiaq, (Uŋasiksilaaŋa?) *mile and a quarter* uŋasiksilaaŋa, tatpagna...? Savikpaglu? Maaŋŋa siñaa. Naŋiaqtuuruaguut uŋalaqpaguġmagu. Aġviġum puigaatigut, puiviksrautaanun, tuvvami mattumani, inillal... nullautilgiññiġitka. [laughter] Aasii taimma nullaqapta, niuqqaqqaaqhuta aniruaguut. Aniiġaluaqaptaasii isiqhuta, anuqqaksiiññaġman. (Ii.) Aasiuvva, isiġmiupasaŋitchugut, nasiqsruqtillugu, ivuniqpaich ataannun   piruaguut,   ulitpaiᵻᵻuni,   ivulaqivluni,   tamanna tuvaġruiññaq unnii, takanuuna arguuraptigun, qaiqsuuram taavruma unanitchiagun, ivuniqpaliḷḷagaruaġluaġniqsuq, (Ii.) itiġapta. (Suŋitkaasi?) Suŋitkaatigut, ivuniqᵻukpaiᵻᵻuni tamanna, qulaulaiññiġai. Aruguqput taamna, qaiqsuuratualugmik paqinnapta tavruŋa, uŋasiksivḷugu uiñiq nullaqtuaguut, aġviġiaqhuta sunauvvauvva. [laughter] Araa, apulaipqaqtakkavuut uvva igliqtuat, araa aġviġich. (Ii.) Ittuallaiqsuaguut, siñiḷḷaiqsuaguut unnii, igliqpaiᵻᵻutiŋ. Apulaitkivut. Apuqsuitchugut. Aasii tavra tatpauŋaqapta, sua qakimna Qaġmak, iñugikkaġaa, (Ii.) taapkuak igḷisillugik, Annaqauramik simmausiqapku, Charlie Nedmik. Malġugnik samma umiaqtuvsaaġisiruŋa. (Ii.) Charlie Nedmik supputitaqtiksralgitchuŋa, aġvaksayuŋulugman nutaukami. (Charlie Ned?) Ii. Tuqutchiḷiġuumman aġviġnik. Iññuktaaġikapku, aasiuvva taavsruma aġviġum puggiqigaatigut.

Aasiuvva umiaptigni, paġnaliqtuqaptigik satkuvut, malġuk naulikkak, malġuk supputik, upaktuqᵻugu, nauliktaksr... (Sikuliaġruakun tainna.) Sikuliaġruakun. Puisapkaqᵻugu tavra, piumman, puigami innatun, sammakiak *one foot*-kiaq aatchaqtillagruaġaġigaa tuvaq tamanna. (Ii.) Qasalaitchuq unnii. Piqakᵻugu tasammaŋŋa. (Ii.) Tavraasii kurraġman tullagruaġaqtuq iviqtitiqhuni. (Ii.) Ilauna puiŋaiḷaaq. Puiḷġiñman supputitquaqsigiga, saniġaanuktiqᵻuŋa aġviġum, (Saniġaanun.) ii, siḷagauraŋanun tamattuma naqtuġniŋan, uvaŋŋa innaġami. (Ii.) Siḷagauraŋanun.

Qanittukkii innaqiuraq samma. (Tainnatun maptutigimmiruaq.) Ii. Bill isigaŋisutkiaq hamma iḷivḷugu, inillaktuaŋaa. (Ii.) Piksaktitparruŋ qugluksaġumi, taamna nauliksallagruaġukługu, qialġutiligmik. (Ii.) Naagga tavra, Annaqauram supputitkaa, Katuavlu, supputignik malġugnik. Quŋusiñġagun tavruuna pisiquaqsigiga, (Ii.) quuŋaiññuraŋŋaan amikḷikpan tavruuna pisiquvlugu, uqautivlugik. Aasii nauliksaġniaġnivḷuŋa uvaŋa. Aasiuvva supputinmatku quġluksaqhuni tamanna siku piksaktillagruaġaa, siḷanmun. (Ii, tuŋignun piŋitkaa.) Ii, tuŋimnun piŋit... pigaluaqtuq igḷiqsiġiga (Ii.). Aasii Charlie Ned una iguunmiñik siqumillagruaqługu paunatchisugruagun imaq... kurraġuaqsaġataaqsiruq immamun. (Ii.) Aasiuvva Katuam papiŋigun tiguvlugu nuqitiqługu imaaqtinŋitkaa. (Charlie Ned.) Annaqauraq (Annaqauraq, Annaqauraq taamna Charlie Ned?) Ii. (*Yeah, okay.*) Aasii taimma nuqitiġmani, tamaani [laughter] pisuġalauraaqsivḷuni.

Taimma ququġaatigut, suutuġnaqsirugurguuq uvva qaugagnik. (Ii.) Suutuġiaqummatigut [laughter] suutuġialiktuaqsiḷgitchugut. (Imma aġviq.) Ii. Aġviq uvva satkuŋagikput, aullaġniaŋitchukkii isumakama. (Tuquŋaruq?) Ii. Satkuvut, nauliksakkaġaa, immuaŋi *eight fathom*-guruat, nuŋummiut... (avataqpagmun) Anmuiññaq nauliksallagruaqtuaŋaa, tavruuna piksaktinmagu inaagun sikum. Sua samna, nuŋummiullu taapkua, mapqatillagruaq... (Qaaqtuq.) Aasiuvva tainnaittuallakhuta atiptigniñ tasamma aulaŋaiññiqsuq, qaaqtuq. (Ii.) Taamna, Airuluuram nauligniġaa iguutaagun. Naulikkamik pimmiruam. (Ii.) Kivruma, iñugikkaġaa Harold-luuraq. Harold Killbear taimña. (Ii.)

Umiaqtuqpaallukhuni uvamniuvaa. Taimmaasii, tainnaitilluta sua pamna kiluptinniñ tavraŋŋa qaaqhuni, qaġruġa. (Ii.) Tavraŋŋa qaaqtiqtuq, kiluptigniñ. Qitiġusiġiaq... tuuqsiḷiġaluaqtuaġuuk Kiasigḷu, Sheldon Siġvan [*Van, like in Chevy van.*] (Ii.) Iñugisuŋaiññakkaġaa tavra taamna umiaqtuqama. Sheldon Siġvan. (Kiasiq?) Ii. Siġvan taivruma iġñiŋa. Sheldon Siġvan. (Ii.) Savaqatiga *weather bureau*-mi, iñuksraqtaaġimmiraġa. Jim Allen-kunni piŋitchuq, allanik iñuqaqtuq amna. (*Oh.*)... pakkaŋani. Umialiptigniitchukpan pigalualgiñmigiga isumaŋatun, uvamnun ataaqtuqtuq. (Ii.) Niŋiviñaqhuniasiikii tavra [laughter] Taim... (Qaaqtuq kiluptigun?) Ii. (Kiluptigun pamuuna?) Ii. Kiluptigun qaiqsuurakun tavruuna qaaqtuq. Qaaqtuq. Tukiqsallagruaġami tavra tatpikuŋanmun saquvluni tavruŋa puktallaġniqsuq. Aulaŋiññiqsuq. (Qaaġman.) Ii. Aullaŋiḷḷagniqsuq. Innatun marra piŋa...tuuqtuqługu tainna samma akuqtutigiruagnik, taiksrumatun katchisun, (Ii.) akuttutigiikhunuk pitaiḷiqtuaguuk, avatqupqaqługuasiuvva pitaiñiqsuguk, iluqanuk. Taimma Kiasik, mitiŋiqqaaqtuaq, mitiŋianigman, savitchaqugaluaġiga, savilaitkaa. (Ii.) Aasiuvva savilaiñmagu, "qitqagun ata tavruuna tuuqsaġiñ" tainnaqtikkaġaa. Qitqapia...qitipiaġataŋakkun tuuqtuq. Pitaktiġmagu taunuŋaŋitchuq maŋuksaġluaġaa, saaviñŋitchuq. (Ii, sua tasamma.) Tasamna. Ullakapku, tigukapku, naqittaallakkaġaa, sua samna aġiñaaġruaqtun inniqhuni. [laughter] "Tavra paqitiġiñ aġviq." Taimma kilak... tavruuna...

(Suutuaniktusiimma.) Aiy? (Suutuaniktusi?) Suutuanikapta (Ii.) niġiqqaaqhuta tuuġiaqtaqput. [laughter] Paqitchaqsakkaqpuut, aullaŋitchukkii iḷisimagikput. (Ii.)

Taimma paqitiqaptigu kilakługu tavruuna, aġviġum iviġviksraŋa, aktilaaŋa naammaksivḷugu mitiŋiqługu, sui... avataiqługu nuqinnaptigu, niaqua qarviqługu, qaqitqaallagruaġikput. (Ii.)

Aasiuvva umiat kiligiaqtitatka Frank Bester-mun, tavrani umiaqtuġman. Frank Bester-lu taapkualu sivulliich, Frank Bester-lu, kiliksiyaqtuqukatka umianik naŋiaqtuuŋaruanik (Ii.) ikayuġiaquvluta. ...tuaq (Aqpaaqtuaq.) Ii. (Immakii naŋiaqtuurut.) Ii. Naŋiaqtuuŋarut niġiuŋitchut. Imaiḷaamigguuq iñuk aġvagniaŋitchuq. (Ii.) Quuttualutkut tamatkua, Aŋasatkut, Aaŋauratkut iglautigiaqsigaarguuq (Ii, aqpaapayuktuaq.) Aqpaapayuktuaq iñugni. Taimmagguuq uqallautigai, nasitchaqtuaquvlugich ivuniġnun, nasiqsruaġviŋiññun, takuyaq tautugnaġnivḷugu tavraŋŋa (Ii.) Yaiy. Arguasuuraġniaŋitchurguuq [laughter] Isumasuuruŋa tavra naksiñasugaluŋa, imaiḷaami aġvakama (Ii.) taavrumiŋa. *Eleven foot*-tanik suqqaqaġniqsuaq (Arahaa!) Tatpaani tuvaqsiusugrulgiññiqsuq uvva. [laughter] Ataagun sikum,

arraa. (Payaŋiññamiuŋ kiimma tainna.) Aġnasalluq. (Payaŋiññamiuŋ.) Pitallaavlugu, puiḷḷaavluni piḷiginñiqsuq. (Aġvaktaġiv-
luguasii.) Ii. Aġvaktiḻḻutaasii tavra taavruma.

A Literal English Translation

When I caught a whale with long baleen, on the ice that have
not melted, on ice this thick [about one foot], the whale
emerged. Using our whaling equipment, we killed it. (On the
ice.) On the ice with no water. (Yes.) The *tuvaq* [locked shore
ice] being about a mile away, (The distance?) the distance
being mile and a quarter away to that up there, the edge of the
shore-locked ice. (The *sikuliaġruaq* [older young ice, about a
foot thick].) We had moved to safety because of the big west
wind. After making camp and after having something to drink,
we went out. After staying out for a while we went back in,
because the wind was picking up. (Yes.) And we didn't stay in
very long. While Annaqauraq (Charlie Ned?) was looking out
on top of the pressure ridge where we had camped under, a
whale emerged where I had chosen to camp.

Getting the *saktu* [whaling equipment] at the boat, two
darting guns, two shoulder guns, we went to it. (Through the
sikuliaġruaq.) Through the *sikuliaġruaq*. While it was still out
of the water, when it emerged, when it emerged out of the
water, it would make the ice to crack open about a foot. (Yes.)
It doesn't even stick together, making it *piqak-* [to be pushed
up and cracked by pressure from below; said of ice] from down
there. (Yes.) And when the whale submerged, the ice goes
back to how it was, (Yes.) just like the whale had not emerged.
When the whale emerged again I told them to shoot it with the
shoulder gun, after I got to the side of the whale, (To the side
of it.) yes, just on the edge of the crack, when it did this, it was
close about this much. (It was that thick.) Yes. I had placed
myself as far as Bill's foot there. (Yes.) I wanted *nauliksaq-* [to
harpoon] it when the ice flew off after they shoot it, with a
qialgun [darting gun with harpoon]. (Yes.) And then Annaqau-

raq and Katuaq shot it, using two shoulder guns. I told them to shoot it on the neck. (Yes.) Just before it *quu-* [to bend] when it gets narrow, I told them to shoot it, and I was going to *nauliksaq-*. And when they shot it, when it *qugluksaq-* [to react by bending], it made the ice flew off, outwards. (Yes, it didn't go toward you.) It didn't... it went toward me but I dodged it. (Yes.) And Charlie Ned, the whale using its *iguun* [something used to suck; in this case, jaws] broke up the ice way over there and he was going headfirst into the water, (Yes.) and Katuaq grabbed him on his *papik* [parka hem] and pulled him up, making him not go into the water. (Charlie Ned.) Annaqauraq. (Annaqauraq, is he Charlie Ned?) Yes. (Yeah, okay.) And when he pulled him out, he just started to walk around there.

Someone called out that it was time to eat duck soup. (Yes.) When they told us to go and eat duck soup, we left to go eat. (And there's the whale.) Yes. Right there, we had shot the whale. It wasn't going to go away, when I thought. (It's dead?) Yes. When I harpooned it, its *immuaq* [rolled rope around the float] was eight fathoms. Just when they were finished, I had aimed the harpoon straight down when the ice went flying off. (Yes.) Just when that roll finished, there was a sound of gun blasting. (Exploding.) And waiting a while, there was an explosion below us, not moving. Harold-*luuraq* had harpooned it on the *iguun*. He was also using the harpoon.

And then, while we were like that, there was an explosion *kilu* [direction away from open water; in this case, south] of us, my *qagruq* [shell]. (Yes.) From there it exploded, south of us. (It exploded south of you!) Yes. (It was south of you.) Yes. It exploded just *kilu-*, it exploded just south of us in that clear area. It exploded. When the whale *tukiqsaq-* [to move forward from a fixed position] it changed its course and went that way and *puktallaq-* [to come to the surface of the water, like a sponge]. It did not move (When it exploded.). Yes. It did not go away.

Kiasik and I had *tuuqsi-* [to put a hole in the ice using an ice chisel]. It is about this thick, making holes about that far apart, like that over there, the wall [about twelve feet]. (Yes.) We made holes that far apart, and just on either side of the whale we made holes, both of us. So Kiasik, who made the *mitiŋiq-* [to chip ice to make a hole in the ice] first, after he made the hole, I told him to try and feel. He couldn't feel it. (Yes.) And when he couldn't feel anything, "Why don't you *tuuq-* [to use an ice chisel to make a hole] right in the middle?" I told him. He made a hole right in the middle of our holes. When he tried to make his lance to go down after making a hole, it didn't go down. He tried to *maŋuk-* [to make it go through]. It didn't go down. (Yes, there it was.) There it was. When I went to him and grabbed and feel it, there it was, like it was soft. "There you have found the whale." Then right there...

(You had your duck soup already!) What? (After your duck soup.) After we had our duck soup, (Yes.) after we ate went to put holes on the ice. We went to find the whale. We knew it didn't go away. (Yes.)

When we found it, we made a hole, *mitiŋiq-,* right there, making it big enough for the whale to come out. When we pulled it, making the head come out of the water, we made it come on top of the ice first. (Yes.)

And then, I let Frank Bester tell the other boats, there when I was whaling. Frank Bester and the first ones, Frank Bester and...to tell others, the ones that had *naŋiaqtuu-* [to camp on the solid shore ice for safety while whaling], (Yes.) to help us. (The one who is running to tell others about catching a whale...) Yes.

(They have *naŋiaqtuu-*.) Yes. They have camped on the solid shore ice for safety. They weren't expecting anything. No one could catch a whale while there is no water. (Yes.) Those— Quuttualuk, Aŋasak, Aaŋauraq—laughed at him. (Yes, even though he was *aqpaaq-* [to run and tell others about a whale being caught].) Even though he was telling them about a whale being caught. So he told them to look on top of where they have their lookout on the pressure ridges, saying that the flag could be seen from there. (Yes.) They did not *arguasuk-* [to disbelieve]. After they saw the flag, they left.

I always think that I *naksi-* [to surpass others], when I caught a whale while there was no water. (Yes.) That one, it had eleven-foot baleen. (Man!) Up there it was staying on the ice, under the ice. *Arraa!* [exclamation of astonishment] (It must not have been strong enough for it.) It was a female. (It did not *paya-* [to lack strength].) Just pushing the ice it emerged, just doing like that. (Catching it then.) Yes. We caught the whale then.

An Interpretive English Translation
The unusual whaling conditions in the spring of 1989 reminded Waldo of the time that his whaling crew caught their biggest whale. The conditions had been unusual for that hunt as well.

The ice had been shaped by a midwinter wind that had blown a large iceberg into shallow water. Moving ice piled up around the iceberg, and the whole mass froze to the ocean bottom, forming a pressure ridge. Usually an easterly wind blows, pushing away the ice not frozen to land, and forming an open lead, where the hunters look for whales. This winter, however, there were no open leads.

A strong westerly wind came up, so Waldo took his whaling crew to a safe area just south of the high pressure ridges. He knew that the shore-locked ice was a safe place to wait out the high winds, so he led them to an area that was clear of pressure ridges, and they set up their camp.

Crew members shot some ducks and began to prepare them for soup. While waiting for the soup, some of the crew went to see how the ice to the north was developing, but there wasn't much activity, so they returned to their tent. Charlie Ned, one of the crew members, stayed up on the pressure ridge, where they had a lookout. Soon Charlie (also known as

Annaqauraq) hollered that he had heard a whale blow and had briefly seen a whale surface through the ice, which was about a foot and a half thick.

The crew quickly ran to the boat and took out two shoulder guns and two darting guns, one of which had forty-eight feet of rope and a sealskin float attached to the harpoon. Charlie Ned and Katuaq grabbed the two shoulder guns, Harold Killbear took one darting gun, and Waldo grabbed the other darting gun with the line attached to it. Someone grabbed the float, and they began to run toward the area where the whale had surfaced through the ice.

When they got there, they saw where the whale had pushed up the ice, forming cracks about a foot wide so that it could breathe. The ice had settled back into its original position, showing only traces of the cracks. Waldo told the others how he wanted them to position themselves when the whale surfaced again. He told Annaqauraq and Katuaq to get in front of the whale and shoot it in the neck before it submerged. He told them that he and Harold Killbear would be at the side of the whale and would use the darting guns from there.

They didn't know exactly where the whale was going to surface again, but they were ready to run to wherever it appeared. Finally, after what seemed like hours, the whale began to push the ice up where it had surfaced before. They quickly positioned themselves according to plan. When Annaqauraq and Katuaq shot the whale, its reaction made the shattered ice fly toward Harold Killbear and Waldo, but they dodged it and got to the edge of the crack, where they threw the darting guns, aiming them straight down. Again the whale reacted and pushed the ice down in front of it. Annaqauraq was sliding into the water when Katuaq grabbed the hem of his parka.

The coil of rope on the float was playing out quickly, and the float had just disappeared under the ice when there was a muffled sound of exploding shells just to the south. Waldo, knowing the length of the coiled rope, estimated where the whale would be. While they were in the process of locating places to make holes in the ice, someone from camp hollered that the duck soup was ready, so the hunters returned to camp to eat and to get the equipment ready for chipping holes in the ice.

After the meal, Waldo and Kiasik went to work making holes in the ice, about twelve feet apart. Kiasik made his hole first, and he put his ice pick through the hole to see if he could feel anything under the ice, but nothing was there. Waldo did the same thing, with the same result, so he told Kiasik to make a hole between the two holes they had made. When Kiasik tested the hole with his ice pick, the pick stopped. Waldo went to the hole and tried to let the ice pick go down, but it went only so far, then stopped. Waldo said it felt like the pick was bouncing, and he told Kiasik that he had found where the whale had died.

Happily they began to make the holes bigger so that they could get the whale ready for butchering on the ice. Waldo told Frank Bester to put up the flag and to go to the other whaling camps and to the village to tell everyone to come help get the whale onto the ice. When Frank Bester went to the first camp to tell them that the crew had killed a whale, the men laughed at him and did not believe him, saying there was no open lead in which to catch a whale. He told them to go to their lookout to see the flag waving. The men were no longer laughing when they saw the flag, and they got ready to go to Waldo's camp to help. Frank Bester carried a flag and continued on to Wainwright, where he put the flag on top of Waldo's house to tell everyone that a whale had allowed itself to be taken by Waldo Bodfish, Sr.

Notes

1. Waldo speaks the North Slope dialect of the Iñupiaq Eskimo language. Iñupiaq refers to the language and to the people (i.e., one speaks Iñupiaq and one is an Iñupiaq). The plural form of Iñupiaq is Iñupiat.

The Iñupiaq-speaking Eskimo inhabit a vast stretch of the Arctic, from the Diomede Islands in the west to eastern Greenland, and from Unalakleet on Norton Sound in western Alaska to Cape Charles on the southern Labrador coast in eastern Canada (Krauss [1974] 1982). There are regional differences in language and customs, but the similarities in language, technology, and hunting methods point to a common origin in the Thule culture about a thousand years ago.

2. Iñupiat customarily begin their accounts by explaining who their relatives are and how they are related. Waldo explains who he is and how he fits into his social network.

3. Riley Ahlook and Eluktuna became reindeer herders through the

apprentice program (see chapter 13). The 1906 report of the Agent for Education in Alaska describes Ahlook and Eluktuna's progress:

> In 1894 he and Elecktoona were sent by the missionaries at Point Hope to Teller to learn reindeer herding. As an apprentice Ahlook showed great interest in the deer. During foggy nights he frequently spent the whole night keeping the herd together. Mr. Kjeelman reported him as the best herder at Teller. He accompanied Lieutenant Jarvis on the famous relief expedition to Barrow. Spent one winter at Unalakleet, another at Point Hope, and moved to Barrow in 1901. He married in 1897. In 1905 he was sent to Wainwright...With Powyun he shares the distinction of driving the first reindeer mail between Barrow and Kotzebue... (Jackson 1906:25)

4. Icy Cape was an important settlement in the early nineteenth century, and it continued to be occupied through the first quarter of the twentieth century. Like Point Hope and Point Barrow, Icy Cape is located on a stretch of land extending out into the ocean along the migration route of the bowhead whales. The population of Icy Cape was largest during the whaling season, although some people lived there year round.

Icy Cape was a coastal settlement of the Siḷaliñarmiut (Siḷaliñigmiut), referred to in the literature as "People of the open spaces" or the Northwest Coast Society. A literal translation means "People away from the mountains." The Siḷaliñarmiut were one of the twenty-five traditional societies identified in Northwest Alaska (Burch 1980: 291).

The Siḷaliñarmiut were adjoined by the Utuqqarmiut (Utuqqaġmiut), who occupied a territory that included the Utuqqaq River drainage and the middle and upper reaches of the Kokolik and Kukpowruk rivers. The Utuqqarmiut were allowed to use the coastal region, which was Siḷaliñarmiut territory, to hunt sea mammals and waterfowl only in the summer. At other times, Utuqqarmiut incursions would probably have led to warfare (Burch, letter, February 13, 1990).

In 1871 whaling ships were caught in the sea ice and abandoned off the coast, in the territory of the Siḷaliñarmiut. Some of the Silaliñarmiut broke into the medicine chests aboard the ships and drank from the bottles, thinking that they contained whiskey. Many people died (Bockstoce 1986:164).

Apparently the Utuqqarmiut were not directly affected by the tragedy, and their society remained intact until the twentieth century. However, the decline in the caribou population, which began in the 1870s, forced the Utuqqarmiut to spend more time on the coast, hunting sea mammals and fishing to compensate for the loss of caribou in their diet (Burch, letter, February 13, 1990).

By the turn of the century, the composition and distribution of Iñupiat in the Icy Cape area was very different from what the Russian explorer Kashevarov had witnessed in 1838 (VanStone 1977:25–26). Regarding the Siḷaliñarmiut, Burch notes that "By the time of the 1900 census, they had lost their old 'tribal' name, and identified themselves as *Kuukmiut* instead. Their major settlement had been moved from Icy Cape to Wainwright Inlet, but there were almost as many at Cape Smythe, quite a few at Pingasugruk, and others were scattered along the coast between Point Hope and Point Barrow." Regarding the Utuqqarmiut, Burch notes that "At the time of the 1900 census, 232 people still identified themselves as *Utuqqarmiut,* but they were spread all over the country, both inland and on the coast, from Point Hope to the mouth of the Colville River; only 10 people lived on the Utukok River" (Burch, letter, February 13, 1990).

The sea continued to erode the site of Icy Cape, and the area became less suitable for hunting. The geologists Philip Smith and J. B. Mertie described the community as it looked in 1924–26 (1930: 103–104). The village was still functioning, although the school had been closed because there were fewer than a dozen students (see chapter 2, note 4). They estimated a population of about forty individuals, for at least part of the year. They also noted a reindeer herd of several thousand.

The establishment of schools, churches, and stores in other villages, along with the closing of facilities in Icy Cape, provided strong incentives for people to move to other settlements, and the site was eventually abandoned (Neakok et al. 1985:15; Burch, personal communication).

5. Leona Okakok: Among the older Iñupiat it is quite rare for someone to have lived only with his parents, thus the need for Waldo to
mention this (personal knowledge; Chance 1966:19–20; North Slope
Borough Commission on Iñupiat History, Language, and Culture
1986).

6. Leona Okakok: It is common among the Iñupiat to name the first
offspring after a deceased spouse; i.e., a first daughter would be
named after her father's deceased wife, or a first son would be named
after his mother's deceased husband. For instance, my half-sister, the
first daughter born after my father's remarriage, was named after my
mother. For general discussions of naming see Chance 1966:20; Burch
1975:68, 142, 158; Heinrich 1963; and Heinrich 1969.

Waldo has mentioned that the spelling of his Eskimo name has
changed from Kusik to Kusiq over the years, and that Kusiq is how
people know him today. Therefore, in writing his name in this book,
we depart from our convention (see chapter 15) and use that spelling.

William Schneider: Naming is very important in Iñupiaq society. Individuals are named after a particular person, and they carry on a part
of that person's personality, assuming certain attributes or qualities of
the person they are named for. They may have the same sense of
humor, mannerisms, or interests. They also simulate the social relations of their namesake. A young boy named after an old man could
be referred to as a grandfather or an uncle by adults who are related
in that way to the boy's namesake.

7. In traditional Iñupiat society, shamans or *aŋatkut* had the power to
do both good and bad, to influence hunting success, to cure people or
make them sick, and to regulate the actions of community members.
They were feared because of their power, but people consulted them
when the need arose. When Christian missionaries came to the North
Slope, they preached against the shamans and, particularly through
their medical skills, convinced people not to use the old power but to
take up Christianity (VanStone 1964:23).

The aŋatkuq who went after Waldo's mother's first husband took a piece of his parka and used it to make Kusiq sicken and die. Waldo says, "My mother tells about it. He took a piece of his parka, on the hem. [He didn't know about it?] He didn't know about it. He died, getting sick" (Review Trip Transcript, p. 111).

Speaking of how people regarded shamans, Waldo said, "They don't bother the shamans too much, but when they find out, when there are no animals, they pay one that has powerful shamanistic powers to perform their powers, to find out. That is how the shamans work in those days. They also know who is going to come and fight them. Then they prepare themselves after the shamans find out for them" (Review Trip Transcript, p. 71; see also pp. 68–71).

8. Captain Hartson Bodfish worked his way up on the whaling crews. He started as a young boy from West Tisbury on Martha's Vineyard, Massachusetts, and eventually became one of the most successful whalers. He helped to pioneer the practice of wintering over at Herschel Island and later at Baillie Island. Although it was a poor anchorage, Baillie Island was believed to be closer to the whaling grounds. Bodfish is reported to have wintered over at Baillie Island in 1900–1901, the year he was master of the steam bark *Beluga*. This is probably where Waldo was conceived. (See Bodfish 1936, Bockstoce 1986: 326–327, and Bockstoce and Batchelder 1977:117.)

On that trip up the Arctic Coast and back, Bodfish had quite a bit of contact with the reindeer station at Teller. According to Bodfish's log books, the *Beluga* was in Port Clarence in July 1900 and at the Teller reindeer station twice before heading north for whaling. On the return, the *Beluga* anchored near the reindeer station on October 18, 1901. Bodfish reports on October 20 that he "paid and discharged the natives." He then steamed to Teller City and back, and on October 21 he started for San Francisco (New Bedford Log Books 952A and 952B). Some of the issues surrounding Bodfish's relationship with Lucy are discussed in Chapter 13.

9. Leona Okakok: Jim Allen, who died in 1944, was a well-known commercial whaler who later turned to trading for H. Liebes and Company. He worked and settled in Wainwright. His story is told in Allen 1978.

10. The ship's logs from the *Beluga* do not mention a stop at Point Hope in the fall of 1900, although they do mention Messrs. Dible and Bayless, two prospectors bound for Point Hope (New Bedford Log Books 952A). It is unclear where these men got onto the ship, and we presume, but do not know, that the *Beluga* stopped at Point Hope to drop them off.

11. When the Reverend Sheldon Jackson was appointed by the Commissioner of Education to the position of General Agent of Education for Alaska in 1875, there was very little money to hire school teachers for Alaska. Jackson successfully enlisted the support of religious groups—the Methodists, Friends, Lutherans, Moravians, Catholics, Episcopalians, and Presbyterians—who got together and divided up the territory. Arctic Alaska went to the Presbyterians, who started a mission in Barrow in 1896 and organized it in 1899. They started another mission at Wainwright in 1922 and organized it in 1923 (Stewart 1908:352, 363–364; Report of the Commission of Education 1908: 374–375; Banks 1974:5).

12. When I called Waldo about this he said he just wanted to mention that there was no difference between their lifestyle, food, and so forth, and that of any other Eskimo settlement.

13. Leona Okakok: *Aġnaqatigiik* is one of the closest relationships in Iñupiat society. It means matrilateral parallel cousins, children whose mothers are sisters or cousins. The term is used mostly by men, who are likely to be of the same age, thus contributing to the closeness of the relationship (as opposed to relationships among siblings, who are younger or older). The term of address *aġnaqaan* is used primarily by men speaking to men, although men and women sometimes use it to address one another. Women never use it to address women.

Aŋutiqatigiik are patrilateral parallel cousins, children whose fathers are brothers. *Iḷḷuġii*k are cross cousins (personal knowledge; see also MacLean forthcoming and Burch 1975:184–190).

Burch, based on his research into kinship terms, has observed changes over time in the uses of terms, and he has found that the terms extend beyond the first cousins. He says:

In the traditional system, the terms were aŋutiqan (aŋutiqatigiik); aġnaqan (aġnaqatigiik) and iḷḷuq (iḷḷuġiik). The
first are patrilateral cousins, the second matrilateral, and
the third cross. If they are first cousins, their parents
were, respectively, brothers, sisters, and brother and sister. If they are second cousins, then the connecting relatives would be their grandparents, etc.; it wasn't only first
cousins who were connected in these ways. Another way
to put it: the children (grandchildren, etc.) of aŋutiqatigiik
(etc.) are also aŋutiqatigiik. Men did not use any of these
terms more or less frequently than women did. In my
experience in the Kotzebue region they still don't, but
men might use one or more of them more frequently on
the North Slope. More important, the term aġnaqan has
come to replace both of the other terms, the system
becoming like our own with aġnaqan meaning any kind of
cousin. Aŋutiqan, in particular, has dropped from usage.
Iḷḷuq is still used sometimes, however. In most cases that
I am aware of, the people who call themselves iḷḷuġiik
don't know why beyond the fact that their parents told
them that's what they were. The people who use the term
for each other definitely understand it to be a joking relationship, however. (letter, January 4, 1990)

Burch spells the Iñupiaq term for singular patrilateral parallel cousins
"aŋutiqan-aŋutiqan" (1975:184), but the relationship is aŋutiqatigiik.

14. Bodfish, on his 1902 trip to the Arctic, anchored off Icy Cape on
July 24 and 25. He also reports staying three days at Icy Cape in 1909
(sometime between July 24 and 29), two days in 1910 (arrived August
3, left August 5), and one day in 1911 (arrived July 25, left July 26).
(New Bedford Log Books 953, 957, 958, 959.)

15. By the 1890s caribou had disappeared entirely from the Seward
Peninsula and the Selawik and Kobuk valleys, and they were scarce
in the other regions mentioned in this book (Burch, personal communication; Burch 1972).

16. Iñupiat people would gather at prominent places like Icy Cape, and when the ice cleared enough for the traders' ships to come, they would trade the winter's catch of fur, particularly white fox skins (see Bodfish 1936:191; Bockstoce 1986:202–203). Independent traders like John Backland, Sr., and C. T. Pedersen specialized in the arctic trade (Bockstoce 1986:204; Cooper 1986:252–253).

Pedersen developed the reputation for being the first to make his way through the ice in the spring. He died in 1962, at the age of ninety-two. Although he sold his shipping interests in 1936, he remained in the fur business until his death (Newell 1977:32–72). Backland, who relied exclusively on sail, died in 1928 at the age of fifty-eight. His son, Captain John Backland, Jr., took over and continued in the sailing tradition. He died in 1961 at the age of fifty-seven (see Newell 1966:393, 656; Sherwood [date unknown]).

17. The term *chief* is best characterized by the Iñupiaq expression *umialik*.

Leona Okakok: *Umialik* literally means "boat owner." This term is used among the Iñupiat to signify a person of wealth, one who can support a lot of people, and therefore is capable of being considered a chief (personal knowledge; MacLean forthcoming).

William Schneider: The term *umialik* was reserved for those men who had both power and wealth. As Burch says, the two attributes are intricately linked. Power was derived from amassing and controlling wealth in the form of resources which could be shared, or used for payment, loans, or gifts (1975a:223–225). Spencer carefully notes that our western concept of "chief" assumes authority over others, but in the Iñupiaq case, men *choose* to associate with the umialik. He leads because others choose to "...cast their lot in with his" (1969:152).

Shaglook's power and wealth derived from his skills in trading. Waldo says, "Foxes, all kinds of foxes they buy with. That is why I was calling him umialik, because he was *store-gnaq*—just like a store. In those days nobody *atanniqsuq*—to rule or boss around anybody. If a person wants to buy something, they buy it" (Review Trip Transcript, p. 105).

18. At the end of July and in early August, when the fawns were about half as big as their mothers, or as Waldo says, "half-way up to their mothers when they stand up," owners marked the reindeer by cutting their ears (Review Trip Notes, May 27–29, 1989).

19. The *qargi,* or men's house, was an important place in each village. This is where the men worked on their equipment, built boats, repaired bows, or prepared harpoons. The qargi was also the primary social setting for ceremonies and feasting. Although in the winter a permanent structure served as the qargi, during the summer, the qargi might consist of the lee side of a large *umiaq* laid on its side to serve as a windbreak. The summer arrangement served as a gathering place for men and was a comfortable spot to work on equipment (Spencer [1959] 1969:182–192).

20. Leona Okakok: *Kauk* is the edible inner part of the walrus skin. *Ugruk* is the bearded seal (see MacLean forthcoming).

21. When Waldo says "canoe," he means umiaq. Umiaq and qayaq are the two primary watercraft used by the Iñupiat. They are both framed with wood and covered with animal skin. An umiaq is a large, open boat used to transport many people and their equipment. A qayaq is a small, narrow, one-man boat with a covered deck. It is highly maneuverable but unstable (Adney and Chapelle 1964:174–211; Burch 1975b:4–5).

Leona Okakok: *Qayaq* is the correct Iñupiaq spelling for what is commonly referred to by non-Iñupiaq speakers as *kayak* (MacLean forthcoming).

22. Leona Okakok: When Iñupiaq speakers use the words "let me," they usually mean "caused me to" or "told me to" rather than "allowed me to." This is because the Iñupiaq postbase *-pkaq-,* while generally translated as "let," encompasses both "allow" and "cause" (MacLean forthcoming; see also chapter 15).

23. In coastal areas of the North Slope, fresh water is obtained in summer from lakes; in winter, lake ice is cut and hauled to the village. Some villages have wells. The well at Icy Cape was quite old. Captain Frederick Beechey, in an early reference to the well, describes Lieutenant Belcher getting water there on his voyage of 1825–28: "He found about twenty natives on the point living in tents, who received him very civilly, and assisted him to fill his water casks from a small well they had dug in the sand for their own use" (1831:275, Vol. II).

Pack ice is also a source of water. During the summer, the salt naturally percolates out, leaving a transparent blue ice called *piqaluyak*. Hunters chop this ice into blocks and melt it to produce potable water (Leona Okakok, personal communication; Nelson 1981:5).

24. Leona Okakok: Scolding in this context probably would have been more of a warning or an explanation of the consequences of bad behavior than a punishment for something he had done. The Iñupiaq word *ayuqiqsuq* means "to give her/him/it moral instruction" and falls between "teaching" and "scolding" (see MacLean forthcoming).

25. Waldo's expression "when the weather gets long" means when the amount of daylight increases in the spring.

26. Arthur Fields, Tom Berryman's grandson, lives in Kotzebue and recalls that his grandfather sent out buyers with cash to purchase furs for his store, the Kotzebue Fur and Trading Company. Arthur says that Berryman was an Englishman who came north over the Chilkoot Trail, then traveled down the Yukon River, up the Koyukuk River, over to the Kobuk River, and down to the coast at Kotzebue. He died in 1943 after having spent forty-seven years in the North (Fields, personal communication, August 23, 1989). Berryman supported the Friends Church in Kotzebue and in Kivalina (Roberts 1978:325–326; see also Marston 1969:146–148 and Alaska Geographic Society 1981: 70–71).

27. Arctic fox (*Alopex lagopus*) has both a blue and a white color phase, although, as Waldo indicates in his narrative, white is much more common. Arctic fox are found in treeless coastal areas and on the sea

ice. The red fox (*Vulpes vulpes*) can also be black, brown, silver, or a cross between two colors. A distinguishing characteristic of the red fox is its white-tipped tail. The red fox is found in most of Alaska (Stephenson and Jenning 1978).

28. After the trading ships came in summer, and before people headed up the river to hunt and fish, families would come together to make donuts from flour and water cooked in seal oil (Review Trip Transcript, pp. 82–85).

29. Waldo noted that the coffee and tea came in 24-pound wooden boxes with tightly braided straw around them (Review Trip Transcript, pp. 80–81).

Notes to Chapter 2

1. The *Bear* is probably the most famous of the revenue cutters. Built in Dundee, Scotland, in 1874, she became a revenue cutter in 1885. The *Bear* patrolled Bering Strait and the Arctic coast until 1926, when she made her last trip to the Arctic, having put in forty years of Arctic service (see Hunter 1986; Rapaport 1962; Bixby 1965; Alaska Sportsman 1963). I have not yet confirmed that the *Bear* stopped at Icy Cape during 1912–1914.

2. The Siberian Eskimos would have spoken Siberian Yupik, a language unintelligible to Iñupiaq speakers unless, of course, they were bilingual; many people were.

3. King Island is located ninety miles northwest of Nome in the Bering Sea. It is two and a half miles long, a mile and a half wide, and is seven hundred to twelve hundred feet in elevation. Sheer cliffs surround the island, and there are only three places where boats can land (Renner in collaboration with Ray 1979:67). Although no one now lives permanently on the island, in 1923 Father LaFortune estimated the population to be two hundred. The islanders depended on

walrus, seal, polar bear, whales, fish, shrimp, and crab. In the summer, they caught seabirds and gathered the eggs (1979:72). The King Islanders were skilled hunters on the sea ice, one of the most dangerous subsistence environments. For more information see Renner in collaboration with Ray 1979; Senungetuk and Tiulana 1987; Kaplan 1988.

4. The development of schools in the Arctic is reported in Vol. 1 of the Reports of the Commission of Education: "In 1890, through the courtesy of the Secretary of the Treasury, permission was granted to Doctor Jackson to accompany the U.S.S. *Bear* on its annual cruise in Bering Sea and the Arctic Ocean and thus extend the school system into Arctic Alaska." As a result of that trip, schools were built at Cape Prince of Wales, Point Hope, and Point Barrow (1908:374–375). Initially, the mission schools were supported by small federal appropriations. By 1895 the Bureau of Education took over full responsibility for running these schools (Lavifischeff 1935:110,160), although teachers were still responsible for religious instruction, medical care, and schooling. Teachers signed contracts for a certain number of years, and when their contracts had expired, they might leave or be reassigned. Many teachers had a difficult time adjusting to life at a remote Alaskan site.

School records housed at the village corporation offices in Point Lay indicate that the Icy Cape school lands were reserved under Executive Order, signed by President Roosevelt on May 4, 1907 (Neakok et al. 1985:23). According to Neakok et al. (1985:10), Ejnar Mikkelsen stated that Mr. F. F. Fellows, a school teacher, was at Icy Cape in August 1906. He was living in a tent waiting for a supply ship. By November 1907, Fellows had a government school house. The Reports of the Commission of Education confirm that a school was built at Icy Cape in the 1906–07 fiscal years and that F. F. Fellows was teacher in 1907. As the following summary indicates, the school operated through the 1912–13 school year.

Year	Teacher	Average Daily Attendance
1906–07	F.F. Fellows	
1907–08	F.F. Fellows	8
1908–09	C.H. Adams	28
1909–10	C.H. Adams	15
1910–11	James V. Geary (DO) Eva W. Geary (DO) Hannah C. Ahnevuk	15
1911–12	James V. Geary Eva W. Geary Hannah C. Ahnevuk	16
1912–13	James V. Geary Eva W. Geary Hannah C. Ahnevuk	23
1913–14	no Icy Cape school listing The Van Valins, teachers from Wainwright, spent part of the spring at Icy Cape.	
1914–15	no Icy Cape school listing	
1915–16	no Icy Cape school listing	
1916–17	no Icy Cape school listing E.M. Forrest, teacher from Wainwright, visited Icy Cape twice.	
1917–18	no Icy Cape school listing	

(summarized from Reports of the Commission of Education for the years noted).

5. The Lomen family owned one of the largest reindeer herds in Alaska. The family had other interests, including a transport company, a store, a lightering service, and a photography shop. Gudbrand J. Lomen and his son, Carl J. Lomen, arrived in Alaska in the summer of 1900. Over the years, the Lomens established a firm place in Alaskan business history (see Lomen 1954; Lomen Collection and tape recordings H86-280 a & b and H87-6 a & b; Stern et al. 1980:38–43).

6. In 1866 Daniel Libby and Otto Von Bendeleben found gold prospects on the headwaters of the Fish River on the Seward Peninsula. In the late 1890s, Libby returned and successfully prospected in this area. In October 1898, the great Nome gold fields were discovered at the mouth of the Snake River. The gold extracted that fall "...was the first gold produced in the Cape Nome mining district," and would lead to the Nome gold rush of 1899–1900 (Cole 1983:43). While the initial rush quickly passed, the Nome economy was able to maintain a modest mining industry in the first half of the twentieth century. Cole notes, "After the richest pockets of gold were exhausted, only large scale mining operations were economical, and a miner without the capital to hire employees or purchase machinery usually ended up working for someone who did" (1983:240).

Alfred Hulse Brooks, the famous Alaskan geologist, traveled to Nome in 1899 to witness firsthand the gold rush conditions. See Brooks [1953] 1973:380–398.

7. Robert Mayokok became a well-known Alaskan artist, specializing in ink drawings of Native life (Ray 1980:29–30).

8. Leona Okakok: In Iñupiaq, people of a certain settlement are called by the name of the settlement plus the postbase -miut, which means "inhabitants of." For example, Utuqqaġmiut means "inhabitants of the Utuqqaq River region." Thus, when an Iñupiaq speaker talks in English about reaching a settlement, he generally talks about reaching people, rather than the place (personal knowledge).

9. This is probably the place identified by Dorothy Jean Ray as "Mizek," 'low swampy place', a small village in the Teller area (Ray 1983:203, 249).

10. They were fishing for salmon, although they also caught arctic char and other fish in the net (Review Trip Transcript, pp. 2–7).

11. T. L. Brevig was a Lutheran missionary who established a mission and school at Teller Mission (see Lund 1974:18–41; Johnshoy 1944).

12. The mission boarding schools served many needs. They provided a home for children whose parents had died or needed help for a few years, and for children who needed medical care. Also, there were children whose parents, like Waldo's, wanted them to receive some schooling while they were living near a school (see also Newman 1978; Cruikshank 1986).

There were only a few boarding schools, but many of today's elders, particularly those from the Nome, Holy Cross, Fort Yukon, and Nenana areas, attended these schools and recall vividly their experiences. They learned reading, writing and practical domestic skills, such as gardening and sewing, and they received religious instruction. Life in the missions was considerably different from being out with families, learning the skills of herding, hunting, fishing, and trapping.

13. Emma Willoya became a well-known seamstress and organizer of the Nome Skin Sewers Cooperative Association in Nome. KICY Radio and Kegoayah Kozga Library have recordings made with Emma. See also Lund 1974:5–9.

14. Leona Okakok: A person who always "listened around" was very perceptive, taking in things which others heard but disregarded (personal knowledge).

15. The messenger feast served a valuable social function in linking people together in a peaceful context for trading. The ceremony was organized around invitations issued by the inhabitants of a host village to their partners in a distant village. Messengers from the host village were sent to issue the invitations. The messengers then listened carefully to the requests of the invited guests and reported back to their home village. Partners tried to fulfill each other's requests at the messenger feast (see Burch and Correll 1971:29–30; Spencer [1959] 1969: 210–228; Wooley and Okakok, n.d.).

16. On the Arctic Slope, *kivgiq-* means "to have a messenger feast" (MacLean forthcoming).

In the Kotzebue Sound area it is called *aqpatat,* after the runners in the Messenger Feast (Burch, personal communication).

17. Leona Okakok: As Vincent Nageak said at the 1978 Elders' Conference (Kisautaq 1981:575), messenger feast customs are different in each area. The terms also differ. In Teller, where Waldo witnessed the dance held in honor of the messengers, the whole feast was called Aqpataq. My understanding from the Arctic Slope is that *aqpatat* were the runners, from both the host and guest villages, who raced into the host village to claim ownership of the qargi. A *kivgaq* was a messenger sent from the host village to announce the messenger feast.

18. Motion dances are the old Iñupiat dances called *aniuraaq,* which means "to go out gradually, dancing," and *kalukaq,* which means "box dance." Part of aniuraaq was performed in connection with the messenger feast (Review Trip Transcript, pp. 100–104).

Leona Okakok: A motion dance is a choreographed dance which is done in only one way (personal knowledge).

19. Waldo is referring to a fishing technique called jigging. A small hole is cut in the ice and a fishing line with a lure on the end is lowered into the water. The lure is made of ivory or bone with an inset metal hook. Before metal was available, the hooks may have been made of ivory, slate, or copper (see Stefansson 1914:84, 348–349). The person fishing moves the line up and down and waits for the fish to bite the hook. John Murdoch described this type of fishing at Barrow in 1881–1883. "The tackle for this fishing consists of a short line of whalebone, provided with a little 'squid' or artificial bait of ivory, and fastened to a wooden rod about eighteen inches or two feet long. The lure which is apparently meant to represent a small shrimp, is kept moving, and the fish bite at it" (1892:279). Edward Nelson provides a detailed accounting of fishhooks and fishing through the ice based on his observations in the Bering Strait area between 1877 and 1881 (1900:175–183).

20. *Taluyak* is a type of fish weir or trap used during heavy fish runs. The weir is made with rocks and willows, and it has three openings where the fish can enter. The trap part is called *puukataq* and resembles a big bag, like a duffle bag (Review Trip Transcript, pp. 10, 49–50).

21. There are rules for dividing up certain types of game (see Spencer [1959] 1969:163–164; Burch 1988c:101–103), but for this type of fishing, the fish were shared equally among those who helped fish. Waldo built the willow-pole enclosure they used to hold the fish. It was about ten feet wide and four feet high. The fish were frozen overnight and then stored in the enclosure for winter use (Review Trip Transcript, pp. 10–14).

22. Although salting fish is a common means of preservation for some people, it was not common for the Iñupiat. In fact, Stefansson reports that the Eskimos he met who had had little contact with Whites had a strong aversion to the taste of salted fish and meat ([1913] 1971:75). Fish and meat were usually split, air dried, and stored in seal oil.

23. Squirrels were usually snared for their fur in April. When caught in the summer, they were probably used for food (Dorothy Jean Ray, personal communication).

24. Pokes are made from an entire sealskin or walrus skin which has been removed intact by means of a special butchering process. The value of the seal poke is that it can hold liquids and is transportable (Nelson 1900:73–74). Pokes are used to store seal oil, meat, vegetable greens, and other foods. Ivory plugs keep the contents from leaking out of the pokes.

25. The salmonberries probably were *Rubus chamacmorus,* also known as cloudberries, and the blackberries probably were *Empetrum nigrum,* also known as crowberries (Richard Nelson, personal communication).

26. Leona Okakok: Waterproof boots are made by using a special stitch on regular sealskin boots while the skin is soft enough to be

shaped around the stitch. The boots are not completely waterproof, although someone wearing them can go through water and then shake off the excess, keeping his or her feet dry (personal knowledge).

For added waterproofing, seal blubber is rubbed on the stitches and other parts of the boot. When double stitches are used, seal oil is put between the seams (Mattie Bodfish, personal communication).

27. Leona Okakok: "Always sometimes" is a common, though hard to explain, expression which stems from the direct translation of the Iñupiaq postbase -suu-. For instance, anisuuruq can mean "He goes out once in a while" or "He goes out all the time" or anything between. If someone says only the word "always," he or she denies the possibility that at some point the person may not do something. On the other hand, if someone says only the word "sometimes," he or she ignores the tendency of the person to do that certain action (personal knowledge).

Notes to Chapter 3

1. Camps and old house sites are located all around Wainwright Inlet (see, for instance, the North Slope Borough's Traditional Land Use Inventory for Wainwright Area, revised 1987). The exact position of Ulġuniq or Wainwright may have been determined by the unloading of the school in 1904. Fred Milan notes that "According to Mr. Pete Hahn, who was the school teacher at Wainwright in 1955, the selection of the site for the schoolhouse and the village was dictated by ice conditions and convenience. The vessel's captain unloaded at a favorable looking site" (1964:21).

2. The boats were on top of the ice, which was being moved by the current and wind. This is one of the most dangerous situations for hunters, because when they are separated from shore they are at the mercy of the currents, which can push the ice together, crushing the hunters' boats (James Nageak, personal communication; see also Burch 1975b:7–8; Nelson 1969:110–115).

3. For a detailed discussion of Iñupiat adaptation to sea ice, see Nelson 1981:1–15.

4. Leads are stretches of open water which form in the sea ice. They are most common in areas where a point of land sticks out and where the current is swift. They continually change as the wind, tide, and currents move the ice around. Leads are where hunters go to get whales, seals, and waterfowl.

5. The safest ice is the grounded shore ice. It is less likely to break loose and be moved by wind and current, and it is closest to the safety of land. The hunters described in this episode couldn't get to the grounded shore ice because leads separated them from it. They were caught between the shore ice and the pack ice on the unstable floe ice. When storms came up and moved the unstable ice, they were forced to go even further off shore to the pack ice.

6. Most adults living on the North Slope grew up hearing stories about relatives or older people who had gotten caught on the ice amid changing conditions and had drifted out to sea. Some never returned. This particular incident was extraordinary because of the distance and time the drifters were gone. (For another telling of this incident by Waldo see Nelson 1981:15; see also Stefansson [1913] 1971:107–109).

7. Leona Okakok: *Nivaat* is the plural form of *nivaaq*, which means "that which was dug" (see MacLean forthcoming).

8. The area between Avvaq Inlet and Icy Cape was favored by herders because the natural features of the land and ocean made it easy to keep the reindeer under control.

9. The bird dart consisted of a shaft with several prongs sticking out from the side (see Murdoch 1892:211).

10. Leona Okakok: *Unaaq* is a pole with an ice pick on one end and a hook on the other. Waldo's use of "follow" here is from *tuvraq-*, which

means "to follow; to track; to imitate; to follow a pattern" (see MacLean forthcoming). It often means "to accompany someone knowledgeable."

11. The logs served as markers to let people know the trap site was a dangerous place.

12. There was a period in the fur trade during which trappers made partnerships with companies or, as in this case, individual ships. A particular trapper would arrange a year ahead for the ship or company to bring certain supplies to him. In exchange, the trapper would trade his fox skins with that "partner" (see Libbey and Schneider 1987:335–358).

13. Leona Okakok: The name Mayaroak (Mayagruaq) comes from the name Mayak plus the postbase -gruaq, which means "something big, huge, unrefined, solid." When -gruaq, is added to a name, one visualizes a person who is either big or tough (personal knowledge; MacLean forthcoming).

14. Waldo described Shaglook as *umialignaq*, which James Nageak translates as "not wanting anything." The old man was a highly successful fox trapper and was effective in buying foxes and selling trade goods. His ability to provide for others contributed to his status and position in the community (see chapter 1, note 17; Review Trip Transcript, p. 104; Ostermann and Holtved 1952:32–42).

15. The Iñupiat whalers distinguish between different types of whales. Waldo said that *iŋutuq*, the young female whales or "small" whales, are the first to travel along the coast in the spring, and if the whalers are late in setting out they can miss them. When he was whaling, he liked to get these and the *qairalliuranik*, the two year olds (Review Trip Transcript, pp. 18–20).

Stefansson was also told that the "inutok" were preferred to the larger whales because the meat was more tender and they were easier to handle (1914:380). Rosita Worl's research also confirms the Iñupiat preference for the "ingutok," although she claims that there are three runs of whales and that these are most likely in the second run (Worl 1980:308).

New research suggests that the iŋutuq is a bowhead whale at a certain stage of development. There is no proof that all are females, although scientists recognize that Eskimos use the term to refer to a short, fat female (Braham, Durham, Jarrell, and Leatherwood 1980:71–72). At this time there is no scientific evidence that sex and age determine when certain whales migrate north, although some scientists believe that since this view is widely held by Eskimos, it will someday prove to be correct (Braham, Fraker, and Kragman 1980:42–43).

16. Before the commercial whalers brought block and tackle, the Eskimos preferred small whales, which were easier to butcher. They were cut up in the water, and then small pieces were pulled up onto the ice. (Review Trip Transcript, pp. 20–21). Waldo talked about some of the rules for dividing shares of the whale (Review Trip Transcript, pp. 24–26), but there are more complete descriptions in the literature (see VanStone 1962:48–53; Worl 1980:316–320).

17. Leona Okakok: This word stems from *aviu-,* which means "to utter a long, loud cry (usually high pitched)," plus *-qtaq-,* which means "repeated action"; therefore, *aviuqtaqtuaq* means "some things which make continual noise" (personal knowledge; MacLean forthcoming).

18. Leona Okakok: Giving away your first kill is very important. It initiates a special relationship between the hunter and the person he gives the food to. The young hunter will continue to give food to the elder and in turn may receive gifts and other forms of support from the elder, cementing their bond. One of the most important gifts the elder provides is to appeal for the hunter's success. The Iñupiaq term is *Ququq,* as in *Ququġniaqtuna,* which means, "I will call upon everything I can for (your) success."

19. Leona Okakok: *Kamatchai-,* a transitive verb which means "to impress, to fill with pride," is often translated by Iñupiaq speakers as "proud." The object of the verb is the speaker rather than the person the speaker is talking about. Thus, Waldo's use of the word "proud" really means that he was filled with pride from having received something from the woman (personal knowledge).

William Schneider: When Waldo was asked to elaborate on how he felt and his meaning of "proud," he said "…because I was so thankful when she called me a good boy—that is what proud is." He went on to say, "When someone great likes you, you have proud feelings, like sometimes in your mind you feel it. Persons feel it when they are included in their praise, at a gathering. That is what I had at that time" (Review Trip Transcript, p. 92).

20. Knud Rasmussen, a Greenlander educated in Denmark, was part Iñuit, part White, and spoke Iñuit fluently. Rasmussen financed the Thule Expeditions based on the profits from an Arctic trading post at Thule, Greenland. The Fifth Thule Expedition focused on the cultural adaptation of Iñuit groups in northern Canada, Greenland, and western Alaska. Rasmussen and two Iñuit companions, Mitiq (Miteq, also known as Qavigârssuaq or Qaavaigarssuaq) and Agnagolook (Anarulunguaq, also spelled Arnarulúnguaq or Arnarulunguaq) traveled from the west coast of Hudson Bay all the way to Alaska, entering the territory in May 1924 (Collins 1984:10; Rasmussen 1927; Ostermann and Holtved 1952; Gilberg 1984:169–171; Burch 1988d:151–170; Mathiassen 1945:12).

21. The Nalukataq, or whaling festival, is held a short while after the whaling season is finished. Sponsored by the successful whaling captains and their crews, it celebrates the success of the season and includes dancing, blanket toss, and feasting. The highlight of the celebration is the distribution of maktak, whale meat, and other food. Special shares of the whale are reserved for elders (Spencer [1959] 1969:350–352).

22. Rasmussen reached Nome on August 31, 1924, after stops in Point Lay, Point Hope, Kotzebue, and Noorvik. He made a brief stop in East Cape, Siberia, but was asked to leave because he didn't have official permission to enter the country (Rasmussen 1927:339, 359).

Notes to Chapter 4

1. When the winds were not favorable for sailing, or when the river

was too narrow for sailing, the umiaq was pulled by dogs in harness. Lines ran from the front of the boat to the dogs, who ran along the bank or in the shallow water. In the western arctic this was an important form of transport (Burch 1975b:4–6).

2. Before the missionaries came to the North Slope, there were no formal ceremonies marking the marriage of a couple. The union of a man and a woman was consummated in the act of sexual intercourse, which established a special social relationship recognized by other community members and by their offspring. Burch and Correll note that "The Eskimos had two basic types of marriage, residential and non residential. Sexual intercourse was all that was needed to establish a union in either case, but in the former type the spouses lived together, whereas in the latter they did not..." (1971:26–27). When the missionaries arrived, they introduced the Christian marriage ceremony and worked to eliminate sexual intercourse outside of the Christian marriage (see Burch 1975a:47–49).

3. Mattie Bodfish is one of the Wainwright dancers. She travels extensively to perform and also teaches dancing to the young people in Wainwright. She has danced in such places as Anchorage, Fairbanks, Los Angeles, Copenhagen, Frobisher Bay, and in Greenland.

4. The Eskimos of the central Canadian Arctic built dome-shaped snow houses from blocks of wind-packed snow. As Burch notes, "The snow house dwellers—the Copper, Netsilik, Iglulik, Caribou and Quebec Eskimos—occupied an immense geographic area, but comprised less than eight per cent of the total Eskimo population" (1988a:45). These were their permanent winter dwellings.

The kind of snow house that Waldo is describing is called *ani-guyyaq,* a temporary structure with a tent inside, with a *talu,* a fur skin door (Review Trip Transcript, pp. 94–97). Nelson did not actually see this type of structure when he was in Wainwright during 1964–1965, but he does mention a type of snow house called "anegiuchak" which was square with a gabled roof of snow blocks (1969:177). Nelson references Brower's description, which is worth quoting:

> The shelter our Eskimos threw up for the duration of the
> hunt was rectangular, the longer dimension providing

comfortable living space for a party the size of ours. The door was in the middle, with sleeping quarters at either end separated by a small open space where the stone oil lamp was kept. It didn't take long to build.

After choosing a snowdrift deep enough to dig out for the body of the house, they cut big blocks of snow and ranged them around the hole, placing one row above another so as gradually to slant towards the center of the house. When the walls were pretty well up, they cut top blocks so as to meet, forming a sort of gable roof. (1942:21)

5. The Meade River is called Kuulugruaq in Iñupiaq. Niġisaqtuġvik is a historic site a short distance downriver from the present site of Atqasuk (Schneider, Pedersen, and Libbey 1980:113–114).

6. Leona Okakok: *Nuna* means "ground; sod; land; country." *Ivruq* is a block of sod (MacLean forthcoming).

7. Leona Okakok: *Niññuq* is the soft snow packed on top of sod to provide extra insulation for the shelter.

8. The stick was used to lift the tail of the fawn to see if it was male or female (Review Trip Transcript, pp. 31–33).

9. Reindeer herding dogs worked much like cattle herding dogs. It appears that the herding dogs were introduced to Alaska by the Lapp or Saami herders who came to teach Eskimos to herd reindeer. Ben Mozee, who was the district superintendent of Alaska Reindeer, Medical and School Services for the years 1920–1928, and then was general reindeer superintendent of Alaska for 1928–1933, has compiled an archival collection of information regarding reindeer herding in Alaska. In the "Reindeer Report, 1926" he (presumed) writes, "The Lapps brought with them five pairs of trained dogs, which were used in the work at the stations and from there have descended the small 'Lapp dogs' seen at various herds along the coast" (Ben Mozee Collection, Box 16, folder 10, p. 2).

The Iñupiaq word for a reindeer dog is *qimmiuraq,* which literally means "little dog."

10. The first Saami herders were brought to Alaska in 1894 by William Kjellmann under instruction from Sheldon Jackson. A second group arrived in 1898 (Stern et al. 1980:25–27).

11. Partners played an important part in Eskimo society and some people still have partners today. Partners make requests of each other and try to fulfill each other's needs. When there were actual boundaries between regional societies, the partnerships meant that you had someone to protect you or watch out for your interests when you traveled into your partner's area (Burch 1970:66). Partners formally exchanged goods at the messenger feasts and the trade fairs. When partners came from different parts of the North Slope, they could call upon each other for protection or for food and equipment unique to an area. For example, an inland man might trade caribou hides and sinew to a coastal man for seal oil and bearded seal skin. Spencer notes that "The ultimate function of the partnership was to extend the process of cooperation beyond the kinship grouping and thus to lend additional stability to the society as a whole" (Spencer [1959] 1969: 171). Burch 1970 also discusses Eskimo trading partnerships.

12. Waldo described Walluk's sinker as a round, grooved rock with a line set in the groove. When Walluk threw it into the water in an open lead, he would watch to see which way the line went. If it drifted away from where he was standing, he knew it was dangerous—the ice might break off and drift out. If the line drifted toward him, he knew the current was pushing the ice toward shore and there was less danger. When there was no open lead, he would make a hole in the ice and lower his sinker into the water to check the current (Review Trip Transcript, pp. 36–38). Burch reports that hunters sometimes drop empty rifle cartridges, open end up, into the water and then watch which way the bubbles of air go to determine the direction of the current (personal communication).

13. Hunting seals at the breathing hole is one of the most sophisticated and highly developed of Iñupiaq hunting skills; it demands patience, timing, and knowledge of the ice and seals.

The literature reflects many variations in technique, level of dependence on this type of seal hunting, and changes brought about by the availability of rifles. The basic principle in all cases is that seals must surface to breath and that patient hunters have a chance to intercept and kill them at that time.

Nelson provides a detailed description (1969:233–240; 1981:58–59) of the breathing hole hunting technique which was practiced on the North Slope, and he also notes Boas's earlier description ([1888] 1964:67–74) from the Central Canadian Arctic, where, in certain areas, there was a high level of dependency on seals and this particular way of hunting. See also Stefansson [1913] 1971:172–173.

Burch notes that "In the Central Arctic, where the sea ice is immobile for several consecutive months each winter, and where there are few alternative resources at that time of year, the Copper Eskimos raised breathing-hole hunting to a high art. First, they moved entire villages on to the ice, several kilometers from shore. When conditions were right, several hunters from each one went out together. The objective was to have one hunter at each of the holes in a particular locality. If a seal was frightened away from one hole before he took a breath, he would be forced to come up at another one nearby or suffocate. If every hole was guarded by a hunter, no matter where the seal emerged it was likely to be caught" (1988a:56–57; see also Damas 1969:51–52).

Before rifles were available, hunters depended on harpooning the seal as it emerged. When the seal came up, the hunter had to judge the right moment and immediately thrust his harpoon into the seal's head, hoping that it would be lodged securely (Burch 1988a:55–57). Murdoch described seal hunting at the breathing hole for the Barrow area, noting that in the 1880s rifles were used to kill the seals, and then harpoons were used to secure and retrieve them (1892:268–269).

14. Leona Okakok: A reindeer that had been trained to pull a sled was called *qimukti*.

15. Tuttuaġvik is the present site of the DEW Line Station but it is also a place where people used to hunt caribou. The caribou were driven into the river, and men in qayat went after them with lances. When they got close enough they would puncture a caribou's dia-

phragm with a quick blow. When they had intercepted as many animals as they could, they hauled them to shore and butchered them (Review Trip Transcript, pp. 40–43).

16. *Umiŋmak* means "musk ox." Waldo noted that the Wainwright people told him that musk oxen used to be at this site, but that now all signs of them are gone (Review Trip Transcript, pp. 40, 43).

Notes to Chapter 5

1. Carrie Eleyuk Kignak, Ernest's wife, was one of the adopted daughters of Michael Keogak.

2. The entrance to an old-fashioned sod house consisted of a hallway that descended from the outside, then went up to the main part of the house. People entered the house from the hallway through a *katak,* a hole in the floor. The hallway trapped the cold and wind and also served as a storage area (see Kisautaq 1981:127).

3. It was common for men to combine reindeer herding and trapping for their livelihood. The two activities did not conflict; herders were able to check their traps in the natural course of watching the reindeer. Burch has noted (1975a:31) that both trapping and reindeer herding kept men out in the country at a time when schools, stores, and churches made living in villages quite attractive. Herders and trappers were thus subject to conflicting pressures: to be out herding and trapping on the one hand, and on the other, to have their families in the village where the children could attend school and family members could attend church services.

4. H. Liebes and Company was a San Francisco-based fur buying business. They had branch stores along the Arctic Coast. The best known of these were the Cape Smythe Whaling and Trading Company run by Charles Brower, the store at Wainwright run by Jim Allen, and the Icy Cape store managed by Upicksoun.

5. Turning the reindeer loose actually meant consolidating individual

herds into company herds, with individual herders maintaining shares in the larger joint herd. Men were hired to watch the consolidated herd. This new style of herding meant that the reindeer were not closely watched or controlled by the owners. The deer were scattered for much of the year, and there was, as Waldo describes, less contact between herders and the deer, hence more opportunities for the reindeer to mix with caribou or be killed by wolves (see Stern et al. 1980: 48–52; Sonnenfeld 1959:82–86). Burch notes that herders were poorly paid during the Depression, and they had to get a permit from the teacher to kill a deer. Herding had become a lot of work with few benefits (personal communication).

6. Waldo means that there were getting to be fewer animals.

7. Reindeer herds were kept on the Arctic Slope until the 1950s, when the last of the herds was finally lost (see Sonnenfeld 1959:78; Arundale and Schneider 1987:68). When the caribou increased in numbers, it became more and more difficult to keep the reindeer from mixing with the caribou and scattering. There are no longer reindeer herds on the North Slope, but there are still some herds on the Seward Peninsula in northwestern Alaska.

8. Jens Forshaug, a unit manager for the Bureau of Indian Affairs, described the three jobs this way. The chief herder was out in the field in change of the herd. The local herd assistant supervised one or more herds associated with a particular village. He would keep the herders supplied. The unit manager was responsibile for all herds in the villages that made up his unit. See also note 13 below.

9. The Native products consisted of finished clothing as well as hides, sinew, and meat.

10. The Native Store was formed in 1916. In 1924 the Wainwright Reindeer and Trading Company was formed by individual herders in Wainwright. The company merged the reindeer operations and the Native Store. The Bureau of Education maintained some control over the stores and the herds until 1930, when the territorial governor's

office assumed responsibility for the reindeer herds. The Bureau of Education continued to have authority over the stores. For a detailed chronology of the reindeer herds in Wainwright before 1925, see "Narrative Re: Alaska Reindeer Herds for Calendar Year 1942, with Supplementary Data" in Alaska Reindeer Herds, Small Collections, Archives, Alaska and Polar Regions Department, Elmer E. Rasmuson Library, University of Alaska Fairbanks, pp. 104–111.

11. Ira Rank's death was reported in the January 1941 issue of *Alaska Sportsman*. He was seventy-six when he died and was described as a "colorful sourdough trader of Nome." He was also remembered for trading on the Siberian coast before the Russian Revolution (pp. 21–22). No references to Pete Brand have been found in the literature.

12. There were three U.S. Department of the Interior vessels called *North Star*. The first was operated from 1932 to 1949, first by the Bureau of Education, and later by the Alaska Native Services. The second was operated between 1949 and 1961, first by the Alaska Native Services, and later by the Bureau of Indian Affairs. The last, *North Star III*, was operated by the Bureau of Indian Affairs from 1962 to 1984. The mission of the *North Star* ships was "to provide life-sustaining resupply of essential goods and services at affordable cost and to enhance the development of alternative local economies" (personal communication, Gerald Taylor, Bureau of Indian Affairs, Seattle). A personal account about serving aboard the *Boxer* and the three *North Star* vessels is preserved in a recording (#H88-62) of Captain Cecil Cole, "Captain Mo," at the Archives, Alaska and Polar Regions Department, Elmer E. Rasmuson Library, University of Alaska Fairbanks. See also Taylor, Hageman, and Allen 1984.

13. Jens Forshaug retired from the Bureau of Indian Affairs in 1973 and lives at Lake Minchumina and in Fairbanks, Alaska. For an account of his activities and travels as unit manager, see recording H 89-2a&b at the Archives, Alaska and Polar Regions Department, Elmer E. Rasmuson Library, University of Alaska Fairbanks.

14. By "rotten," Waldo means that the ice had started to melt, creat-

ing holes or places where there was open water.

Leona Okakok: The Iñupiaq name for the rotten, unsafe ice is *aunniq* (MacLean forthcoming).

15. The barrier island and lagoon systems to the west and south of Wainwright are prime nesting areas for many types of birds, including eider ducks, King Eiders, terns, and wrens. Waldo said that when the eggs are taken (in June), some birds will lay a second time (Review Trip Transcript, pp. 57, 58, 60).

Notes to Chapter 6

1. The 1940 census was the sixteenth census. For detailed information, see Truesdele 1943.

2. At Qagluġruaq the water doesn't freeze to the bottom of the river, and the fish congregate in the deep places. *Qaglu* means "deep water place in the river."

3. Leona Okakok: In the North Slope dialect of Iñupiaq, *aanaakłiq* is broad whitefish, *sulukpaugaq* is grayling, *qaaktaq* is Bering cisco whitefish, and *pikuktuuq* is humpback whitefish (MacLean forthcoming). The terms are different in the Kotzebue Sound area.

4. Leona Okakok: *Arraa!* is an exclamation of amazement.

Notes to Chapter 7

1. Taboos regulated the behavior of Iñupiat families and communities, and observance of the taboos helped insure success in the food quest. When game supplies were low or people were sick, they tried to determine if a taboo had been violated (see Burch 1988a:96–97; Ostermann and Holtved 1952:117–120; see also chapter 1, note 7).

Notes to Chapter 8

1. Waldo refers to him as Jack here, but I assume he is referring to Aarnout Castel, who, like Jim Allen, spent his life in the North (*Anchorage Times,* December 28, 1968, p. 2; see also chapter 10, note 11).

2. Ben Eielson was one of the most famous pilots in Alaskan history. At the time of this story, 1926–1927, Eielson was attempting to reach Spitzbergen by flying over the North Pole. For a gripping account of the preparations and flight, see Potter [1945] 1983:38–50.

3. The *Baychimo,* a Hudson's Bay Company ship, was frozen in during the fall of 1931 (see Allen 1978:203–209).

4. Stefansson (1914:8–9) did not think that coal would be a satisfactory answer to the people's fuel needs. He was correct, in that most people on the North Slope now burn oil or natural gas, but for the first half of the twentieth century coal was important. It was mined from exposed seams on the banks of the Kuuk River, and families in the Barrow, Wainwright, and Icy Cape areas used many other sources of coal when out camping. Historic settlement after the introduction of iron stoves was influenced by the location of fuel, including driftwood, dry willows, and coal.

5. Sea ice is subject to the forces of wind, tide, and current. In the winter months the ice builds up from shore and becomes grounded on the ocean bottom, forming shore-fast ice. Then new ice forms between the shore-fast ice and the pack ice. The shore-fast ice and the pack ice are relatively stable compared to the new ice, where leads and open water are most common (see Nelson 1981:10–14; La Belle et al. 1983:143).

6. Leona Okakok: The boat sled is called *umiiraun,* and the ridge formed by the pressure of moving ice is called *ivuniq* (MacLean forthcoming).

7. Leona Okakok: Sometimes when the ice becomes dangerous, the hunting parties have to retreat to safe, shore-fast ice. This retreat is called *naŋiaqtuu-* (MacLean forthcoming).

8. Point Hope is a good place to hunt whales because the point sticks far out into the ocean, close to where open water or leads develop in the ice (see Burch 1981:23–25).

9. In 1913, Fay Delzene came in first in the Sixth All Alaska Sweepstakes from Nome to Candle and back, a distance of 408 miles (see Darling n.d.).

10. The USS *Boxer* was a Department of the Interior vessel. It was acquired by the Bureau of Education in 1920 to transport school supplies (Stern et al. 1980:46–47; see also chapter 5, note 12).

11. The Icy Cape store was owned by H. Liebes and Company and was managed by Upicksoun, brother of Jim Allen's wife (Neakok et al. 1985:37).

12. In this account it is unclear how many people were still living at Icy Cape, and why those there didn't play more of a part getting the supplies up to the store. According to Waldo (letter, August 29, 1989), some people had moved to Wainwright, Point Hope, Point Lay, and Barrow but there was, presumably, still a resident population.

Notes to Chapter 9

1. David stayed at Jim Allen's house for a while because Jim and his wife, Eleanor, wanted to adopt him. Waldo did not consent (Review Trip Transcript, p. 51).

2. The crew varied each year. Members not mentioned in the narrative include Waldo's uncle Charlie Ned, his brother Stephen, Paul Patkotak, old Kakmak, Frank Bester, Sheldon Segevan, and Harold Killbear (Review Trip Notes, May 27–29, 1989).

3. Waldo and Mattie's children are named after people who are important to them. Iñupiaq names are not gender specific. Boys and girls often have the same name.

4. Leona Okakok: In Iñupiat society, sometimes a child takes on a name on his own. This practice still goes on today.

William Schneider: William Shoudla gave the name Ekilalook to Marietta, Waldo and Mattie's daughter. Ekilalook, who was married to Takpak, was Shoudla's sister from Barrow. Nimrod, who is Waldo and Mattie's son, was named Kuksoo after Mattie's stepmother, Dorothy Nakaak (Review Trip Notes, May 27–29, 1989).

5. A snowshirt is a parka cover. Women make them from brightly colored calico. They also use white fabric to make snowshirts for hunters so that they won't be seen by the animals (Review Trip Transcript, p. 52).

Notes to Chapter 10

1. Richard Webb was the teacher at Wainwright (see Webb n.d.). We do not have any further information on Dr. Sinefelt.

2. Stanley Ross Morgan was a United States Army radio engineer. He was working for the Alaska Communication System at Point Barrow and was a second lieutenant in 1943. He retired from the Army in 1946 (Tewkesbury and Tewkesbury 1947:54).

3. Today, village health aides receive regular medical training and are qualified to serve as first responders for medical care in rural Alaska. During the time that Waldo describes, aides would work with doctors when they came to the village, or they would confer over the radio in emergencies. The village health aides' radio, and in some cases the schoolteachers' radio, was the only direct link with doctors and hospital care. The severity of many medical emergencies was lessened by the efforts of radio operators.

4. In 1946, Dr. E. S. ("Stu") Rabeau was appointed medical officer to the Alaska Native Service (BIA) hospital in Kotzebue. He held the position for eleven years and traveled to the villages and the hospitals at Nome, Barrow, and Tanana. Dr. Rabeau was well known for his shortwave radio "sched" in which he discussed medical problems. He died in 1984 (Fortuine 1984:95–96).

5. Waldo refers to cocaine, but it may have been codeine

6. The role of Eskimo doctors in curing people was important. In recent years the work of these experts has been documented. Iñupiat healers like Della Keats and Andrew Skin have shared their knowledge freely with interested researchers (see Kirchner 1982; Lucier, VanStone, and Keats 1971). The Eskimo doctors used their hands to manipulate organs, and they depended on their knowledge and skills to make people well. Shamans or aŋatkut, on the other hand, depended on supernatural powers, which they invoked to do both good and bad, to predict the future, and to influence the availability and movement of game. Eskimo doctors were welcomed into communities and actively sought out, whereas the shamans were often feared and were consulted only as a last resort.

7. Leona Okakok: *Saptaq* means "to feel, to palpate the body in order to determine what is wrong" (MacLean forthcoming).

8. Sig Wien became a commercial pilot in 1937 (Harkey 1974:290), and in that year flew along the Arctic Coast for the first time, on a trip to pick up a big game hunter in Wainwright. Sig made regular trips to Barrow starting in 1943, providing Barrow's first year-round transportation (Potter [1945] 1983:174–182). He is well known and respected by villagers along the coast from Nome to Barrow, and at Anaktuvuk Pass in the Brooks Range (Joling 1988:9).

9. Other mail carriers not mentioned were Ernest Kignak and Howard Leavitt. (See Ernest Kignak's life history in IHLC files, North Slope Borough, Barrow, Alaska).

10. John Cross came to Alaska in 1934 and flew for Cordova Air Service. He then flew for Wien Consolidated Airlines in Kotzebue and became owner-operator of Northern Cross, Inc., out of Deering

(Tewkesbury and Tewkesbury 1947:16; Atwood and DeArmond 1977:20).

11. According to Warren and Dorcus Neakok of Point Lay, Aarnout Castel (Castelaruk) and Ira Rank might be considered partners. Castel took over from Rank when he died. Both men dealt in raw fur and finished fur clothing. Castel is also remembered for having transported schoolchildren to school by boat, and he was a member of Stefansson's 1914 expedition (Neakok et al. 1985:29; Hunt 1986: 95,135). He is also mentioned as a visitor to Flaxman Island sometime after 1920:

> In the summer of 1921, ten-year-old Josephine Panningona Itta moved from Barrow to Flaxman Island...At first they lived in Leffingwell's house which, as indicated by the remains of the sod foundation, had two relatively large rooms. According to Josephine, her immediate family and her father's parents were the only ones living in the house at this time. Henry Chamberlain, Costello, and other non-Natives occasionally visited, staying with them at Leffingwell's (Libbey and Hall 1981:10).

Castel died in 1968 and is buried in Nome, where members of his family still live (*Anchorage Times,* December 28, 1968, p. 2; Chapman n.d.).

12. The hunters use a wooden or ivory plug to keep the air from escaping (Review Trip Transcript, pp. 53–55). Nelson mentions the use of a hand-operated tire pump to assist in inflating the walrus and says that hunters used a piece of blubber or a shell wrapped in cloth to plug the opening (1969:369–370).

13. The hunter gave Waldo four hundred dollars more than Waldo would have gotten if he had sold the fur to the store.

Notes to Chapter 11

1. Helge Larsen and Froelich Rainey were working on the history of

Eskimo culture. At Point Hope they had uncovered prehistoric artifacts of a culture they called Ipiutuk. They were eager to see where else this culture manifested itself, and Larsen turned his attention inland. The comparison of inland and coastal adaptation intrigued Larsen and prompted his 1942 trip to the Utuqqaq River (see Larsen and Rainey 1948:17; Larsen 1973).

2. They were collecting the eggs of arctic terns, old squaws, and eider ducks. Waldo said he put the eggs into water to help him decide which to take. Those that sank were unformed embryos; those that floated were forming into chicks, and he returned them to the nest (Review Trip Transcript pp. 57–58, 60; see also chapter 5, note 15).

3. Leona Okakok: This type of towing is called *ukamaq-*. The dogs or the people walk along the beach towing the boat, usually against the wind or current (MacLean forthcoming).

4. Leona Okakok: The term *sullivik,* by itself, means "a time or place for making a lot of things" (personal knowledge).

William Schneider: Sullivik may have been a special preparation site for people going inland from the coast. Samuel Agnasagga speaks about its strategic location: "That what they call it, Sullivik, many people understand it is the name for sewing place. It's not that mean(ing) only, more people gather in this place that need to do much work, like qayaq, umiaq, sled, new skin to put on their canoes, for next trip...This area is pretty safe from any enemy, that's why more people gather here in order to do something they need to be done" (Ivie and Schneider [1978] 1988:93).

According to Larsen, "From Pingalo, where they stored their umiaks, the Utorqarmiut sailed to Tulareaq near the mouth of the Utorqaq River. Here they made additional equipment to be used at the coast, but before they could use the clothing, tools, and hunting gear which had been made inland, certain ceremonies had to be performed" (1973:124).These examples tend to point to specific places where there was a separation and transition from inland to coastal activities and vice versa. However, this was not true in areas such as the Noatak River, where people worked on inland caribou skins at sites in the Noatak Delta. Burch reports that Nuatagmiut (Nuataaġmiut) of the Upper Noatak River made all of their caribou-skin clothing in the Noatak Delta (personal communication).

At this point, sites like Tulaaġiak and Sullivik are best viewed simply as places where people prepared to travel inland or to the coast, and not as "type" sites whose meaning can be generalized beyond the local area. Further research on how sites were categorized (e.g., work sites, umiaq storage sites, gathering sites) may lead to a better understanding of inland/coastal adaptation, a subject of considerable interest (see Burch 1976).

My early documentation of historic sites in Wainwright was influenced by both Burch's paper and Larsen's earlier work (1973). Although not well described in the literature, adaptation along the Utuqqaq and Kuuk rivers, both historically and at present, illustrates how people use both coastal and inland areas according to seasonal availability of particular resources. The Chipp-Ikpikpuk and Meade River areas also illustrate these dynamics, at least for the more recent historic periods (see Arundale and Schneider 1987). The number of fishing sites on these rivers also attests to the continuing importance of fish in the diet of North Slope people, and the rivers provide seasonal access to caribou, although caribou have not been as reliable a resource as fish.

5. Waldo uses "riffle" to designate shallow places where a swift current creates small rapids.

6. By "elevation," Waldo means places where the river descends sharply.

7. Kirgavik is the place of the hawks. According to one story, a friendly medicine man put the hawks there to warn the people when enemies were coming (Ivie and Schneider 1988:54–55).

8. In traditional Eskimo society, intersocietal relations were strained at best. A member of one group who was found in another group's territory was at risk of losing his life unless he could gain local support through kinship or partnership (Burch and Correll 1971:24). Revenge warfare was also practiced: a member of one group would enter another group's territory to seek out an individual who had

killed a relative or other member of his own group. When he found the person (or, according to some sources, a relative of that person, or sometimes even another member of that group), he would attempt to kill him and escape back to his own territory (Libbey, personal communication).

According to the Russian explorer A. F. Kashevarov, who traveled along the Arctic Coast in 1838, an old man near Cape Dyer said that "...two of his comrades had set out about a month ago for caribou that had been killed not very far away in the tundra. He assumed that they (his comrades) had been killed by 'Utukagmiuts' whom they sometimes meet in the tundra; they don't know any other people there" (VanStone 1977:57).

Intersocietal warfare could involve many people. Burch's data lead him to suggest that, for at least part of the nineteenth century, enough grudges and resentments built up to spark a war somewhere in Northwest Alaska at least once a year (1974:3). Kashevarov's expedition came across a burial site at Cape Lisburne which was apparently the result of a war between the Point Hope and Kotzebue Society people (VanStone 1977:54; Burch 1981:15; see also Burch 1988b:230, illustration 305).

A number of factors contributed to the decline in warfare at the end of the nineteenth century. According to Burch,

> In all areas, the incidence of warfare declined as a result of depopulation following the introduction of European epidemic diseases (and the often attendant famines), the breakdown of traditional native political boundaries, and the self-conscious interference by Europeans in native affairs. By the end of the nineteenth century—several decades earlier toward the south—warfare had essentially ceased as a dominant theme of interregional relations among different native groups. (1988b:232)

9. Waldo said that the Utuqqaq houses were framed with willows and the remains looked like a *paamaraq*, a temporary sod shelter (MacLean forthcoming). The perimeter of the qargi was square (Review Trip Transcript, p. 64). A structure found by Larsen on his Utuqqaq River trip resembles this description, although it is referred to as an

"ivrulik" (Larsen and Rainey 1948:35,45; see also Corbin, 1975:26, figure 7).

Waldo's description of the qargi is of interest, since they were such an important part of the social and ceremonial life, and so few are described in the literature. Waldo identified another qargi at the site of Kaŋich, about thirty-seven miles inland from Wainwright, at the juncture of the Kuuk, Kaolak, and Avalik rivers (Ivie and Schneider 1988:46). His identification was based on the structure's large size in comparison to the other structures.

James Corbin recently brought to my attention another description of a qargi which was provided to him by Helge Larsen from his field notes. Larsen learned about the qargi from Aqsheataq, who was identified as a Tulugarmiut. Larsen apparently worked with him in Fairbanks in 1950. Aqsheataq's description to Larsen indicates that the qargi was rectangular and was covered with caribou skins. It was not heated (letter, Corbin to Schneider, April 1, 1990; letter, Larsen to Corbin, April 19, 1972).

10. The presence of prehistoric animals on the North Slope is a source of continuing interest and discussion among Iñupiat travelers (see Arundale and Schneider 1987:27–30).

11. Leona Okakok: *Masu* is a form of edible root (*Hedysarum alpinum*), commonly called "potato" (MacLean forthcoming).

12. The location of this material is in question. It is not at the University of Alaska Museum or at the American Museum of Natural History. The collections at the National Museum of Denmark are, at present, only partly accessible, so a definitive statement is not yet possible. Jørgen Meldgaard, the curator, Department of Ethnography, wrote "As far as I know, Helge Larsen's field trip to the Utukok River was a reconnaissance where old sites were mapped and notes made on oral history, but only few, if any, artifacts were collected" (letter, October 24, 1989). Other types of records may exist. James Corbin visited Larsen in 1972, and it is Corbin's impression that, at that time, Larsen had at the museum his slides, notes, and photographs from the Utuqqaq River trip (letter, April 1, 1990).

13. Major Marvin (Muktuk) Marston and Ernest Gruening, who was governor of Alaska during World War II, were the two primary forces behind the establishment and success of the Alaska Territorial Guard (ATG). Beginning in 1942, the governor and the major traveled to remote village sites to enlist recruits for the guard (Marston 1969:4).

14. Otto Geist served under Marston as chief quartermaster for the western division. He was a good choice because he had traveled extensively in the territory and was known by many of the Native people. Geist was a professor at the University of Alaska, and by 1943 he had made contributions in the fields of natural history, archaeology, and ethnography. Geist remained in the Territorial Guard until 1947 when he returned to the university to resume his research (Keim 1969:246–255).

15. I think the trip that Waldo describes was made in 1959, although there are discrepancies in the written reports by Geist and geologist Paul Sellmann, and it is difficult to correlate these with Waldo's story. See Geist Collection, Series XIV, Expeditions, Box 3, Archives, Alaska and Polar Regions Department, Elmer E. Rasmuson Library, University of Alaska Fairbanks.

16. Under the provisions of the 1971 Alaska Native Claims Settlement Act, regional profit-making corporations were established. The Arctic Slope Regional Corporation includes the villages of Point Hope, Point Lay, Wainwright, Atqasuk, Barrow, Anaktuvuk Pass, Nuiqsut, and Kaktovik. The Corporation literally extends across Arctic Alaska. The land selection committees in each village made the selections of land for the villages to own. The Land Selection Committee in Wainwright continued to operate after land selection and advised on matters such as historic sites. For a comprehensive discussion of the Alaska Native Claims Settlement Act, see Arnold 1978.

17. Flossie Hopson Andersen designed and researched the *Traditional Land Use Inventory,* which is the first comprehensive inventory of Native historic sites on the North Slope. This document, which is organized by village area, serves as the foundation for more recent work sponsored by the North Slope Borough.

Notes to Chapter 13

1. Waldo's relationship to Captain Hartson Bodfish is documented in other written sources. One of the earliest references appears in the C. L. Andrews Collection. Sandy Bodfish, from Indialantic, Florida, is married to George Bodfish, an adopted son of Hartson Bodfish, Jr., who was the son of Captain Hartson Bodfish and Clara Howes. She brought to my attention an article titled "Nine Polar Bears," by Waldo Bodfish (1947) as told to J. Lester Minner. In this article, Minner identifies Waldo as the son of Captain Bodfish. Waldo is also identified this way in Allen 1978:205.

Arthur Railton, editor for the Dukes County Historical Society, provided me with a copy of an article titled "Waldo Bodfish, Son of Vineyard Whaler, Respected Member of His Alaskan Village" (*Vineyard Gazette*, August 15, 1975). The article is based in part on a letter from Dr. Michael Halberstam, a Public Health Service doctor who was stationed in Barrow. The letter was written in 1959 and identifies Waldo as the captain's son. The article perhaps contains some inaccuracies. For instance, the claim is made that when Captain Bodfish came North, Waldo's mother hid Waldo so the captain wouldn't take him. I asked Waldo about this, and he did not recall that being the case.

Finally, Arthur Railton knows people still living on Martha's Vineyard who knew Captain Bodfish, and they recall that it was common knowledge that he had an Eskimo family, although it wasn't publicized.

2. Through the years, the Revenue Cutter Service provided transportation not only to the Reindeer Service, but also to whalers and schoolteachers traveling to their stations or Outside. Eskimos also used the cutters to travel along the coast.

3. Ahlook is not mentioned in Lieutenant Jarvis's 1899 report on the overland expedition to rescue the stranded whalers (U.S. Revenue Cutter Service 1899), although he is specifically mentioned in the 1906 Report of the Agent for Education in Alaska.

4. Seveck (1973) also describes this period of reindeer herding his-

tory. He discusses traveling with the herds and taking reindeer herding officials around to the herds, and he also tells about shipping reindeer meat out on the USS *Boxer.*

5. The extensive Lomen Collection provides a good picture of the effort the Lomens put into producing and marketing reindeer meat. See also Lomen 1954.

6. See also "Narrative RE: Alaska Reindeer Herds for Calendar Year 1942, with Supplementary Data." For a comprehensive overview of reindeer herding history in Alaska, see Stern et al. 1980.

7. The achievements of the pioneer aviators laid the groundwork for commercial companies to develop the polar routes. Einar Sverre Pedersen played an instrumental role in developing the gyro, the maps, and the transmitting stations necessary to make commercial transpolar flight feasible. See Pedersen 1958 and Pedersen 1962. See also recording H-85-18.

8. I am indebted to Margaret Blackman for first suggesting this point to me. I am now very conscious of the several places in his account where Waldo reminds the reader of our travels together and what he showed me.

Notes to Chapter 14

1. Fred Milan conducted demographic studies; Richard Nelson studied subsistence activities; John Burns studied sea mammals; Dale Slaughter researched archaeological sites; Barbara Bodenhorn researched family structure; and David Libbey investigated Native use of historic sites.

2. The North Slope Borough is a regional governmental body that provides a variety of services from public works to historic documentation. Funds for the Borough come from taxes paid by the oil companies who have holdings in Prudhoe Bay, Kukparuk, and other areas on the North Slope.

3. Under provisions of the National Petroleum Reserve Production Act of 1976, a series of studies were conducted to determine resources within the reserve, including subsistence, recreational, wildlife, and mineral values. The National Petroleum Reserve in Alaska was originally established in 1923 by President Harding and designated National Petroleum Reserve #4. For a chronology of oil exploration and development events in NPR-A, see U.S. Department of the Interior 1982, Table I-1, "Overview of Events Leading to EIS."

4. Pilot biscuits are a staple on camping trips, and they often substitute for bread at mealtime. Meat is a staple in the diet, and those who leave home for schooling or work often comment on how they miss wild game, such as caribou, seal, and whale.

5. Edna Ahgeak MacLean has devoted many years to documenting and describing Iñupiaq language and culture. She is a faculty member at the Alaska Native Language Center, University of Alaska Fairbanks, and is currently working for the Alaska State Department of Education.

6. Anyone interested in the changes made can retrace the steps from the completed narrative back to the archival manuscript to the transcripts, to the recordings, and finally to the narrator.

7. For other approaches to this challenge see Blackman (1982) and Blackman (1989).

Bibliography

Adney, Edwin Tappan, and Howard I. Chapelle.
1964   *The Bark Canoes and Skin Boats of North America.*
         Washington, D.C.: Smithsonian Institution Press.
The Alaska Geographic Society.
1981   *The Kotzebue Basin.* Edited by Robert Henning et al.
         Vol. 8, no. 3.
Alaska Sportsman
1941   "From Ketchikan to Barrow." January:20–22.
1963   "From Ketchikan to Barrow." June:28.
Allen, Arthur James.
1978   *A Whaler and Trader in the Arctic, 1895–1944: My
         Life with the Bowhead.* Anchorage: Northwest Pub-
         lishing Company.
Anchorage Times
1968   December 28, 2.
C. L. Andrews Collection.
         "Journal, Kivalina, Alaska, 19 February, 1924 to 4
         July, 1924, Barrow." Box 4, folder #42. Notebooks,
         No. 2, Arctic. Archives, Alaska and Polar Regions

Department, Elmer E. Rasmuson Library, University of Alaska Fairbanks.

"Annual School Census Report."

n.d.   Records Group 75. Bureau of Indian Affairs, National Archives, Sand Point, Washington.

Arnold, Robert.

1978   *Alaska Native Land Claims.* Anchorage: Alaska Native Foundation.

Arundale, Wendy H., and William S. Schneider.

1987   *Quliaqtuat Iñupiat Nunaŋiññiñ: The Report of the Chipp-Ikpikpuk River and Upper Meade River Oral History Project.* Barrow: North Slope Borough Planning Department.

Atwood, Evangeline, and Robert DeArmond.

1977   *Who's Who in Alaskan Politics: A Biographical Dictionary of Alaskan Political Personalities, 1884–1974.* Portland: Binford and Mort for the Alaska Historical Commission.

Banks, Phyllis Eileen Davis, ed.

1974   "Echoes from History." *The Alaska Presbyterian* 9 (1):5 (Spring).

Beechey, Frederick W.

[1831] 1968   Narrative of a Voyage to the Pacific and Beering's Strait to Co-operate with the Polar Expeditions: Performed in His Majesty's ship Blossom, under the Command of Captain F. W. Beechey, R. N., F .R. S. & C., in the Years 1825–28. New York: Da Capo Press. Originally published by Authority of the Lords Commissioners of the Admiralty. Vol. 1 of 2. London: Colburn and Richard Bentley. Bibliotheca Australina #34.

Bixby, William.

1965   *Track of the Bear.* New York: David McKay Company, Inc.

Blackman, Margaret B.

1982   *During My Time: Florence Edenshaw Davidson, A Haida Woman.* Seattle: University of Washington Press.

1989   *Sadie Brower Neakok: An Iñupiaq Woman.* Seattle: University of Washington Press.

Boas, Franz.
[1888] 1964   *The Central Eskimo.* Lincoln: University of Nebraska Press. First published as Sixth Annual Report of the Bureau of Ethnology. Washington, D.C.: Smithsonian Institution Press.

Bockstoce, John R.
1977   *Eskimos of Northwest Alaska in the Early Nineteenth Century: Based on the Beechey and Belcher Collections and Records Compiled During the Voyage of the H.M.S. Blossom to Northwest Alaska in 1826 and 1827.* Monograph Series No. 1. Oxford: Pitt Rivers Museum.

1986   *Whales, Ice, and Men: The History of Whaling in the Western Arctic.* Seattle: University of Washington Press.

Bockstoce, John R., and Charles F. Batchelder.
1977   "A Chronological List of Commercial Wintering Voyages, 1850–1910." In *Steam Whaling in the Western Arctic,* by John R. Bockstoce, 111–123. New Bedford: New Bedford Whaling Museum.

Bodfish, Hartson H.
1936   *Chasing the Bowhead.* Cambridge: Harvard University Press.

Bodfish, Mattie.
n.d.   Personal communication with William Schneider.

Bodfish, Waldo.
1947   "Nine Polar Bears." As told to J. Lester Minner. *Alaska Sportsman,* September:22–23, 41–42.
1989   Letter to William Schneider, August 29.
1989   Letter to William Schneider, December 25.

Braham, Howard W., Mark A. Fraker, and Bruce D. Kragman.
1980   "Spring Migration of the Western Arctic Population of Bowhead Whales." *Marine Fisheries Review,* September–October:26–46.

Braham, Howard W., Floyd E. Durham, Gordon H. Jarrell, and Stephen Leatherwood.

1980   "Ingutuk: A Morphological Variant of the Bowhead Whale, Balaena mysticetus." *Marine Fisheries Review,* September–October:70–73.

Brooks, Alfred Hulse.

[1953] 1973   *Blazing Alaska's Trails.* Fairbanks: University of Alaska Press.

Brower, Charles D.

1942   *Fifty Years Below Zero: A Lifetime of Adventure in the Far North.* New York: Dodd, Mead, and Company.

Burch, Ernest S., Jr.

1970   "The Eskimo Trading Partnership in North Alaska: A Study in 'Balanced Reciprocity'." *Anthropological Papers of the University of Alaska* 15 (1):49–80.

1972   "The Caribou/Wild Reindeer as a Human Resource." *American Antiquity* 37 (3):339–368.

1974   "Eskimo Warfare in Northwest Alaska." *Anthropological Papers of the University of Alaska* 16 (2):1–14.

1975a   *Eskimo Kinsmen: Changing Family Relationships in Northwest Alaska,* edited by Robert F. Spencer. Monograph #59, The American Ethnological Society. St. Paul: West Publishing Company.

1975b   "Inter-Regional Transportation in Traditional Northwest Alaska." *Anthropological Papers of the University of Alaska* 17 (2):1–11.

1976   "The 'Nunamiut' Concept and the Standardization of Error." In *Contributions to Anthropology: The Interior Peoples of Northern Alaska,* edited by Edwin S. Hall, Jr., 52–97. Mercury Series Archaeological Survey of Canada, Paper #49. Ottawa: National Museum of Man.

1980   "Traditional Eskimo Societies in Northwest Alaska." In *Alaska Native Culture and History,* Senri Ethnological Studies #4, 253–304. Papers presented at Second International Symposium, August 1978. Osaka: National Museum of Ethnology. Kyoto: Nakanishi Printing Company.

1981   *The Traditional Eskimo Hunters of Point Hope, Alaska: 1800–1875.* Barrow: North Slope Borough.

1988a   *The Eskimos.* Norman: University of Oklahoma Press.

1988b   "War and Trade." In *Crossroads of Continents, Cultures of Siberia and Alaska,* edited by William Fitzhugh and Aron Crowell, 227–240. Washington, D.C.: Smithsonian Institution Press.

1988c   "Modes of Exchange in North-west Alaska." In *Hunters and Gatherers 2: Property, Power and Ideology,* edited by Tim Ingold, David Riches and James Woodburn, 95–109. Oxford: Berg Publishing.

1988d   "The End of the Trail: The Work of the Fifth Thule Expedition in Alaska." *Etudes/Inuit/Studies* 12 (1–2):151–170.

1989   Letter to William Schneider, November 9.

1990   Letter to William Schneider, January 4.

1990   Letter to William Schneider, February 13.

n.d.   Personal communication with William Schneider.

Burch, Ernest S., Jr., and Thomas C. Correll.

1971   "Alliance and Conflict: Inter-Regional Relations in North Alaska." In *Alliance in Eskimo Society,* edited by D. L. Guemple, 17–39. Published as Proceedings of the American Ethnological Society Supplement. Seattle: University of Washington Press.

Cassell, Mark S.

1989   "An Archaeological Reconnaissance of Commercial Whaling Period Sites in the Vicinity of Point Belcher, Alaska." Fairbanks: Bureau of Land Management, Fairbanks District Office.

Chance, Norman A.

1966   *The Eskimo of North Alaska.* Case Studies in Cultural Anthropology. New York: Holt, Rinehart, and Winston.

Chapman, Judy.

1989   "Arctic Pioneer Unknown: Aarnout Castel." Unpublished paper.

Cole, Cecil.
 n.d.   "Captain Mo." Recording H88-62. Archives, Alaska
                and Polar Regions Department, Elmer E. Rasmuson
                Library, University of Alaska Fairbanks.

Cole, Terrence.
 1983   "A History of the Nome Gold Rush: The Poor Man's
                Paradise." Ph.D. diss., University of Washington.
                Ann Arbor: University Microfilms International.

Collier, Arthur J., Frank L. Hess, Philip S. Smith, and Alfred Hulse
Brooks.
 1908   *The Gold Placers of Parts of Seward Peninsula,
                Alaska.* U.S.G.S. Bulletin #328. Washington, D.C.:
                U.S. Government Printing Office.

Collins, Henry B.
 1984   "History of Research Before 1945." In *Arctic,* vol. 5
                of *Handbook of North American Indians,* edited by
                David Damas, 8–16. Washington, D.C.: Smithsonian
                Institution Press.

Cooper, Paul Fenimore, Jr.
 1986   "Herschel Island and the History of the Western Arc-
                tic." In *Living Explorers of the Canadian Arctic,*
                edited by Shirley Milligan and W. O. Kupsch, 245–
                254. Yellowknife: Outcrop, The Northern Publishers.

Corbin, James Evans.
 1975   "Aniganigaruk: A Study in Nunamiut Eskimo Archae-
                ology." Ph.D. diss., Washington State University.
 1990   Letter to William Schneider, April 1.

Cruikshank, Moses
 1986   *The Life I've Been Living.* Recorded and compiled by
                William Schneider. Oral Biography Series, #1. Fair-
                banks: University of Alaska Press.

Damas, David, ed.
 1969   "Environment, History, and Central Eskimo Society."
                In *Contributions to Anthropology: Ecological Essays,*
                40–64. National Museums of Canada, Bulletin #230.
                Ottawa: Queen's Printer.

Darling, Esther Birdsall.
n.d.   The Great Dog Races of Nome, Held Under the Aus-
                pices of the Nome Kennel Club, Nome, Alaska. Offi-
                cial Souvenir History.

Fields, Arthur, Sr.
1989   Personal communication with William Schneider,
                August 23.
1989   Letter to William Schneider, November 24.
Forshaug, Jens.
n.d.   Recording H29-2 a & b. Archives, Alaska and Polar
                Regions Department, Elmer E. Rasmuson Library,
                University of Alaska Fairbanks.
Fortuine, Robert.
1984   "E. S. ('Stu') Rabeau, M.D. 1920–1984." *Alaska Medi-
                cine* 26 (3):95–96 (July/August/September).

Geist, Otto.
n.d.   "Collecting Pleistocene Fossils and Natural History
                Material in Arctic Alaska River Basins, 1959, 1960,
                and 1961." Series 14, Expeditions, Box 3, Geist Col-
                lection. Archives, Alaska and Polar Regions Depart-
                ment, Elmer E. Rasmuson Library, University of
                Alaska Fairbanks.
Gilberg, Rolf.
1984   "Profile: Knud Rasmussen, 1879–1933." *Polar Record*
                22 (137):169–171.

Harkey, Ira.
1974   *Pioneer Bush Pilot: The Story of Noel Wien.* Seattle:
                University of Washington Press.
Heinrich, Albert Carl.
1963   "Personal Names, Social Structure and Functional
                Integration." *Anthropology and Sociology Papers,* no.
                27. Department of Sociology, Anthropology and
                Social Welfare, Montana State University, Missoula,
                Montana.
1969   "Social Integration and Personal Names in an
                Eskimo Group." *The Journal of Karnatak Univer-
                sity—Social Sciences* 5:1–14.

Hunt, William R.

1986   *Stef: A Biography of Vilhjalmur Stefansson, Canadian Arctic Explorer.* Vancouver: University of British Columbia Press.

Hunter, Kathy.

1986   *Tracking the Bear, 1873–1963.* Palmer: Lazy Mountain Press.

Ivie, Pamela, and William Schneider.

[1978] 1988   *Wainwright: Land Use Values Through Time in the Wainwright Area.* Barrow: North Slope Borough Planning Department. Originally prepared as a report for the North Slope Borough for the NPR-A Planning Team and published as *Occasional Paper No. 13* by Anthropology and Historic Preservation, Cooperative Park Studies Unit, University of Alaska Fairbanks, and the North Slope Borough.

Jackson, Sheldon.

1906   *Fifteenth Annual Report on the Introduction of Domestic Reindeer into Alaska.* Washington, D.C.: U.S. Government Printing Office.

Johnshoy, Walter J.

1944   *Apauruk in Alaska: Social Pioneering Among the Eskimos.* Philadelphia: Dorrance and Company.

Joling, Dan.

1988   "Nunamiut Eskimos: Return of Pilot Sig Wien." In Heartland, *Fairbanks Daily News-Miner,* June 12, 8–11.

Kaplan, Lawrence D.

1988   *Ugiuvangmiut Quliapyuit, King Island Tales.* Fairbanks: Alaska Native Language Center and University of Alaska Press.

Keim, Charles J.

1969   *Aghvook, White Eskimo: Otto Geist and Alaskan Archaeology.* Fairbanks: University of Alaska Press.

Kignak, Ernest.

n.d.   Ernest Kignak's Life History. On file with the North Slope Borough Commission on Iñupiat History, Language, and Culture, Barrow, Alaska.

Kirchner, Scott.
1982   "Andrew Skin, Sr.: Eskimo Doctor." *Alaska Medicine,* November/December:101–105.

Kisautaq (Leona Okakok).
1981   *Puiguitkaat, The 1978 Elders' Conference.* Barrow: North Slope Borough Commission on Iñupiat History, Language, and Culture.

n.d.   Personal communication with William Schneider.

Krauss, Michael E.
[1974] 1982   *Native Peoples and Languages of Alaska.* A map. Fairbanks: Alaska Native Language Center.

La Belle, Joseph, Robert H. Schulze, Richard P. Voeker, James L. Wise, and Gary M. Wohl.
1983   *Alaska Marine Ice Atlas.* Anchorage: University of Alaska, Arctic Environmental Information and Data Center.

Larsen, Helge.
1972   Letter to James Corbin, April 19.

1973   "The Tareormiut and the Nunamiut of Northern Alaska: A Comparison Between Their Economy, Settlement Pattern, and Social Structure." In *Circumpolar Problems: Habitat, Economy, and Social Relations in the Arctic,* edited by Gosta Berg, 119–126. A symposium for Anthropological Research in the North, September 1969. New York: Pergamon Press.

Larsen, Helge, and Froelich Rainey.
1948   "Ipiutak and the Arctic Whale Hunting Culture." *Anthropological Papers of American Museum of Natural History,* vol. 42. New York: American Museum of Natural History.

Lavifischeff, Tikhon I.
1935   "History of Education in Alaska." Ph.D. diss., University of California.

Libbey, David.
n.d.   Personal communication with William Schneider.

Libbey, David, and Edwin S. Hall, Jr.
1981   *Cultural Resources in the Mid-Beaufort Sea Region.* A

Report for the North Slope Borough's Coastal Zone Management Plan (May 1981). Barrow: North Slope Borough Planning Department.

Libbey, David, and William Schneider.

1987   "Fur Trapping on Alaska's North Slope." In *Le Caster Fait Tout: Selected Papers of the Fifth North American Fur Trade Conference, 1985,* edited by Bruce G. Trigger, Toby Morantz, and Louise Dechene, 335–358. Montreal: Lake St. Louis Historical Society.

Lomen, Allen.

n.d.   Recordings H86-280 a & b and H87-6 a & b. Archives, Alaska and Polar Regions Department, Elmer E. Rasmuson Library, University of Alaska Fairbanks.

Lomen, Carl.

1954   *Fifty Years in Alaska.* New York: David McKay Company, Inc.

Lomen Family Collection.

Archives, Alaska and Polar Regions Department, Elmer E. Rasmuson Library, University of Alaska Fairbanks.

Lucier, Charles V., James VanStone, and Della Keats.

1971   "Medical Practices and Human Anatomical Knowledge Among the Noatak Eskimos." *Ethnology* 10 (3):251–264.

Lund, Henriette.

1974   *Of Eskimos and Missionaries: Lutheran Eskimo Missions in Alaska 1894–1973.* Minneapolis: Division for Service and Mission in America, The American Lutheran Church.

MacLean, Edna Ahgeak.

Forthcoming *Iñupiaq Dictionary.* Fairbanks and Barrow: Alaska Native Language Center, Iñupiaq Language Commission.

Marston, Marvin (Muktuk).

1969   *Men of the Tundra: Eskimos at War.* New York: October House, Inc.

Mathiassen, Therkel.
1945   "Report on the Expeditions." In Report of the Fifth
                Thule Expedition 1921–24. The Danish Expedition to
                Arctic North America in Charge of Knud Rasmus-
                sen, Ph.D, vol. 1, no. 1. Copenhagen: Gyldendalske
                Boghandel, Nordisk Forlag, 1–119.
Meldgaard, Jorgen.
1989   Letter to William Schneider, October 24.
Milan, Frederick.
1964   "The Acculturation of the Contemporary Eskimo of
                Wainwright, Alaska." *Anthropological Papers of the
                University of Alaska,* no. 2, 1–95.
Ben Mozee Collection.
                Archives, Alaska and Polar Regions Department,
                Elmer E. Rasmuson Library, University of Alaska
                Fairbanks.
Murdoch, John.
1892   "Ethnological Results of the Point Barrow Expedi-
                tion." *Ninth Annual Report of the Bureau of Ethnology
                to the Secretary of the Smithsonian Institution, 1887–
                88,* 3–441. Washington, D.C.: U.S. Government Print-
                ing Office.
Nageak, James.
n.d.   Personal communication with William Schneider.
"Narrative Re: Alaska Reindeer Herds for Calendar Year 1942, with
Supplementary Data."
n.d.   Alaska Reindeer Herds, Small Collections. Archives,
                Alaska and Polar Regions Department, Elmer E. Ras-
                muson Library, University of Alaska Fairbanks.
Neakok, Warren, Dorcus Neakok, Waldo Bodfish, David Libbey,
Edwin S. Hall, Jr., and the Point Lay Elders.
1985   *To Keep the Past Alive: The Point Lay Cultural
                Resource Site Survey.* Barrow: North Slope Borough
                Planning Department.
Nelson, Edward William.
1900   *The Eskimo About Bering Strait.* Extracted from the
                Eighteenth Annual Report of the Bureau of Ameri

can Ethnology, 1899. Washington, D.C.: U.S. Government Printing Office.

Nelson, Richard K.

1969   *Hunters of the Northern Ice.* Chicago: University of Chicago Press.

1981   *Harvest of the Sea: Coastal Subsistence in Modern Wainwright.* A Report for the North Slope Borough's Coastal Zone Management Program. Barrow: North Slope Borough.

1987   Recording H87-53 A-B. Archives, Alaska and Polar Regions Department, Elmer E. Rasmuson Library, University of Alaska Fairbanks..

New Bedford Log Books.

#952A, Beluga (Steam Bark) Whaling Voyage: Arctic Ocean, 7 April 1900 to 31 December 1900; #952B, Beluga (Steam Bark) Whaling Voyage: Arctic Ocean, 1 January 1901 to 6 November 1901; #953, Beluga (Steam Bark) Whaling Voyage: Arctic Ocean, 2 April 1902 to 7 November 1902; #957, Herman (Steam Bark) Whaling Voyage: Arctic Ocean, 27 April 1909 to 1 November 1909; #958, Herman (Steam Bark) Whaling Voyage: Arctic Ocean, 1 May 1910 to 25 October 1910; #959, Herman (Steam Bark) Whaling Voyage: Arctic Ocean, 22 March 1911 to 9 November 1911. Old Dartmouth Whaling Museum. New Bedford, Massachusetts.

Newell, Gordon, ed.

1966   *The H. W. McCurdy Marine History of the Pacific Northwest.* Seattle: The Superior Publishing Company.

1977   *The H. W. McCurdy Marine History of the Pacific Northwest, 1966–1975.* Seattle: The Superior Publishing Company.

Newman, Turak.

1978   *One Man's Trail: An Old-Timer Tells the Story of His Life.* Anchorage: Adult Literacy Laboratory, with funds from the Alaska Historical Commission.

New York Times
    1945   February 2, 19.

North Slope Borough Commission on Iñupiat History, Language, and Culture.
    1986   "Traditional Law Conference Transcripts." Elders' Conference. Barrow: North Slope Borough Planning Department.
    n.d.   Genealogy files, an ongoing compilation at Commission Office. North Slope Borough, Barrow, Alaska.

North Slope Borough Planning Department.
    1977   Traditional Land Use Inventory. Point Lay. October. Prepared by the North Slope Borough Commission on Iñupiat History, Language, and Culture.
    1978   Traditional Land Use Inventory. Barrow/Atkasook. January. Prepared by the North Slope Borough Commission on Iñupiat History, Language, and Culture.
    1987   Traditional Land Use Inventory. Wainwright/Utuqqaq. Revised November 1987. Prepared by the North Slope Borough Commission on Iñupiat History, Language, and Culture.

Okakok, Leona (Kisautaq).
    n.d.   Personal communication with William Schneider.

Ostermann, H., and E. Holtved, eds.
    1952   *The Alaskan Eskimo as Described in the Posthumous Notes of Dr. Knud Rasmussen.* Vol. 10, no. 3, of the Report of the Fifth Thule Expedition, 1921–1924. Copenhagen: Gyldendalsk Boghandel, Nordisk Forlag.

Pedersen, E. S.
    1958   "Airline Navigation in Polar Areas." *Journal of the Institute of Navigation* 6 (4):356–360.
    1962   "Transpolar Jet Navigation." *Canadian Aeronautics and Space Journal* 8 (4):71–77 (April).
    n.d.   Recording H-85-18. Archives, Alaska and Polar Regions Department, Elmer E. Rasmuson Library, University of Alaska Fairbanks.

Pedersen, Theodore "Teddy."
1944   "Call All Hands." *Alaska Sportsman,* April:12, 13,
                26–30.
Potter, Jean.
[1945] 1983   *The Flying North.* New York: Bantam Books.
Rainey, Froelich.
1941   "Native Economy and Survival in Arctic Alaska."
                Applied Anthropology 1 (1):9–14.
Rapaport, Stella.
1962   *The Bear, Ship of Many Lives.* New York: Dodd,
                Mead, and Company.
Rasmussen, Knud.
1927   *Across Arctic America: Narrative of the Fifth Thule
                Expedition.* New York: G. P. Putnam's Sons.
Ray, Dorothy Jean.
1980   *Artists of the Tundra and the Sea.* Seattle: University
                of Washington Press.
1983   *Ethnohistory in the Arctic: The Bering Strait Eskimo.*
                Kingston: The Limestone Press.
n.d.   Personal communication with William Schneider.
1989   Letter to William Schneider, October 17.
Renner, Louis, in collaboration with Dorothy Jean Ray.
1979   *Pioneer Missionary to the Bering Strait Eskimos: Bel-
                larmine Lafortune, S.J.* Portland: Binford and Mort,
                for the Alaska Historical Commission.
Reports of the Commission of Education, U.S. Bureau of Education
                Reports 1908–1919 (inclusive of school years 1906–
                1918). Washington, D.C.: U.S. Government Printing
                Office.
Roberts, Arthur.
1978   *Tomorrow Is Growing Old: Stories of the Quakers in
                Alaska.* Newberg: The Barclay Press.
Schneider, William.
1989   Review Trip Notes, 17–19 May. Archives, Alaska and
                Polar Regions Department, Elmer E. Rasmuson
                Library, University of Alaska Fairbanks.
1989   Review Trip Transcript, 17–19 May. Archives, Alaska

and Polar Regions Department, Elmer E. Rasmuson Library, University of Alaska Fairbanks.

Schneider, William, Sverre Pedersen, and David Libbey.

1980   *Barrow-Atqasuk: Land Use Values Through Time in the Barrow-Atqasuk Area,* Occasional Paper #24. Barrow and Fairbanks: North Slope Borough and Cooperative Park Studies Unit, University of Alaska Fairbanks.

Senungetuk, Vivian, and Paul Tiulana.

1987   *A Place for Winter: Paul Tiulana's Story.* Anchorage: Cook Inlet Region Incorporated Foundation.

Seveck, Chester Asakak.

1973   *Longest Reindeer Herder.* Arctic Circle Enterprises.

Sherwood, Alan.

n.d.   "Arctic Sea Coast Just Another Mainstreet." Copy found in Episcopal Church Collection, Box 4. Archives, Alaska and Polar Regions Department, Elmer E. Rasmuson Library, University of Alaska Fairbanks.

Simpson, Thomas, Esq.

1843   Narrative of the Discoveries on the North Coast of America; Effected by the Officers of the Hudson's Bay Company During the Years 1836–39. London: Richard Bentley, New Burlington Street.

Slaughter, Dale.

1979   "Excavations at the Site of Siraagruk." Appendix C in *Cultural Resource Survey and Clearance: National Petroleum Reserve in Alaska,* edited by E. S. Hall, Jr. Anchorage: United States Geological Survey.

1982   "The Point Barrow House Type: Analysis of Archaeological Examples from Siraagruk and Other Sites in Northern Alaska." *Anthropological Papers of the University of Alaska* 20 (1–2): 141–158.

Smith, Philip S., and J. B. Mertie, Jr.

1930   "Geology and Mineral Resources of Northwestern Alaska." U.S. Department of the Interior, *U.S. Geological Survey Bulletin #815.* Washington, D.C.: U.S. Government Printing Office.

Sonnenfeld, Joseph.
1959   "An Arctic Reindeer Industry: Growth and Decline."
               The Geographical Review 49 (1):77–94.
Spencer, Robert.
[1959] 1969   *The North Alaskan Eskimo: A Study in Ecology and
               Society.* First published by Bureau of American Eth-
               nology, Bulletin #171. Washington, D.C.: Smithso-
               nian Institution Press.
Stefansson, Vilhjalmur.
1914   *The Stefansson-Anderson Arctic Expedition of the
               American Museum: Preliminary Ethnological Report.*
               Anthropological Papers, vol. 14, part 1. New York:
               American Museum of Natural History.
[1913] 1971   *My Life with the Eskimos.* New York: Collier.
Stephenson, Bob, and Larry Jenning.
1978   *Wildlife Notebook Series.* Juneau: Alaska Department
               of Fish and Game.
Stern, Richard O., Edward L. Arobio, Larry L. Naylor, and Wayne C.
Thomas.
1980   *Eskimos, Reindeer, and Land.* Fairbanks: Agricultural
               Experiment Station, School of Agriculture and Land
               Resources Management.
Stewart, Robert Laird.
1908   *Sheldon Jackson, Pathfinder and Prospector of the Mis-
               sionary Vanguard in the Rocky Mountains and
               Alaska.* New York: Fleming H. Revell Company.
Stuck, Hudson.
1920   *The Alaskan Missions of the Episcopal Church.* New
               York: Domestic and Foreign Missionary Society.
Taylor, Gerald.
n.d.   Personal communication with William Schneider.
Taylor, John N., Andrew Hageman, and Beth Allen.
1984   "Supply Patterns in Western Alaska: A Secondary
               Source Analysis." Final Report, School of Manage-
               ment, University of Alaska Fairbanks.
Tewkesbury, David, and William Tewkesbury.
1947   *Tewkesbury's Who's Who in Alaska and Alaska Busi-
               ness Index,* vol. 1. Juneau: Tewkesbury Publishers.

Truesdele, Leon.
1943   *Sixteenth Census of the United States: 1940 Popula-*
                tion Characteristics of the Population (with Limited
                Data on Housing) Alaska. Washington, D.C.: U.S.
                Government Printing Office.
U.S. Department of the Interior.
1982   *Draft Environmental Impact Statement on Oil and*
                Gas Leasing and Development in the National Petro-
                leum Reserve in Alaska. Anchorage: Bureau of Land
                Management.
U.S. Revenue Cutter Service.
1899   "Report of the Cruise of the U.S. Revenue Cutter
                Bear and the Overland Expedition for the Relief of
                the Whalers in the Arctic Ocean from 27 November
                1897 to 13 September 1898." Treasury Department,
                Division of Revenue-Cutter Service. Washington,
                D.C.: U.S. Government Printing Office.
VanStone, James.
1962   *Point Hope: An Eskimo Village in Transition.* The
                American Ethnological Society. Seattle: University of
                Washington Press.
1964   "Some Aspects of Religious Change Among Native
                Inhabitants in West Alaska and the Northwest Terri-
                tories." *Arctic Anthropology* 2 (2):21–24.
VanStone, James, ed.
1977   "A. F. Kashevarov's Coastal Explorations in North-
                west Alaska, 1838." *Fieldiana Anthropology* 69, Field
                Museum of Natural History.
The Vineyard Gazette.
1975   "Waldo Bodfish, Son of Vineyard Whaler, Respected
                Member of His Alaskan Village." August 15. Also ref-
                erenced in Dukes County Historical Society
                Archives, Box 70, 1B, Envelope 3.
Willoya, Emma.
n.d.   Recording H83-408. Archives, Alaska and Polar
                Regions Department, Elmer E. Rasmuson Library,
                University of Alaska Fairbanks. Additional record-

ings at KICY Radio and Kegoayah Kozga Library in Nome.

Wooley, Chris B., and Rex A. Okakok.

n.d.   "Kivgiq: A Celebration of Who We Are." Paper presented to the Sixteenth Annual Meeting of the Alaska Anthropological Association, March 3–4, 1989, Anchorage, Alaska.

Worl, Rosita.

1978   "The North Slope Iñupiat Whaling Complex." In *Alaska Native Culture and History,* Senri Ethnological Studies #4, 305–320. Papers presented at Second International Symposium, August 1978. Osaka: National Museum of Ethnology. Kyoto: Nakanishi Printing Company.

Author Index

Subject Index

For clarification, this index identifies Iñupiaq terms in italics. Spelling variations of Iñupiaq words are further distinguished. The text spelling of personal names follows an older spelling style; the reader is referred to text spellings by "*See.*" The current orthographic spelling is given in parentheses. For place-names, the current orthography is used. Alternative and U.S. Geological Survey spellings are given in parentheses. Maps are identified by "m" after the page number. Photographs are identified by "p" after the page number.

313